The Journal of

William Beckford

in Portugal & Spain

The Journal of
William Beckford
in Portugal & Spain

1787 – 1788

Edited by Boyd Alexander

NONSUCH

First published 1954
Copyright © in this edition 2006
Nonsuch Publishing Ltd

Nonsuch Publishing Limited
The Mill, Brimscombe Port, Stroud, Gloucestershire, GL5 2QG
www.nonsuch-publishing.com

Nonsuch Publishing Ltd is an imprint of Tempus Publishing Group

British Library Cataloguing in Publication Data.
A catalogue record for this book is available from the British Library.

ISBN 1-84588-010-2

Typesetting and origination by Nonsuch Publishing Limited
Printed in Great Britain by Oaklands Book Services Limited

CONTENTS

INTRODUCTION TO THE
MODERN EDITION

When William Beckford arrived in Lisbon at the end of March 1787 he was a dashing and immensely rich young man of twenty-six. The journey had not been planned to end in Portugal: he had set sail from England to visit his sugar plantations in Jamaica from which the family derived its immense fortune. But, seasick or merely whimsical, Beckford decided to break the journey in a country whose seafaring explorers had become boyhood heroes in the stillness of his father's library at Fonthill in Wiltshire. If Beckford was impressed by his first view of the city floating on the estuary of the great Tagus, Lisbon society was equally taken by the attractive and princely Englishman who arrived with a retinue of thirty servants. If cooks, footmen, carriers and grooms were not enough, before long fine antique furniture and a library of rare books were to follow. It appeared that Beckford intended to stay for some while and to take a place at the very pinnacle of Portuguese society.

In fact, Beckford's sojourn in Lisbon lasted until the winter; at the end of November he left for Spain, where he stayed for six months before moving to Paris, eventually returning to England in 1789. Beckford left two accounts of his summer in Lisbon. One of these, the *Sketches of Spain and Portugal*, he published in 1834 when he had retired to a reclusive life in Bath, but was enjoying something of a revival as a writer. Beckford claimed that his *Sketches* were based on certain notes that he had made while on his continental travels. They are written in a faultless, flowing prose in which the episodes of daily life are rounded off in polished, story-like fashion. They were intended to show off the author cavorting in the houses and at the tables of the courtly and grand. So far as Portugal was concerned, they were meant to relate the "happier times" of the *ancien régime*, a halcyon and lost "golden" age before the horrors of the Napoleonic war descended upon Iberia.

But, alongside the *Sketches*, there existed another literary work, a private diary or journal which only saw the light of day in 1954 when it was exhumed from the Beckford papers by Boyd Alexander and published under the title of *The Journal of William Beckford in Portugal and Spain 1787–1788*. This *Journal*, republished in this current edition in full for the first time since 1954, has a quite different tone and character from the *Sketches*, although it relates the events of the same summer. In an early entry, Beckford reveals that he is anxiously waiting for news from England to hear if his aunt, Lady Effingham (a courtier), has had any success in managing to get a recommendation for him so that he can be presented to the Portuguese queen, despite the opposition of the "malevolent cuckold, Walpole". The malevolent cuckold was none other than the Hon. Robert Walpole, British envoy at Lisbon from 1772 to 1800, who, whether acting from official instructions or merely out of personal spite, opposed Beckford's presentation at court throughout his tenure as envoy. Walpole's obstinacy did not deter the Marquis of Marialva, Beckford's friend and champion, from pursuing the matter to the highest level. One diary entry describes a visit to the Prime Minister's office: unable to get his way, the impetuous Beckford storms out of the room, leaving the loyal Marialva to placate a ruffled Prime Minister.

There are other aspects of Beckford's life in the *Journal* which are less fraught than the affair of presentation. One is his abortive romance with Dom Pedro de Marialva, the Marquis' teenage son, which is then replaced by an affair with another "inflammable" Portuguese youth, Gregorio Franchi, who became Beckford's lover and lifelong friend. There are lighthearted moments as well—in the agreeable company of literary friends in umbrageous Sintra—or peaceful explorations on horseback (often alone) in the lush hinterland around Colares or nearer at hand in the Alcântara Valley, then on the outskirts of the city. Nevertheless, despite these more relaxed moments, the abiding mood of the *Journal* is a sad, reflective one, in which a young Englishman manages to express the very Portuguese sentiment of *saudades*, or feeling of loss and nostalgia for what has been lost.

When he prepared his edition in 1954, Boyd Alexander had the advantage of the sole guardianship of the Beckford Papers, which subsequently found their way to the Bodleian Library (the diary pages are now to be found in Beckford Papers MS c 43 and d 5). Certain jottings and unexplained variants made Boyd Alexander's task of editing the manuscripts a difficult one; he explained that his object was to produce a text acceptable to the general reader rather than one addressed to the scholarly world. There is therefore no cumbersome critical apparatus to his edition. However,

Boyd Alexander did add a series of important footnotes, which, by describing the key players in the story and the various locations in and around Lisbon, remain an invaluable source of biographical material as well as of contemporary Portuguese society. For that reason, Boyd Alexander's edition remains a significant reference point for scholars as well as a good story for the general reader. Its re-appearance in this Nonsuch edition is very welcome.

MALCOLM JACK
London
August, 2005

INTRODUCTION

William Beckford, born on 29 September 1760, was the only legitimate child of Alderman William Beckford, twice Lord Mayor of London, one of the richest men in England, and the principal City friend of the Earl of Chatham, who became godfather to his son. The Beckfords were the wealthiest and most powerful family in Jamaica, owners of many sugar plantations and countless slaves. They had risen from obscurity in Maidenhead early in the seventeenth century. By the close of it, the Alderman's grandfather had been in turn Jamaica's Commander-in-Chief, President of the Council and Lieutenant-Governor; he died in a fit of anger in 1710 when contradicted by a member of the Council—as a family, the Beckfords had violent tempers. The Alderman's father was Speaker of the Jamaican House of Assembly; the Alderman himself, after an education at Westminster, settled in England as a London merchant. He was an able, ambitious and aggressive man with a strong colonial accent and impetuous speech which provoked uncharitable laughter in the House of Commons, where he sat first for Shaftesbury and then for the City. He bought the estate of Fonthill, near Salisbury, where he was surrounded by long-entrenched landowners who did not relish his proximity, for he was much richer than they and did not fail to show it. It is not surprising that he became a noisy Whig, a fire-eater supporting Wilkes and Chatham against the Court and the King's Party.

The Alderman's wife was a Hamilton, grand-daughter of the Earl of Abercorn, a relationship which she permitted no one to forget, although her first husband had been a Jamaican planter named Marsh (by whom she had one child, Elizabeth— Beckford's half-sister). She indoctrinated her son with her snobbery, and had him all to herself when the Alderman died in 1770 at the age of sixty. She was tyrannous, possessive and spoiling; she denied him the rough-and-tumble of education at boarding schools by making him live with tutors at home, surrounded by her own generation and by aunts with a religious turn of mind ("methodistical dowagers", as he called them).

It happened that several of his mentors knew something of the Orient; their tales and experiences fired his lively imagination, already stimulated by his Jamaican family background. His drawing-master, Alexander Cozens, an important early English water-colourist, was born in Russia and had known Persians. Sir William Chambers, who taught him the principles of architecture, had sailed before the mast to China, and was an authority on Chinese gardening. Beckford read everything he could (even in Arabic and Persian) about the Arabs, the Chinese and the Indians, and gloated over the whimsical caprices of Oriental sultans. In 1777 he was, like Gibbon, sent to Geneva to finish his education, and stayed with his uncle, Colonel Hamilton, formerly of the East India Company. There he was regarded as a precocious genius, and began, under the influence of Rousseau, to display a morbid loneliness and self-absorption, with arrogant contempt for his elders and hatred of their interest in politics and money: "fat bulls of Basan encompass me around; tubs upon two legs, crammed with stupidity, amble about me," he wrote to Cozens. Periodically in Switzerland, and in London or Paris in the 1780s, he emerged from his musing solitude to take Society by storm, drawing attention to himself by mimicking everyone from dowagers downwards, by singing Italian arias with the voice of a soprano, and by all kinds of foolery in which there was an element of downright bad manners.

But these noisy bursts of frivolity concealed a steady ambition to be a writer—he was always scribbling, and to good purpose. It was, however, on this chosen ground that he met with his first serious reverse. After Switzerland, his first tour in Europe was in 1780 and 1781, when he went via Holland to stay with Sir William Hamilton near Naples. This journey inspired an original travelbook entitled *Dreams, Waking Thoughts, and Incidents; in a Series of Letters from various parts of Europe.*[1] It was printed and ready for publication in April 1783, when his family forced him to withdraw it. They wanted him to be a politician, but he never would have been taken seriously in the House as the author of a romantic travelbook which began:

> Shall I tell you my dreams? To give an account of my time is doing, I assure
> you, but little better. Never did there exist a more ideal being. A frequent
> mist hovers before my eyes, and through its medium I see objects so faint and
> hazy, that both their colours and forms are apt to delude me … All through
> Kent did I doze as usual; now and then I opened my eyes to take in an idea
> or two of the green, woody country through which I was passing; then closed

them again; transported myself back to my native hills; thought I led a choir
of those I loved best through their shades; and was happy in the arms of
illusion. The sun set before I recovered my senses enough to discover plainly
the variegated slopes near Canterbury.

The book was permeated by a romantic atmosphere distasteful to his elders,
who perceived his instability of character and temperament, and rightly feared
his friendship for high-spirited and dissolute people like Lady Craven and Lady
Archer. Moreover, by fits and starts he was in love with his first cousin's wife Louisa
Beckford, an affair which had dragged on since 1780. She was six years his senior
and destined for a consumptive's grave; she spoiled and flattered him in order
to maintain her precarious hold. But worst of all, he was ridiculously partial to
an effeminate youth, William Courtenay, later Viscount Courtenay and Earl of
Devon, whom he had first met in June 1779 at Powderham Castle when the boy was
nearly eleven (Beckford's junior by almost eight years). At first no flights of fancy
were too much to project upon the pretty youth, who was the only boy in a family
of fourteen. It was the strongest attachment Beckford had yet developed. In time
he grew genuinely concerned about the youth's education and tried to counter the
pampering of Powderham.

In order to exorcise these bad influences, Beckford's family married him off,
in May 1783, to the twenty-one-year-old Lady Margaret Gordon, daughter of the
impoverished Earl of Aboyne. For a time he was torn between Louisa, Courtenay
and his wife. But his wife's simple affection and candour won him over, and
Louisa faded into the background. In 1784 all was set fair. He was elected MP
for Wells, but not finding the House to his taste, he sought a barony through the
influence of Lord Thurlow, the Lord Chancellor, his former guardian. The patent
was actually made out, and his name was mentioned in the press as a recipient in
the coming Honours, when, from September to October 1784, the young couple
stayed at Powderham at the same time as Lord Loughborough, Chief Justice of the
Common Pleas, who had married young Courtenay's aunt. We may never know
what happened. The upshot was that from the end of November a press campaign
(apparently instigated by Loughborough) was launched against Beckford,
accusing him of misconduct with young Courtenay, then in his seventeenth year.
Readers of this Journal will have to judge for themselves what their relationship
was likely to have been and whether (or to what extent) it exceeded the bounds of
the romantic and the sentimental. At least his own wife, writing to her aunt Lady
Gower shortly after the scandal, stated that she still loved him, believed in his
innocence and fully supported him against her own relatives.[2] But his reputation
had gone for ever. Henceforth he was a social outcast wherever Englishmen were
to be found.

Beckford and his wife went into enforced retirement at Fonthill. But becoming bored by their painful situation in England, in July 1785 they went to Vevey in Switzerland, where Lady Margaret died on 26 May 1786, after giving birth to her second daughter, Susan. Beckford's enemies in England launched further press attacks against him, suggesting that he was responsible for her death. Thereafter his bitterness knew no bounds and became his most marked characteristic:

> I have been hunted down and persecuted these many years. I have been stung and not allowed opportunities of changing the snarling, barking style you complain of, had I ever so great an inclination. No truce, no respite have I experienced since the first licenses was taken out at Nebuchadnezzar's office for shooting at me. If I am shy or savage you must consider the baitings and worrying to which I allude—how was I treated in Portugal, In Spain, in France, in Switzerland, at home, abroad, in every region. You was in Turkey or in Lubberland when the storm raged against me and when I was stabbed to the heart by the loss of Lady Margaret. And what was the balm poured into my wounds—a set of paragraphs accusing me of having occasioned her death by ill-usage. Allowances were to be made for former attacks, but none for this, and I will own to you that the recollection of this black stroke fills me with such horror and indignation that I sigh for the pestilential breath of an African serpent to destroy every Englishman who comes in my way.[3]

He had no time to recover from this black stroke before another cruel blow was dealt to his literary aspirations. In 1782, under the inspiration of an extraordinary Christmas party of young people at Fonthill, he had composed in French his most remarkable work, for which he is still best remembered, the Oriental tale *Vathek*. He polished it over a long period, and slowly added further tales known as *The Episodes of Vathek*. Meanwhile a friend of his, a clergyman named Samuel Henley, was translating it into English under his supervision. For this purpose Henley retained the original French manuscript, apparently the only copy. Six weeks after Lady Margaret's death, Henley published his English translation, contrary to Beckford's strict injunctions. Moreover, he published it anonymously, alleging that it was a mere translation of a current Oriental tale. Beckford's best work had been stolen from him. In far-off Switzerland he was powerless. Since he evidently had no copy of his French original, which he now wanted to publish as quickly as possible, it is thought that he had to obtain a copy of Henley's translation and have it hastily retranslated into French.

Such is the sad background of the Journal. But what was Beckford doing in Portugal in 1787? In January he had returned to England as a widower. But the dust of the Powderham scandal had not been allowed to settle. His family decided to relegate him to his Jamaican sugar estates—the most inappropriate place for such a man:

> No one ever embarked even for transportation with a heavier heart. The more I hear of Jamaica, the more I dread the climate, which I fully expect will wither my health away.[4]

He sailed on March 15 and the first stop was at Lisbon nine days later. Having been seasick most of the time, he refused to go any further, and remained there for eight months. His stay might have been very short, and we should have missed the Journal. For Robert Walpole, the British Minister, aware of his reputation, refused to receive him or to present him to the Queen of Portugal, Maria I. This automatically excluded him from official functions and from English society.

But events took an unprecedented turn. Somehow Beckford was introduced to the Queen's favourite, Diogo, the "young" Marquis of Marialva, Grand Master of the Horse, a man twenty-one years his senior.[5] Marialva at once became deeply attached to him, and they were inseparable. This put Beckford on an equal footing with half the grandees in Lisbon, who were mostly related to each other and formed an exclusive circle. As friends and relations of Marialva, they called on Beckford in great numbers and took sides over his unusual case, which became the talk of the town. There was the added attraction of his good table, fine taste, immense wealth and lively, exotic company. Marialva left no stone unturned to get him presented to the Queen. The affair began to assume some importance, since the Marquis daily had her ear, and his prestige, as well as Walpole's, was at stake. Court etiquette was quite clear: a foreigner had to be presented by his ambassador. Marialva first tried to circumvent this by persuading the Queen to allow him or the Prime Minister, Melo, to present Beckford. But she was by nature timid and irresolute. And Melo dissuaded her, for he had no wish to antagonise the powerful and arrogant ambassador; as a former diplomat himself, he respected etiquette, and he was a political opponent of the devout and Pombal-hating nobility.

As in every Court, there were political cliques struggling against each other for power. The Portuguese whom Beckford met were divided into those who hated the memory of the dictator Pombal (who had fallen at the beginning of Maria I's reign in 1777), and those who had been influenced or trained by him. He had done his best to exclude the nobles from the Government, had harried them whenever he could, and had decreased the wealth and prestige of the Church. He had engineered or made use of the Tavora-Aveiro conspiracy of 1758, and thrown many nobles and priests into prison, where some had died and the rest languished until the new reign. The nobles never forgave him and wished to undo his policies and exclude all Pombalites from power. Contrary to expectation, they remained in office under Maria I and even grew more powerful. São Caetano, the Queen's Confessor, was advanced step by step as titular Archbishop of Thessalonica, Inquisitor-General, special adviser of the Sovereign in the Cabinet, and Prime Minister in all but name. By Beckford's time, most of the business of government was executed by Melo, who, influenced by Pombal, scoffed bitterly at "the pompous, vain and expensive establishment of the Patriarchal Church and its attendants."[6] Pombal's heir (the second Marquis), a notoriously dissolute man, became Gentleman of the Bedchamber to the Queen and retained the Presidency of the Lisbon Senate, which he owed to his father's nepotism. Worst of all, the dictator had supervised the education of Maria's heir, Dom José, Prince of Brazil, who was also influenced by the radical modern ideas of Joseph II of Austria; he and his wife (who was also his aunt) formed a rallying point of opposition to the Court. Even the Queen's principal female adviser and friend, Madame Arriaga, was the widow of one of Pombal's collaborators.

One can imagine the caballing, and the daily pressure exerted on the poor Queen.[7] This gave Beckford's case some importance, once he had become intimate with the Marialvas. São Caetano, virtual ruler of the country, gave him audiences; Seabra, the wily lawyer who liked to be on the winning side, discussed his case for hours with the leaders of the nobility; the Marquis of Pombal called, hoping to improve his precarious position by currying favour with the friend of Marialva; the Prime Minister was obliged to fight a rearguard action; and the Prince of Brazil awaited a favourable opportunity to see him. All very gratifying to the outcast ignored by his own ambassador. But the weakness of his position became apparent when his relatives failed to send him letters of recommendation which Walpole could not overlook. The rulers of Portugal began to lose interest in him; there was no alternative but to depart. The roundabout way Marialva had to work in order to gain his point is rather pathetic. When he found that the Queen and the Prime Minister insisted on the presentation being made by Walpole, he tried unsuccessfully to make Luis Pinto de Sousa Coutinho, Portuguese Ambassador in London, persuade our Government and Court to instruct Walpole to present Beckford. (It is satisfactory to learn that in 1795, during Beckford's second visit to Portugal, he defeated Walpole, who wrote an angry note to the same Pinto, then Foreign Minister, asking why Beckford had been presented. Evidently the usual etiquette was set aside in Beckford's favour. This may have been because, owing to the Queen's madness, the reins of government had been assumed by her surviving son Dom João, who liked Beckford and openly commended him.)

The struggle with Walpole is not the sole plot in the Journal, nor is the human interest centred only on the unexpected intimacy with Marialva.

Beckford's appearance on the scene caused two other complications in the Marialva family. His second struggle was to prevent his friend marrying him off to his eldest child Henriqueta, then fifteen years old; she was already practically engaged to the sixty-eight-year-old Duke of Lafões, styled "Uncle to the Queen" and the first man in the land after the Royal Family, and she did in fact marry him soon after Beckford's departure. Marialva's plan betrays the strength and unusual nature of his attachment; he hoped by this scheme to keep his friend at his side in Portugal. But Beckford, although sometimes ready to intrigue with a woman, was not the man to marry her. He was far more interested in Henriqueta's thirteen-year-old brother Dom Pedro. The Journal opens with his first meeting with the pair, and we can follow the whole course of their friendship. Quite apart from his innate tendencies, he enjoyed improving the minds and tastes of growing boys.

Beckford's account of the Marialvas gives the most intimate picture on record of the family of a Portuguese grandee of the period. His sympathetic study is independently echoed by the contemporary traveller Murphy:

> The nobility ... are not very rich; for tho' their patrimonies are large, their rents are small. I doubt if any of them has ever seen a map of his estate or exactly knows its boundaries ... In a country wherein there are no racehorses, licensed gambling-houses or expensive mistresses, a gentleman may live splendidly upon a moderate income ... Nor do they excite the envy of the poor by midnight orgies or gilded chariots. Their time is spent between their duty at Court and the social enjoyments of private parties. The fine arts ... are almost entirely neglected by the nobility of this country ... Their lives are an even tenor of domestic felicities, not remarkable for brilliant actions, and but rarely stained by vice ... they possess many amiable qualities. They are religious, temperate and generous, faithful to their friends, charitable to the distressed and warmly attached to their Sovereign; whose approbation, and a peaceful retirement, constitute the greatest happiness of their lives.[8]

Since Beckford could not defeat Walpole, he regretfully travelled on to Madrid at the end of November 1787. Here he was caught up in a whirl of gaiety in aristocratic and diplomatic circles and fell into an ever more confused state. He became simultaneously entangled with an older married woman, a young married girl and a twelve-year-old Mahometan boy—a repetition of his dilemma during his honeymoon. Here too his social position was unique and unbearable: unlike other foreigners of private station and no rank, he had the entry to some of the first palaces in the capital, but his ambassador refused to present him at Court. Once more, against his will, he was plunged into a "Walpolian contest"; once more he left defeated (in June 1788), after creating havoc with the hearts of both sexes.

He did not return to Lisbon until November 1793, but then he stayed nearly two years. We do not know much of interest about this stay except for his presentation at Court, the renting of Monserrate (outside Sintra), and the tour of the monasteries of Alcobaça and Batalha in June 1794, of which he kept a journal, expanded forty years later into the book Recollections of an Excursion to the Monasteries of Alcobaça and Batalha.[9] It was not realised that this Journal had been written, and had survived, until Beckford's biographer, Professor Guy Chapman, discovered two of its pages, written on the torn-off boards of books or notebooks. I have discovered another twelve manuscript pages in the Hamilton Papers, which may complete it.

In October 1795 he set sail for Naples from Lisbon, but his ship was intercepted by a Barbary privateer and had to flee to the safety of Alicante on the Spanish coast. He then spent two days touring the Royal Palace and grounds of Aranjuez, jotting down his impressions in a green pocket-book, and published them, practically without alteration, thirty-nine years afterwards as Letters 17 and 18 of Spain. Later he returned overland to England, which he reached in June 1796. Dom João, the Regent of Portugal, had entrusted him with some kind of diplomatic mission, but the English Cabinet, which contained his old enemies Pitt and Loughborough (now Lord Chancellor and first Earl of Rosslyn), would not listen to him. From time to time he passed on the Cabinet's views to the Portuguese Regent, probably through Marialva, and these two may have wanted him to be made British Ambassador in Lisbon. He arrived there for the third and last time in October 1798, after his mother's death, and stayed until about July 1799. Next to nothing is known of this visit.

Except for comparatively short trips to France and one to Switzerland, he remained in England, first at Fonthill and, after its sale in 1822, in Bath, where he died in 1844. Over a period of many years, with James Wyatt as architect, he built an immense pseudo-Gothic abbey at Fonthill, where he moved when in 1807 he pulled down his father's eighteenth-century classical mansion by the lake. Here he formed fabulous collections of books, pictures and *objets d'art*. His expenditure on collecting and the steady depreciation of sugar and of his Jamaican property obliged him to offer his estate (with some of its contents) for sale by Christie in 1822. People flocked to see and to buy. But shortly before the promised auction, the house and grounds with some of the contents were sold privately for £330,000 to Farquhar, a self-made millionaire. The tower collapsed in 1825, and Farquhar, disgusted with his unsuccessful speculation, sold the ruins and its grounds next year. At Fonthill Beckford lived like a recluse, except for the visits of his family. One of his principal consolations was writing in Italian almost every day (and sometimes a "3rd Edition" in one day) to his most intimate friend, the Chevalier Gregorio Franchi, whom he had met as a choir-boy in the Patriarchal Cathedral at Lisbon in 1787. Franchi was for many years his general factotum and his chief agent for the purchase of pictures and antiques, so this correspondence covers every aspect of life at Fonthill between 1807 and 1819.

Besides his building, gardening, planting, collecting and scribbling at Fonthill and Bath, and his friendship with Franchi, almost his only pleasure came from his younger daughter Susan, who in 1810 had very properly married the tenth Duke of Hamilton, her father's junior by seven years. Her elder sister Margaret made a runaway marriage with Colonel Orde, a relatively poor man without great prospects. She was cut off without a penny, and her father's property devolved upon the Hamiltons. We owe to them the careful preservation of Beckford's papers, which lay unexamined in their ducal vaults until this century.

BOYD ALEXANDER
1954

1.   Beckford published this book, with alterations, in 1834 as Vol. I of *Italy; with Sketches of Spain and Portugal.* The Iberian sections are hereafter referred to as *Spain* and *Portugal.*

2.   Lady Margaret Beckford to Lady Gower, Fonthill, 22 November 1784: "I was not to abandon a man who had always behaved to me with the greatest tenderness and affection. The satisfaction I feel at having acted in the manner I did, is not to be expressed; I every hour see fresh proofs of gratitude and affection from my dear husband." (*Granville Papers* in Public Record Office). She asks her aunt to show that she does "not believe the half of what has been said" against Beckford, and wants to tell her about Lord Loughborough's behaviour, and how much to blame her own brother has been in the affair.

3.   *H.P.* draft to Lady Craven, n.d., but *c.* 1790: quoted (not quite correctly) in Oliver's *Life of William Beckford,* 1932, p. 258.

4.   *H.P.,* fair copy of undated draft letter to Wildman, Falmouth, March 1787.

5.   The entry for Friday June 8 suggests that it was through Beckford's devotion (real or assumed) to St. Anthony and the Mass, which might have brought him into contact with the old Abbé Xavier and so with the devout Marialvas. For Beckford writes of Xavier: "It was he who first pointed me out to them [the Marialvas] in the most glowing colours, and who may be said to have sown the seeds of an attachment now springing up so vigorously."

6.   Walpole's despatch of 27 September 1788. (In Public Record Office).

7.   On Monday October 22 Beckford wrote: "[Marialva] told me in the strictest confidence that the Queen had thoughts of retiring from government, that she was worn out with the intrigues of the Court and sick of her existence."

8.   James Murphy, *Travels in Portugal in the years 1789 and 1790*, pp. 197–9.

9.   A few details of this stay and of his last one are contained in Portuguese documents collected in *Lisboa de Outrora* by J. Pinto de Carvalho, edited by G. de Matos Sequeria and L. de Macedo, Lisbon, 1938: Vol. I, article on Beckford.

NOTE ON THE MANUSCRIPT

The manuscript of the Journal, all in Beckford's hand, consists of:

(a) For the most part, quarto sheets of two leaves (except when one leaf has been torn off). Occasionally other pieces of paper have been used, for example, the backs of Marialva's letters received in Madrid. The Journal actually begins on the last page of a quarto sheet which is otherwise filled with a fair but unfinished copy of a letter by Beckford from Fonthill dated "28 Février 1785".
(b) Preliminary jottings on two foolscap sheets.
(c) A green pocket-book.

One of the foolscap sheets, used in Madrid, has preliminary jottings for the dates Monday 24 to Friday 28 December 1787, and Wednesday 2 to Saturday 12 January 1788, none of which Beckford had time to write up later. The other sheet[1] has three jottings which Beckford did not afterwards write up (Saturday July 28, Thursday August 2, and an undated entry beginning "Lisbon feels hot and fusty"), and thirteen jottings for Monday July 9 to Saturday July 21 inclusive, which Beckford afterwards wrote up more fully in his Journal. To lessen production costs, these preliminary jottings have not been printed, except in the few instances where they contain worthwhile details which Beckford did not include in his Journal, and then I have given them in footnotes. There is no serious difference between these jottings and the corresponding Journal entries. From the existence of this one foolscap sheet of preliminary jottings which were afterwards written up, we cannot assume that there were other similar jottings, now lost or destroyed, which covered other dates.[2] On the contrary, the fact that Beckford, an inveterate preserver of scraps (even when compromising or rubbishy), kept this sheet suggests that that there were no others; we may conclude that he did not normally make preliminary jottings, and that they are a sign of his being rushed.

The green pocket-book is one of the most interesting items in the whole vast mass of the Beckford Papers. He carried it about on his person in Switzerland, France, Portugal and Spain between 1778 and 1795, and jotted in it on the spot, in pencil or ink, his impressions and Journal entries—it contains one of his earliest attempts to keep a diary. As we might expect, the jottings in this notebook for 1787–8 were made during special expeditions, those to Mafra,[3] the Cork Convent, Pedra de Alvidrar and the Escorial. It will be noticed that the entry Tuesday 11– Wednesday 12 December simply runs "In the Book." The green pocket-book has many pages torn out, which may have contained these two entries; if not, there was another notebook. Fortunately, Beckford's *Spain* prints as Letter 6 an entry for each of these dates and the text there may be that of the original entries.

Although we cannot be certain, I do not think that much of the Journal has been lost or destroyed. The first obvious gap is at the undated entry (about Tuesday July 31) which begins in mid-sentence ("regions of chalk and pasture, where I may sleep") at the top of the first leaf of a quarto sheet. This loss corresponds with a break in the keeping of the Journal caused by Beckford's return for a few days from Sintra to Lisbon in hot weather. The written-up entries stop after July 27 and begin again on August 3 (there are jottings for July 28 and August 2). Accordingly, Beckford inscribed his paper cover for later entries: "P[ortuguese] J[ournal]. From Augst the 3d: [1787 added later] to Augst the 30th." He then found a further entry or entries (which obviously included the whole or part of the above undated, incomplete entry); so he altered the cover inscription from "August the 3d:" to "Tuesday July 31st." This does not help us to date our entry exactly, since we cannot assume that it was the only one which he found. But it does show that there was some break in the keeping of the Journal at the end of July and beginning of August; it is therefore reasonable to assume that little of the manuscript is missing at this point.

The next break in the Journal is from September 10 to 20 inclusive. But since Friday September 21 begins at the top of the first leaf of a quarto sheet, there is no evidence that previous entries were made and lost. The second ascertainable loss of a manuscript page is at the undated fragmentary entry "I could make nothing of my voice" written at the top of the first leaf of a quarto sheet, and immediately followed on the same leaf by the entry for Sunday November 18. The previous entry was for Monday November 12, which, together with several of the earlier entries, was hastily scrawled in a tiny hand in every available corner of a quarto sheet of two leaves (already filled with earlier entries). At this time Beckford was evidently hurried or tired, and not much of the manuscript is likely to be missing.

The third place where a page is missing corresponds with Beckford's journey from Lisbon to Madrid. Beckford wrote on the cover of this section "From Wednesday Novr. 28 to Sunday Decr. 16th, 1787." But there is only one quarto sheet of four completed pages with entries for December 10–14 inclusive; the entry for December 10 begins in mid-sentence "heavy sands,"[4] at the top left corner of the first leaf. This fragmentary entry corresponds word for word with Letter 5 of *Spain*, so the missing parts of the Journal may have approximated more or less to Letters 1–5 of *Spain*. Professor Guy Chapman[5] gives a short extract from a supposed entry for Sunday December 16; but it is not in the manuscript of the Journal, nor can I find it elsewhere in the papers. In short, there are three points at which portions of the manuscript are missing, but one may be supplied from *Spain*, and the other two may represent only an entry or so each.

In transcribing the manuscript, there are two pitfalls: Beckford's alterations and erasures, and his later additions which were often written on blank spaces in the original quarto sheets and incorporated in the Journal before he became an old man. The latter are easily detected, but it is difficult to be sure when they were written; since they seem to be genuine accounts of events (however late their composition), they have been retained,[6] but this occasionally leads to discrepancies. The entry for the Cork Convent expedition on September 9 is an example: the last paragraph contradicts the first because it was added later, when Beckford was unwilling to describe his disappointment with Dom Pedro (and hence his attachment to him). But such discrepancies have no bearing on the truthfulness of entries made at the time. There are twelve additions, three of which are single paragraphs added at the end of the original entry (September 9, October 31, and November 4). Of the eight additions which form complete entries, all but two (November 23 and 24) can be compared with original preliminary jottings, three of which I have printed in the text or in footnotes.[7] I have excluded all the additions, mostly in the Spanish section, made towards the end of Beckford's life.

Beckford's alterations and erasures over a period of years make it difficult in places to restore the original (which is my aim), for it is hard to be sure which were made at the time and which later, when he was considering publishing extracts in letter form (an idea he may have had from the beginning). From the point of view of scholarship, at least two alternative versions of some much cut-about passages might be given, so as to include the version as it stands and the earliest supposed version as far as it can be reconstructed. But this would involve a paraphernalia of critical apparatus objectionable to the general reader (for whom this text has been prepared), and so has been avoided. The only alternative has been to try to reconstruct the original version. Beckford sometimes wrote in an alternative phrase or sentence and deleted neither variant; his alternative is usually more stilted and literary. I have not troubled the reader with it,[8] the number of footnotes being already too great. For largely literary reasons Beckford often changed a word or phrase as he was writing, and at the same time deleted what he had first put. Occasionally the original phrase adds something to his description or makes the text clearer; in these few cases I have taken the liberty of adding his earliest but deleted phrase (where I could read it) to the text in square brackets. To give two examples: at the opening of July 22 I have restored *Went to Sintra* in order to avoid adding a footnote to elucidate the text; in the description of Monsignor Acciaioli on July 26 I have restored the adjective *round*, which is so descriptive. There is another type of alteration by Beckford: occasionally he wrote something which would have been best not committed to paper; he subsequently deleted it heavily. I have tried to restore such phrases, but I have not used a square bracket. For example, on August 19 Beckford wrote *I loaded Franchi with childish caresses and* (followed by a line too heavily deleted to be legible). Almost certainly at the time, Beckford erased *I loaded*, and inserted *kept loading me* after *Franchi*. I have ignored Beckford's alteration. I have only noted his undecipherable deletions where I thought it worth doing so without increasing the footnotes too much: even where deletions are very heavy, it cannot be assumed that they conceal something unusual.

For the sake of the general reader, I have re-paragraphed, re-punctuated, expanded abbreviations where necessary,[9] and I have normally given modern and correct spelling, especially of proper names. The grandees had long strings of Christian and family names, but in the footnotes I have usually cut them down to the minimum. Beckford's dating of entries has been standardised to cardinal numbers of the month.

It only remains to compare the Journal with the corresponding section of the travel-book *Italy; with sketches of Spain and Portugal*, which Beckford published in 1834, at the age of seventy-four, nearly forty-seven years later. This book is a carefully edited series of extracts from the Journal, cast into letter form and excluding almost everything personal and the leading themes and plot; it also contains fresh material. When he came to publish, Beckford was in a difficult situation; he had never given up hope of being re-admitted to society and of acquiring the peerage so nearly won in 1784; he was also the father-in-law of a Duke, to whose family he was genuinely devoted, despite moments of explosive exasperation. It was therefore essential for him to suppress all reference to his invidious position abroad and to his contest with Walpole, and perhaps also to conceal his sympathy for Roman Catholicism.

If he had been content with this negative policy of suppression, his reputation for truthfulness would not have suffered so much. But having been ostracised by the rulers of England, he attempted to show in his book that he had been welcomed by those of Portugal. This is the purpose of most of the new material in Portugal, of which no early manuscript versions exist, namely his presence at the rehearsal of a Royal Council (Letter 21); his dinner with the Archbishop-Confessor (Letter 27); his last affecting interview with him (Letter 33, which should be compared with Monday October 8); and his interview with the Prince of Brazil (Letter 31 dated October 19). The latter was not improbable, for the Journal shows that the Prince was anxious to see Beckford and took his side (June 23 and October 17), and that Beckford was on familiar terms with Colonel Luis de Miranda Henriques, who was one of the Prince's intimates and who in Portugal is said to have arranged the meeting. But in view of the other additions in the book about the Archbishop, and since the meeting with the Prince is not mentioned in the Journal, its occurrence is questionable. Incidentally, the Journal for October 19 does, like the letter, mention a ride in the Colares neighbourhood, but makes no closer reference. The dates given in the printed letters are often quite arbitrary, being sometimes altered and arranged for literary convenience, so that we are not confined to October 19 in our search for this incident in the Journal.

The same problem arises over the alleged interview on Monday December 24 with the Spanish Infante Gabriel and his Portuguese wife (Letter 13 of *Spain*). There is nothing inherently improbable in it, since it could have been arranged through either of Beckford's friends—Marialva's cousin the Portuguese ambassador, or Prince Masserano, Captain of the Flemish troop of the Royal Bodyguard, who had an apartment in the Royal Palace; Marialva might even have written to his cousin to arrange it. As to its occurrence on December 24, the Journal does not help, since the first entry for that day is a preliminary jotting (and therefore cannot necessarily be expected to mention it), and the written-up entry was unfinished. Most of the other fresh material in Spain (which Beckford incorporated in his Journal in his old age) represents what probably took place, but was not written down at the time because Beckford was too busy and was bored with his diary; for example, he never finished his original account of his trip to the Escorial (Thursday December 20 and Letters 10 and 11), and did not have time to describe the sinister Count Beust (Letter 14) or to descant at great length upon Pacheco's party (Saturday December 29 and Letter 12).

There is one large item at the beginning of Portugal which is not in the Journal—the first six letters, written from Falmouth while he was waiting to sail to Lisbon. In manuscript they are original copies of letters written (or purporting to be written) to various people—his mother, his half-sister Mrs. Hervey, his former tutor Lettice, and his agent Wildman. There are one or two Falmouth jottings in journal form, made at random and usually undated. Then two months and ten days elapsed before the Journal at Lisbon suddenly began; it would spoil its unity to include these earlier scraps.

In *Portugal* there is one characteristic alteration of detail which has troubled the critics and made them question Beckford's veracity. In Letter 30 (dated November 8) he describes how his dining-table was graced by the poet Bocage, who at that date may have been in Goa and was probably not on speaking terms with its former Viceroy, Sousa, another supposed guest. The entry for Monday October 29 resolves all these difficulties. The appreciative bard was not Bocage, but the lesser-known Caldas; moreover, Beckford met the Viceroy on another occasion (November 18): the two accounts were strung together in the book for literary convenience and effect. The falsifications in the book do not affect the trustworthiness of the Journal.

This brings us to Beckford's treatment of passages in the Journal which he extracted for his book. Sometimes he reproduces the whole, or almost all, of an entry to form one Letter, and the style may or may not be polished up (compare the Corpus Christi procession on June 7 and in Letter 10). Sometimes the same incident is used, but there is little similarity in the two accounts (compare the breakfast with the Penalvas on June 6 and in Letter 17). Sometimes the narrative has to be compressed in the book and all sorts of touches are omitted (compare the visit to the Carthusian monastery on June 21 and in Letter 13). Sometimes a scissors-and-paste method is used, events and phrases being gathered into one letter from different entries. For example, Letter 14 strings together in a continuous and false narrative, with alterations of detail, calls by Pombal (June 30), Teles (June 6), Almeida and Aguilar (June 16); the invitation from the nuns of the Sacrament (June 14); the visit to the theatre (undated entry about July 31) and to the Lacerdas (July 19); the Archbishop's career (July 4), and Vila Nova's religious mania (July 18). The loss of vivid detail that sometimes occurs in the book may be illustrated at random by comparing the passages which open the account of Gildemeester's unfortunate dinner party on July 25 (Letter 20):

JOURNAL

Grand gala at Court, and the Marquis gone to attend it, for this blessed day not only gave birth to Gildemeester but to the Princess of Brazil. I felt aguish shiverings after breakfast, and basked in the sun. M. Verdeil has had the kindness to uncripple me by paring away my cursed corn in a workmanlike manner. We went to dine with the Marchioness. I never saw D. Pedro appear to such advantage. He begins to grow childish and engaging. A band of regimental music on the march to Gildemeester's began playing in the court, and drew forth a swarm of servants. D. Henriqueta and I sat on the steps which lead up to the great pavilion. She bent gracefully forwards talking to one of her favourite attendants. The children sat at our feet playing with some flowers I had gathered for them, and often looking up at my countenance with engaging fondness that recalled to my mind the sweet smiles of my own little ones, and brought tears into my eyes. etc.

BOOK

Grand gala at Court, and the Marquis gone to attend it, for this blessed day not only gave birth to Guildermeester but to the Princess of Brazil.

We went to dine with the Marchioness.

A band of regimental music on the march to Gildermeester's began playing in the court, and drew forth one of those curious swarms of all sexes, ages and colours which this beneficent family are so fond of harbouring. Donna Henriqueta was seated on the steps which led up to the great pavilion, whispering to some of her favourite attendants who, like the chorus in an ancient Greek tragedy, were continually giving their opinion of whatever was going forward.

1.   One side of which is also occupied by the words of a Portuguese song copied earlier for Beckford.

2.   Six other jottings were written on the usual quarto sheets (i.e. not on detached sheets) in the body of the Journal, and from them Beckford made much later compositions; see pp. 25–66. Two entries (for the Cork Convent and Escorial trips) in the green pocket-book, described below, are also preliminary jottings.

3.   Not in my text, because Beckford wrote it up; but the others are included.

4.   I have started the sentence in my text with the corresponding phrase from Letter 5 of *Spain* (for which book see p. 28).

5. *Beckford,* 1952, p. 221
6. They are all asterisked and printed under the following dates: September 9; October 3, 4, 20, 31; November 4, 5, 8, 23, 25 and 26.
7. The jottings for October 3 and 4 are not printed because the later version follows them very closely; the jotting for November 8 is not worth printing as well as its later version.
8. Unless it adds to the description, in which case I have sometimes included it. For example, in his description of Street Arriaga (Monday 11 June) Beckford added above *a ruddy countenance,* which I have included.
9. But I have contracted titles like Dom and Donna to "D.", as is usual.

ACKNOWLEDGMENTS

The transcription of this Journal for the first time from the original manuscript would not have been possible without the generosity of its owners, His Grace the Duke of Hamilton and Brandon, and Hamilton & Kinneil Estates Ltd., who placed it at my disposal over a long period of time. I cannot be too grateful to them and to His Grace's Curator, Miss Bruce Johnston, who has at all times given me the most sympathetic encouragement.

My next warmest thanks are due to Dr. Maurice Ettinghausen, of Messrs. A. Rosenthal of Oxford. He generously spent much time and effort in Lisbon, searching out rare books and illustrations not in the British Museum and making essential contacts for me; without his vital help in many directions I could not have assembled the large mass of material in my footnotes. I am also grateful to his friend, Senhor António de Aguiar. His Grace the late Duke of Alba, President of the Royal Spanish Academy of History, was wonderfully kind in clearing up points not ascertainable over here; in the matter of Spanish Voyages he was ably assisted by his colleague Capitan de Navío Julio Guillen, Director of the Naval Museum in Madrid, who took great trouble to go into those detailed questions.

I am also much indebted to Mr. Marcus Cheke of the Foreign Office, who spent much time in trying to answer some of my questions; to Mrs. Walter Kingsbury of Sintra, who helped me with the tangled problems of some of the Sintra properties; to Prof. Dr. Virginia Rau of Lisbon University, who lent me some indispensable books otherwise unobtainable; to the eminent Lisbon topographer, Dr. Gustavo de Matos Sequeira, who looked up the baptism registers of Loreto Church and several other points; to Prof. C.R. Boxer of London University, and to His Grace the Duke of Lafões, who sent me a photograph of the unrecorded portrait of the second Duchess, and who gave me other information.

I am most grateful to all those who helped me on one or more points, which often must have cost them much time and trouble—the Librarian of the Music Department of the Bibliothèque Nationale; Miss Bridgwater, Assistant Reference Librarian of Yale University Library; the Saxon State Archives at Dresden; Dr. Marchetti of the Biblioteca Nazionale, Rome; Mr. Neil MacLaren of the National Gallery; the Earl of Ilchester and Viscount Sandon; Mr. A.R. Walford, Secretary of the Lisbon branch of the Historical Association; Mrs. Hartcup; Dr. George West of the British Council; Mr. Graham Blandy of Madeira, and Dr. Cabral do Nascimento, Keeper of Archives at Funchal, Madeira.

My thanks are also due to Mr. Sacheverell Sitwell and Mr. Peter Quennell, who read my typescript at an early stage, and gave me much needed encouragement during my long-drawn-out task; to Viscount Bearsted, who, together with the National Trust, allowed me to photograph and reproduce the head and shoulders of Romney's portrait of Beckford; to the Deputy Keeper of the Public Record Office, who permitted me to quote from the unpublished despatches of our ambassadors Walpole and Listen, and from an unpublished letter in the Granville Papers. The kindness of all these persons, and others, added greatly to the pleasure of this work and was indispensable to it.

I also much appreciate the care which the publishers have taken over the production of this book.

B.A.

GLOSSARY
OF FOREIGN WORDS NOT EXPLAINED IN NOTES

Açafata	Lady of Queen's Wardrobe.
Aviso	(Usually) order signed by Secretary of State in Sovereign's name.
Bacalhao	Codfish.
Burra	She-ass.
Camareira-mor	Principal Lady of the Bedchamber.
Carrinho	Cabriolet.
Coração	Heart.
Corregedor	The chief civil magistrate in a city.
Criada	Servant.
Menino	Little boy.
Merenda	Collation.
Quinta	Country-house.
Scalera	Barque, galley, etc.
Seguidillas	Spanish dance with singing.
Tertulia	Evening party in private house.
Tirana	Song-dance popular in Andalusia.
Volterete	Card game, called in England *ombre*.

SIGNS AND ABBREVIATIONS

Almanacs	*Almanach para o anno de MDCCLXXXVI [etc.] Lisboa.*
H.P.	Hamilton Papers (Beckford Section).
< >	Editorial insertion. When there are no words inside, a word, or occasionally a phrase, is illegible in the manuscript.
[ ]	Editorial restoration of phrases erased by Beckford.
*	Additional passages written by Beckford much later.
(?)	Indicates that the reading of the preceding word is uncertain.

PORTUGUESE JOURNAL 1787

Lisbon, 25 May 1787

We drove in the evening as usual along the sea shore by the venerable arcades of the Convent of Belem.[1] The old Abbade Xavier[2] was upon the watch at the door of the Marialva Palace.[3] He invited us in to view the apartments and the manege where the Marquis[4] displays great feats of horsemanship. The rooms are meanly furnished with English coloured prints and indifferent drawings of saints and madonnas. The Marquis has a decided taste for clocks, compasses and timekeepers. I counted no less than ten in his bedchamber. Four or five were in full swing and made a sad hissing. I left them striking away, for it was exactly six o'clock, and followed my venerable conductor up and down half a dozen staircases and along several terraces into a large saloon hung with rusty red damask.

There I found D. Pedro di Marialva,[5] a young stripling not inelegantly made but disfigured by a preposterous pig-tail. He received me with great attention as the object of his dear Father's[6] peculiar predilection. Polycarpo,[7] the first tenor singer in the Queen's Chapel, was playing on a harpsichord placed in the middle of the room. The door of a dark apartment adjoining, being ajar, gave me a transient glimpse of D. Henriqueta,[8] D. Pedro's sister, advancing one moment and retiring the next, eager to approach and examine the exotic being she had probably heard so much of, but not daring to set her foot in the saloon on account of her mother's absence. She appeared to me a lovely girl with eyes full <of> youthful gaiety and a turn of shape remarkably graceful. But of what do I talk? I only saw her as in a dream: perhaps her charms might vanish in open daylight. My imagination, lighted up by this romantic apparition, inspired me to play and sing in a manner that surprised the whole herd of precentors, priests, musicians and fencing masters that were in waiting upon the heir of the Marialvas. He accompanied me along the loggias called verandas in Portugal, which command a tolerably fresh and shady view of a garden well watered and filled with fresh looking vegetables—not common objects in this sultry climate. Seeing in him a sort of unwillingness to quit me so soon, I pressed him to accompany us the rest of our drive, so he jumped into the coach. His slight knowledge of French prevented our conversation from becoming very interesting. The evening was glorious and a fresh breeze from the sea tempered the heat. Many vessels were in sight at the entrance of the harbour. We returned about 8 o'clock after landing D. Pedro at his Palace. I slept ill owing to the yowling and yelping of dogs and puppies. The sad idea of my sufferings this day twelvemonth[9] rushed into my mind and renewed all my agonies.

Saturday 26 May

Dreadfully hot. I attempted to write to my sister[10] but was obliged to leave off after scrawling two pages. About one o'clock arrived the old Abbé open-mouthed with stories of the Marialvas etc. etc. He stayed dinner and talked unmercifully. We set him down at the Marialva Palace and proceeded on our drive as usual. The view of the sea with the Tower of Belem rising out of it and the rich tints of a western sky in this climate still gives me pleasure; but I am very low and melancholy. No wonder, when I reflect upon what I lost the fatal 26 of May '86. As we drove by the Marialva Palace on our return, D. Pedro appeared on the veranda to make his bow to me. We stopped the coach. He coloured up to his eyes, I know not why, nor he neither perhaps. I found Polycarpo waiting for me, and sung from 8 till ten without ceasing, like a simpleton. I make myself ill by these proceedings.

Sunday 27 May

At nine, off in state to the Patriarchal.[11] Verdeil,[12] Bezerra[13] and that turkey poult Mr. Sill[14] with me. We mounted into the music gallery. Singers settled about me like flies upon sugar and yet I give them no encouragement. Polycarpo begged me to return tomorrow to hear one of the boys play,[15] marvellously as he pretends. Well, we shall see. The music of the mass indifferent, except two sublime motets of Jommelli,[16] worth going two leagues in the sun to hear. I was exalted into heaven whilst they were executing, and will certainly return tomorrow. Much staring at me as I went out and great demonstrations of respect etc. etc.

I dined at Horne's:[17] wretched messes neither English nor Portuguese, bad veal, neither ox nor cow but something between, both inexpressibly carrionish and flabby. D. José de Mateus,[18] Bezerra and Lousana composed the company. D. José may have good sense but has slow ideas and a still more drawling manner of expressing them. This climate does not agree with me, noise and heat would soon send me out of the world, and I fear both are to be apprehended at Lisbon where 30 or 40,000 dogs prowl all night long in the streets making themselves of use and importance by gobbling up all that falls from the windows. I have half a mind to sleep in peace and coolness at Sintra; but then the Patriarchal and Polycarpo's young friend——. I shall get into a scrape if I don't take care. How tired I am of keeping a mask on my countenance. How tight it sticks—it makes me sore. There's metaphor for you. I have all the fancies and levity of a child and would give an estate or two to skip about the galleries of the Patriarchal with the *menino* unobserved. D. Pedro is not child enough for me. I did not see him this evening on his veranda as we drove by the Marialva Palace as usual. <The> Miss Sills[19] were of the party. They think me rather inclined to fall in love with D. Henriqueta; so I am. Old Horne, who is a capital builder of airy castles, has already settled the whole plan, obtained the Quinta dos Bichos[20] from the Queen[21] for my residence, and has already fixed upon the contracts he shall ask for under my auspices. God knows what may happen! I am very anxious to learn how Lady Effingham[22] has conducted herself in the affair of procuring such recommendations for me to this Court as may confound that malevolent cuckold Walpole.[23] D. José <de> Mateus and Bezerra at tea. I played a little but felt ennuied and jaded.

Monday 28 May

Went to the Patriarchal but not in such state as yesterday. I am in better spirits, having slept tolerably and not heard so much yelping. The Patriarch officiated. I knelt near the altar with much devotion. My piety I believe caught the eyes of the high priest,[24] a good old man but a determined bigot I hear, and so orthodox that the Queen, who is clemency itself, would not trust him with the office of Grand Inquisitor lest his zeal might thin her kingdom, depopulated enough o' (?) my conscience. The same music of Jommelli was repeated and filled me with the same thrilling sensations. During sermon time I slipped away with Polycarpo and ran up a flight of wide easy steps at the top of which stood the *menino* who plays so well on the harpsichord. He took hold of Polycarpo's hand and seemed beside himself with joy at this opportunity of showing his talents. Several youths came around us. Only one was admitted into a tolerably neat room where the harpsichord was placed. The others applied their large eyes alternately to an aperture in the door, which was carefully closed and watched by a priest. The *menino* has surprising abilities and did ample justice to the glorious compositions of Haydn he played. I could have passed an hour agreeably in hearing of him and was in fact delighted; but rose up, after I had listened about a quarter of an hour, with dignity and apparent coldness. A weather-beaten, one-eyed architect Polycarpo presented to me conducted me back to my old station near the High Altar where I knelt out the remainder of the Mass with elevated eyes and hands crossed on my breast. I wish much to hear the *menino* again and will return tomorrow, please the Patriarch! Polycarpo in behalf of his disciple hinted that my pianofortes would set off his talents to greater advantage. I suppose he wants me to send for him. All in good time.

Horne and his family dined with me. Very stupid in the evening. I take airings as regular as an old Dowager. The Abbade as constantly lies in wait for me as I go by with some gossiping story or other of the Marialvas. Mr. Horne went to Seabra,[25] the quondam Secretary of State whom Pombal in a fit of jealousy banished to Angola, where he would have fallen a victim to the climate had not an old negro woman taken care of him. Seabra is much my friend and calls the Ministry here complete fools for being cowed out of shewing me attentions by such a blundering puppy as Walpole. He thinks the Marquis of Marialva has not managed my business well; nothing more likely. This Seabra is as subtle as the Old Serpent. I wish to see him. He is to pay me a visit as soon as the Packet arrives, whether it brings me credentials or no. I am sick of forming the chief subject of conversation at all the card tables, office Boards, and Counting Houses in Lisbon. It seems the Marquises of Angeja[26] <and> Lavradio[27] talked of little else but my concerns this evening with Seabra, who did not return from them till 8 o'clock. Horne, who went out at half past six, waited for him at his house with exemplary patience.

Tuesday 29 May

Thermometer at 72 at 8 o'clock in the morning. It will be at 82 or 86 in the middle of the day and reduced to 60 most probably at night and by sharp winds that raise clouds of dust and set dogs a-barking. I have been again to the Patriarchal, but was ill rewarded for my pains. The Patriarch being absent, Mass was performed in a most slovenly manner and the fine motets of Jommelli barbarously murdered. To add to my misfortunes the one-eyed architect prated to me incessantly in wretched French, and a succession of priests plied me with their snuff-boxes. I could not help taking a civil pinch or two and I have almost sneezed myself dead. I longed to have heard a little more tinkling on the harpsichord upstairs, and to have stretched my legs in those cool corridors I told you of the day before yesterday. But the fear of scandal kept me in prudent silence and gravity. I am at the last gasp with heat; no doubt these hot climates play the devil with me.

Mr. Horne is just come in to dinner and tells me there was a mighty banquet yesterday at the Duke de Lafões':[28] 50 or 60 covers, all the Ministers etc. etc. I dare say Mr. Walpole rejoiced not a little in the idea of having put me out of the way of being present at these festivals. The duration of his triumph depends upon the wind I hope, and must cease with the arrival of the Packet, unless my relations and friends are more impotent and slothful than ever I imagine. Mr. North[29] was at the Duke's and the young Marialva with his uncle, the Grand Prior.[30]

After dinner I sat in the veranda talking over the Patriarchal with M. Verdeil and enjoying the fresh breeze that played very agreeably amongst the vine leaves of our little garden. At half past six we drove according to custom along the shore of Belem. The old walls of the convent reflect intolerable heat. Aloes which spring from the sands on the sea shore begin shooting up into flower. They have a stiff formidable appearance. Three or four withered beldames were hanging out bibs and muckenders[31] on the leaves of these gigantic vegetables. To vary our airing we struck out of the common track and visited the convent of S. José de Ribamar.[32] The building is irregular and picturesque, rising from a craggy eminence and backed by a thick wood of elm, bay and *arbor judea*. We were shewn by simple, smiling friars into a small court with cloisters supported by low Tuscan columns. A fountain playing in the middle and sprinkling a profusion of gillyflowers gave an oriental air to this little court that pleased me exceedingly. The friars seem sensible of its merits, for they keep it tolerably clean. Not so their garden. Bindweed and dwarf aloes almost prevented my getting across it in my way to the wood, a delicious place, the refuge and comfort of half the birds in the country. The trees, though bent by the winds into very grotesque shapes, still retain a luxuriance of foliage very seldom to be met with in the neighbourhood of Lisbon. Thanks to monkish laziness the underwood remains unclipped and intrudes wherever it pleases upon the alleys, which hang over the sea in a bold romantic manner. I looked down the steep on the smoothest beach imaginable. The waves, impelled by a cool wind, broke softly on the shore. How I should enjoy stretching myself on its sands by moonlight and owning all my frailties and wild imaginations to some love-sick languid youth reclined by my side and thrown by the dubious light and undecided murmurs into a soft delirium. Alas, will my youth pass away without my feeling myself once more tremblingly alive to these exquisite though childish sensations?

The friars would show me their flower garden, and a very pleasant terrace it is, neatly paved with chequered tiles interspersed with knots of carnations in a style I should conjecture as ancient as the dominion of the Moors in Portugal. Espaliers of citron and orange cover the walls and have almost got the better of some glaring shell work with which a reverend Father ten or twelve years ago was so idle as to encrust them. Shining beads, china plates and saucers turned inside out compose the chief ornaments of this decoration. I observed the same propensity to shell work and broken china in a Mr. Devisme,[33] whose garden at Bemfica about a league from Lisbon eclipses all the glories of Bagnigge Wells, White Conduit House and Marylebone in leaden statues, Chinese temples, serpentine rivers and dusty hermitages. We got home late. In our way back I had almost forgotten to tell you we met the Abbade with a nosegay and some new stories about the Marialvas ready cut and dried for me. He told me about D. Pedro and his uncle's intending to come and see me etc. and a deal more I but half understood—he mumbles so. At ninety-two however I shall be mighty well contented to speak as intelligibly.

Wednesday 30 May

I was awakened in the night by a horrid cry of dogs; not that infernal pack, which Dryden tells us in his divine tale of Theodore and Honoria[34] went regularly a-ghost hunting every Friday, could yowl more dreadfully. I wished them at hell for breaking my dreams which were very agreeable. Methought I was walking with William Courtenay[35] on the declivity of green hills scattered over with orange trees in blossom. Our eyes were bathed in tears of affection and forgiveness, our hands were joined, and we seemed to have entirely forgotten the miseries we had occasioned each other. If I believed in presentiments I should expect good news by the Packet. My spirits were lighter than usual this morning. I had strength to support the continual talk, talk, talk of the Abbade who came to dinner and announced the visit of the Grand Prior of the Order of Aviz, a natural brother of the old Marquis of Marialva. He arrived at six, a good portly prelate-like figure, very cheerful and cordial. I like him extremely. He told me that in the province of Minho about sixty leagues off there were vast green pastures enclosed with hedges and rows of lofty trees, verdant hillocks—such as I dreamt about perhaps—and copses of flowering shrubs. O the blessed region! Would to Heaven I was creeping about it under the shade of luxuriant sweet-scented broom, rills gushing around me, and the leaves of fullblown wild roses floating down the rippling waters. Are not these rare fresh pastoral ideas of a hot dusty day? Such imaginations cool me a little. The Grand Prior would have stayed chatting with me till night had not the Abbade hinted to him that I never missed taking what air there was every evening. This was a great joy to Horne who wanted to be moving.

He persuaded me much against my will to go to the Gardens <of> Palhava,[36] the residence of John the Fifth's bastards, instead of following my usual track by the sea shore. I never will be so taken in again. I was jolted and heated and put out of humour. The roads to this blessed garden are abominable and more infested by beggars, flies, dogs and mosquitoes than any I am acquainted with. The Palace Palhava which belongs to the Marquis of Lourical, now Ambassador at Madrid, is placed in a hollow, and the tufted groves which surround it admit not a breath of air; so I was half suffocated the moment I entered their shade. A great, flat space before the garden front of the villa is laid out in dismal labyrinths of clipped myrtle hedges, with lofty pyramids rising from them, and reminded me of that vile Dutch maze planted by King William at Kensington and rooted up 10 or 12 years ago by King George the Third. Beyond this puzzling-ground are several long alleys of stiff dark verdure, called *ruas*, i.e. literally streets, with great propriety, being more close, more formal and not less dusty than High Holborn. I deviated from them into plats of well-watered vegetables and aromatic herbs, enclosed by neat fences of cane, covered with an embroidery of the freshest and most perfect roses, quite free from insects and cankers, worthy to have strewn the couches and graced the bosom of Lais, Aspasia or Lady Craven.[37] You know how every mortal of taste delights in these lovely flowers; how frequently and in what harmonious numbers Ariosto has celebrated them. Has not Lady Craven a whole apartment painted over with roses? Does she not fill her bath with their leaves, and deck her idols with garlands of no other flowers? And is she not quite in the right of it? The perfume of roses affects me too, poor childish animal, more than I can express. I could hang over them for hours, and find out every instance some new charm in their form, in their colour, in their fragrance.

Whilst I was poetically engaged with the roses, Horne entered into conversation with a sort of Anglo-Portuguese Master of the Horse to their Bastard Highnesses. I took an aversion to this fellow the moment I came up to him. He had a snug well-powdered wig, a bright silver sword, a crimson full-dress suit, and a gently bulging paunch. With one hand in his bosom and the other in the act of <taking> snuff, he harangued copiously on the temperance, holiness and chastity of his august masters, who live sequestered from the world in dingy silent state, abhor profane company, and never cast a look upon females. Being curious to see the abode of these royal sober personages, I entered the Palace. Not an insect stirred, not a whisper was audible in the principal apartments which consist in a suite of lofty coved saloons, nobly proportioned, and uniformly hung with damask of the deepest crimson. The upper end of each room is distinguished by a ponderous canopy of cut velvet. To the right and left appear rows of huge elbow-chairs of the same materials. No glasses, no pictures, no gilding, no decoration but heavy drapery; even the tables are concealed by cut velvet flounces, in the style of those with which our dowagers used formerly to array their toilets. The very sight of such close tables is enough to make one perspire, and I cannot imagine what demon prompted the Portuguese to invent such a fusty fashion, hideous everywhere, but peculiarly so in a climate as sultry as their own. This taste for putting commodes and tables into petticoats is pretty general, at least in royal apartments. At Queluz[38] not a card or dining table has escaped, and many an old court dress, I should suspect, has been cut up to furnish these accoutrements, which are of all colours, plain and flowered, pastorally sprigged or gorgeously embroidered. Not so at Palhava. Crimson alone prevails, and casts its royal gloom unrivalled upon every object. Stuck fast to the wall, between two of the aforementioned tables, are two fauteuils for their Highnesses; and opposite, a rank of chairs for those reverend fathers in God who from time to time are honoured with admittance.

How mighty is the force of education! What pains, what application it must require on the part of nurses, equerries and chamberlains to stifle every lively and generous sensation in the princelings they educate, to break a human being into the habits of impotent royalty! Dignity without power is the heaviest of burdens. A sovereign may always employ himself; he has the choice of good or evil; but princes like these of Palhava, without credit or influence, who have nothing to feed on but imaginary greatness, must yawn their souls out, and become in process of time as formal and inanimate as the evergreen pyramids of stunted myrtle in their gardens.

Happier were those babies King John did not think proper to recognize, and they are not few in number, for that pious monarch

> Wide as his command,
> Scattered his Maker's image through the land.[39]

They perhaps, whilst their brothers are gaping under rusty canopies, tinkle their guitars in careless moonlight rambles, wriggle in gay fandangos, or enjoy sound sleep, rural fare, and merriment in the character of jolly village curates.

I was glad to get out of the Palace; its stillness and gloom sunk my spirits, and a confined air impregnated with the smell of burnt lavender almost made me sick. I am just returned gasping for air. I told Miss Sill she might as well be in bed with a warming-pan as in a Portuguese cabriolet with her uncle Horne. He carries a noble belly, set off in this season with a satin waistcoat richly spangled. I must go to Sintra or I shall expire.

Thursday 31 May

'Tis in vain I call upon clouds to cover me and fogs to wrap me up: the sun glares fiercer and fiercer every hour. I cannot get to Sintra till to-morrow. There is such a fuss when I move, so much packing and carting, such a to-do with cooks and maîtres d'hôtel and the Lord knows who. What a fool I am to suffer all these conveniences. M. Verdeil has been reading to me his description of our miseries at sea, our joy at first sight of the Rock,[40] and our adventures with a string of jackanapes that hopped on board to scrutinise the ships upon our first entering the Tagus.[41] I laughed heartily. The one-eyed architect came this morning. He turns out a complete bore. Instead of admiring the elegant form and antique ornaments of the furniture I brought with me from England, he pointed all his applause at the gilding and varnishing. I never was more tired of a man in my life.

10 o'clock p.m. My prayers are heard. It is grown cooler, the wind is changed and I shall be saved the trouble of going to Sintra. Till it rains I have no great desire for scaling rocks and brushing out clouds of dust from shrubberies half withered. Horne and his family dined here as usual. I continue much satisfied with the eldest Miss Sill. She has an excellent heart and a clear judgment with infinitely more taste and imagination than falls in general to the share of prudent, reasonable personages. We did not stir out till half past six. The shore of Belem—for we returned to our old drive—appeared in all its evening glory—the sky diversified by streaming clouds of purple edged with gold, and innumerable vessels of various sizes shooting along the Tagus. The sea at the entrance of the harbour seemed in violent agitation, all froth and foam. We prolonged our drive as far as the Convent of Ribamar and were fanned by refreshing breezes which I hope will bring in the Packet. The Abbade stopped us upon our return to deliver me a most affectionate letter from the Marquis of Marialva. Are not you tired of hearing of the Abbade? I have more patience than you. The Marquis comes on in his French—his last epistle is very tolerable both as to style and grammar. Where will all this corresponding end, this lively friendship so suddenly conceived and so rapidly grown up to perfection? D. Pedro did not make his appearance on the veranda. The poor boy is most strictly confined and educated. He has but a slender frame and they work him to death at the rate of 8 or 9 lessons a day. Instead of encouraging him to row upon the river, play at cricket or run about the garden with children of his own age, he is cooped up with a herd of toothless duennas and superannuated chaplains, equally narrowing his mind by their threats and their praises. It would be curious to overhear the evening conversation of such <a> group when D. Pedro is allowed to unbend his mind by listening to their gossipings.

Friday 1 June

A total change has taken place in the atmosphere. The sun is concealed and the horizon darkened by distant storms. If they would but approach and wash the dust off the thick laurels in the Quinta dos Bichos what a pleasant walk I should take there this evening. A clumsy handed fellow of a Portuguese with ghastly clockwork eyes is tuning or rather bedevilling my pianofortes. There was another a few days ago who had also a touch at them. Ten to one but the instruments, like D. Pedro, will be rendered good for nothing by too much mending. I am writing in answer to the Marquis' letter and falling foul of Mr. Walpole and other diplomatic coxcombs with a vengeance.

Old Horne, who has a colt's tooth, entreated me to walk in the Botanic Garden[42] where in general are to be found certain youthful animals of the female gender called *açafatas* in Portuguese, of a species between a bedchamber woman and a maid of honour. The Queen has kindly taken the ugliest with her to the Caldas.[43] These that remain have large black eyes sparkling with the true spirit of adventure, a vast flow of dark hair, softer than it looks—for I fingered it by chance an hour ago—and pouting lips of the colour and size of full-blown roses. All this, you will say, does not compose a perfect beauty; certainly not, I never meant to give you that idea. I only wish you to understand that the nymphs we have just quitted are the flowers of the Queen's flock and that she has four or five dozen more at least in attendance on her sacred person with larger mouths, smaller eyes, coarser hair and swarthier complexions. I felt much out of sorts this evening and had not spirits to jabber Portuguese. My conversation was chiefly addressed to a lovely blue-eyed Irish girl of fifteen, lately married to a Portuguese officer. Spouse goes a-pilgrimaging to Nossa Senhora do Cabo;[44] little madam whisks about the Botanic Garden with the *açafatas* and a troupe of sopranos who teach her to warble, speak Italian etc. She is well worth their pains: her hair of the loveliest auburn, her straight grecian eyebrows and fair complexion form a striking contrast to the gypsy-coloured skins and jetty tresses of her companions. She looked like a visionary being skimming along the alleys and leaving the potbellied sopranos and dowdy *açafatas* far behind, wondering at her lightness.

The Garden is pleasant enough, situated on an eminence, planted with planes, acacias, catalpas and other light-green trees clustered with flowers. Above the tops of these airy groves rises a broad, majestic terrace, with marble balustrades of shining whiteness. They design wretchedly in this country, but execute with great neatness and precision. I never saw balustrades better hewn or chiselled than those bordering the stairs which lead up from the wood to the terrace. Its ample surface is laid out in oblong compartments of marble containing no very great variety of vanillas, aloes, geraniums, China roses and the commonest plants of our greenhouses. Such ponderous divisions have a dismal effect. They give this part of the garden the air of a place of interment, and it struck me as if the deceased inhabitants of the adjoining palace were sprouting up in the shape of prickly pears, Indian figs, gaudy holly-oaks and peppery capsicums. The terrace has about fifteen hundred paces in length. Three large basins of clear water give it an air of coolness, much increased by the waving of planes and acacias exposed by their lofty situation to every breeze which blows from the entrance of the Tagus. The azure of the sea and river appears to great advantage between the quivering foliage.

The Irish girl and your humble servant coursed each other like children along the terrace and when tired reposed under a group of gigantic Brazilian aloes and palmettos by one of the basins. The swarthy party detached one of its guardians, a priest, to observe all the motions and resting of us white people. This Argus, a gawky young man whose complexion might suit the taste of a lascar or a Hottentot, cut a mighty foolish figure whilst prying into our looks and attitudes. Our language luckily was beyond his comprehension, but I daresay he saw by our countenances that we wished him in a ducking-stool for his intrusion. The sun set before I took my departure. Black eyes and blue eyes seem horridly jealous of each other. I fear the Irish girl will suffer for having more alertness than the *açafatas*. She will be pinched if I <am> not mistaken as the party return through the dark passages which join the Palace of the Ajuda to the garden. I don't like the thought of leaving such a fair little being in the hands of fiery Portuguese females, so much her inferiors in complexion and delicacy. They will take special care, I warrant them, to fill the husband's head with suspicions less charitable than those inspired by Nossa Senhora do Cabo.

The Abbade and D. Pedro will think me lost: not one of the family has heard or seen anything of me today. D. José de Mateus and Bezerra came in with the tea. Bezerra, who posted home from Sintra at two o'clock in the morning with his black hair frizzling over his ears and his eyes like coals of fire, bounces about like a cracker. He is a most squibbish being and I could really blow him into the air at any time with some of my desperate Arabian stories. I must not give him a sight of *Barkiarokh*[45] lest he should go quite mad. *Vathek* has more than half done his business. D. José—though much his friend—laughs in his sleeve at such extravagancies. These two men form a perfect contrast and yet they are continually together.

Saturday 2 June

The dogs spared me and it was tolerably cool, so I am better this morning and should like another race with the Irish girl or the *meninos* at the Patriarchal, whichever would most please Providence. I am resigned to whatever I meet with. Silly dreams last night: I was dancing a jig with Mary Queen of Portugal and had got a monstrous toupee fringed with small saletting. I have finished my epistle for the Caldas[46] and will deliver it into the Abbade's snuffy fingers this evening. If anything it is too complimentary. I don't know yet exactly how much froth and flattery will sit on a Portuguese stomach. Horne tells me a monstrous deal, and he ought to know, he has been studying their constitutions almost half a century. D. José <de> Mateus and Bezerra at dinner. We drove to Ribamar and saw the Packet coming in full sail.

Sunday 3 June

I went to the Convent of the Necessidades[47] belonging to the Oratorians to see the ceremony of consecrating a friar of that Order Bishop of Algarve.[48] I was placed in a gallery fronting the altar, crowded with nobility in shining raiment, the relations of the new prelate. The floor being spread with rich Persian carpets, it was pretty good kneeling and I was very devout and attentive. The Count de Val de Reis, Viceroy of Algarve,[49] lent me his prayer book. I thought the ceremony would never finish. The chapel being small and choke full of people, the figurants about the altar were lost in a confused group of profane greasy faces. There was a mighty glitter of copes, censers, mitres and croziers continually in motion, for several bishops assisted in all their pomp. The music was simple and pathetic, it affected the grandees in my neighbourhood very profoundly, for they put on woeful contrite countenances, thumped their breasts and seemed to think themselves miserable sinners. I too looked very humble and penitent. The Grand Prior who was there as a relation entered into a long conversation with me. His manner is full of mildness and dignity. I like him better than any Portuguese I have seen, spiritual or temporal. Father Theodore <de> Almeida,[50] one of the luminaries of Portuguese literature, was introduced to me. He descanted in a truly monkish style upon the episcopal duties and the peculiar merits of the person who was now on the verge of entering upon them. I suspect His Reverence put on more sanctity than he feels.

Upon my return from church I found no letter by the Packet. I am thunderstruck. Three mails arrived and not a line for me. I am more than half inclined to suspect Walpole of intercepting my letters. I keep up my spirits however wonderfully. Horne looks quite down in the mouth. I went to condole with him upon our mutual disappointment and found him in the rueful act of shaving. We sat conjecturing, wondering and fretting till dinner. A heavy fall of newspapers at coffee time. In one of 8th May, I learn the decision of the Saltash Committee in favour of the sitting Member, Major Lemon.[51] I fought his battles you know, and am to have the disposal of this seat for life. How could Mr. Wildman,[52] the sole adviser, manager and abetter of the petition etc., neglect giving me intelligence of our success. This is the third time of my disputing this point, and it has cost me many a thousand. I am at length victorious, and nobody writes me word of it. Is that possible? There must be foul play.

At six we went to the Marialva Palace to pay a visit to the Grand Prior. The great courtyard spread with dunghills and filled with shabby two-wheeled chaises put me in mind of the entrance of a French post-house. We made the best of our way between heaps of filthiness, up the great staircase, and had near tumbled over a swingeing sow and her numerous progeny which escaped from under Mr. Horne's feet with bitter squeakings. This hubbub announced our arrival, so out came the Prior, D. Pedro and a troop of shambling blear-eyed domestics and chaplains. Every great Portuguese family is infested with herds of these ill-favoured dependents. I hate the sight of them, it always puts me out of humour. There is no shaking them off—move where you will they follow you, laugh when you laugh, and one cannot say a droll thing without setting some hundreds of dirty teeth a-grinning, and being poisoned with a stream of garlic and bacalhao. A stranger, you may easily suppose, is the peculiar object of their speculations. The Grand Prior had shed his pontifical garments and did the honours of the house, and conducted me with great agility all over the apartments and into every hole and corner where the old Marquis his brother deposits watches and knick-knacks. D. Pedro is mighty fond of me, he looks very puny and peaking, with a countenance as long as one's face in a spoon. The old Abbade seemed overjoyed to find me upon such friendly terms with the Grand Prior. All the rarities of the family were brought out for my inspection, curious shellwork, housings embroidered with feathers, ebony crucifixes admirably carved, models of horses and the Lord knows what besides, stinking of camphor enough to strike one down.

Whilst we were staring with all our eyes and holding up our handkerchief to our noses, the Count de Val de Reis made his appearance in grand gala, straddling as if he had p-ss-d himself. I complimented him on his hopeful relation the new Bishop, and received much foul breath and many speeches in return upon my exemplary behaviour at Mass. He has little pigs' eyes that try to look cunning, <and> the jaw of a baboon forever munching. I soon grew tired of his flattery, wished to have given him some barley sugar and so sent him sucking away. There exists not a more thorough-paced bigot than this worthy Governor of Algarve. He abhors the memory of Pombal and entertained Verdeil all this morning with anecdotes of John the Fifth's piety, whom he esteems the greatest monarch that ever existed. To get rid of the long narrations he kept pouring warm into my ear, I took refuge at the harpsichord in the crimson damask saloon. The door of D. Henriqueta's apartment was thrown wide open tonight and the curtain only half drawn. I could distinguish her features in spite of the darkness into which the inviolable custom of Portugal obliges her to retire in her mother's absence upon the approach of male animals. A group of lovely children, her sisters, sat at her feet upon the ground and looked like genii tumbling out of the folds of a curtain in some grand allegorical picture by Rubens or Paul Veronese.

9 o'clock. Would you believe it, it is grown so cold that I wish for a fire. The wind whistles and showers descend. We have closed all doors and windows so that the neighbourhood will not be alarmed by my squallings. Here is Jeronimo <de> Lima,[53] one of the Queen's first composers, and I am going to sing with all my main.

Monday 4 June

You are all busy I suppose in crisping, curling and powdering yourselves for St. James'. I am sitting meekly and reverently with two holy Fathers from St. Anthony's Convent,[54] talking of martyrdom and miracles. I begin to make myself pretty well understood in Portuguese and shall soon acquire the right twang. The language is full of terminations in -oins and -ong, like the Chinese, or rather, like the sound of a hollow tub when beaten upon. This day three years ago I little dreamt of ever having a conference with friars in Portugal. I was then on the high road to fame and dignity, courted by Mr. Pitt, fawned upon by all his adherents, worshipped and glorified by my Scotch kindred, and cajoled by that cowardly effeminate fool William Courtenay.

As the sky was overcast and the dust laid by the rain which had lately fallen, we sallied out after dinner to pay visits. Never did I behold such cursed ups and downs, such shelving descents and sudden rises as occur at every step one takes in going about Lisbon. I thought myself fifty times on the point of being over-turned into the Tagus or tumbled into sandy ditches amongst rotten shoes, dead cats and negro beldames who retire into such dens and burrows for the purpose of telling fortunes and selling charms for the ague. The Inquisition too often lays hold of these wretched sibyls and works them confoundedly. I saw one dragging into light as I passed, whether by a Familiar of the Inquisition or no I will not pretend to answer. Be that as it will, I was happy to be driven out of sight of this hideous object whose howlings struck me with horror. The more I am acquainted with Lisbon the more I dislike it. Its appearance announces neither the wealth nor dignity of a capital, but rather a succession of ugly villages awkwardly tacked together. The churches in general are contemptibly small and so totally deficient in point of architecture as to resemble nothing I ever beheld except certain imaginary views of Mexican temples to be found in a Dutch atlas. Most of these have turrets in the delectable taste of old-fashioned French clock cases, such as Boucher designed with many a scrawl and flourish to adorn the apartments of Mme de Pompadour.

We traversed the city this evening in all its extent in our way to the Duke de Lafões' villa. There was much staring at the height of the coachbox, the short jacket of the postillion and other anglicisms of the equipage. Not finding the Duke at home, we continued our drive on the shore of the Tagus under the walls of the garden of Marvila[55] which belongs to the old Marquis of Marialva. Rows of thick elms render this spot very delightful, and the irregular hillocks in its neighbourhood are covered with Spanish broom. Dark clouds mottled with stormy red hung over the river—at this extremity of Lisbon above nine miles broad—and the opposite shore, dimly discovered, received a pale though many coloured gleam from a faint rainbow which the setting sun had hardly strength to form. The vast expanse of waters, the variegated sky, the coolness of the air and the blue range of distant mountains brought full into my mind the scenery of the Lake of Geneva and a thousand circumstances attending the loss of her I loved more than my existence. That dreadful gulf which now is fixed between us arose before my imagination in all its terrors. I returned home gloomy and comfortless, calling in vain upon her who can hear no more, the companion of my happiest hours, once so lively and blooming, now lying cold and ghastly in the dark vaults at Fonthill, the loveliest and most unaffected of beings who doted on her poor William with such excessive fondness, and pardoned with such a sweet endearing cheerfulness his childish errors. That tutelary angel it has pleased the Great Being to take away from me, and I am now left almost without a friend wandering about the world, the object of the vilest calumnies and the most capricious persecution. But it is Englishmen alone who behave to me with such malevolence: the first characters in other nations know how to excuse my past faults and respect my present conduct. In Portugal particularly many persons in the highest stations and of the worthiest as well as noblest families treat me not only with politeness but affection.

Tuesday 5 June

The weather still continues temperate and the sun overcast. I have been hanging over the jasmines I brought out of the garden of the Necessidades, and inhaling their soft perfume. Mr. Horne has a species of Cape Jasmine[56] which bears double flowers of the size of a common white rose, and more deliciously scented than any flower I thought our globe could produce. They tell me shady days are very uncommon in this climate. I availed myself of the sun's absence to walk in the valley of Alcantara amongst orchards of orange and lemon brightened up by the showers which have lately fallen. Across this valley stretches that enormous aqueduct[57] you have heard so often mentioned as the most colossal edifice of the kind in Europe. It has only one row of pointed arches, and the principal arch, which crosses a rapid brook, measures near three hundred feet in height. The Pont du Gard and Caserta, if you recollect, have several rows of arches one above the other, which by dividing the attention take off from the size of the whole. There is a vastness in this single range that strikes with astonishment. I sat down under the great arch on a fragment of rock and looked up to the stone-work so high above me with a sensation of awe bordering on fear, as if the building I gazed upon was the performance of some unmeasurable Being endued with gigantic strength, who might perhaps take a fancy to saunter about his work this morning and in mere awkwardness crush me to atoms. Hard by the spot where I sat are several enclosures crowded with canes ten or twelve feet in height; their fresh green leaves, waving with the feeblest wind, form a perpetual murmur. I am very fond of this rustling, it half lulls me asleep, and helps me to forget every care for a few moments.[58]

Soon after I came home from my walk the Grand Prior and his nephew arrived to dine with me. D. Pedro amused himself highly with my books and gems and shewed a great sensibility for music. We sung and played and paused over prints alternately. Night drew on before we dreamt of its approach. I accompanied the uncle and nephew home in my carriage and we parted with great reluctance. I was just come back when the Count de Val de Reis was announced. It was near ten and I gaped unconscionably. The Count has a moistness of mouth rather disgusting and drivels at every syllable. Our conversation was limpingly carried on in a great variety of broken languages—Italian, Portuguese, French and English succeeded each other at every period. About eleven, thank God, he took his departure, and I bowed him out to the edge of the staircase with great complacency. One must not decide too hastily upon outward appearances. This dawdling, slobbering, canting personage is one of the most distinguished officers in Portugal, one of the few who have seen actual service and given unquestionable proofs of their military prowess and capacity.

Wednesday 6 June

I breakfasted at the Marquis of Penalva's[59] and met with a most cordial and friendly reception. The apartments are hung with pictures by the greatest masters, many of which if they had not been retouched would merit a place in the first collections. I am afraid some indifferent artist not sparing of brilliant colours has been allowed to dab out the rubs and scratches contracted in the confusion of the earthquake. A Holy Family in the best manner of Raphael seems to have been very lately emblazoned with ultramarine. It is placed in great state under a cut velvet canopy between two flounced tables garnished with silver vases and artificial flowers. The whole suite of rooms opened for my reception had an air of good taste and opulence that surprised me not a little. There was likewise a frankness and good humour in the attentions of my hosts quite engaging. I felt perfectly at home and stretched myself on a sofa to hear some delightful music composed and executed on the harpsichord by Antonio Leal, one of the Chapel Masters at the Patriarchal church.[60] Every door was clustered with priests, servants and pages according to the invariable custom of Portuguese families; all of them were more splendidly dressed than their masters, which struck me as a further mark of refinement in the Penalva family. The collation, consisting of chocolate, sweetmeats, tea and very excellent coffee, was served in Dresden china admirably painted. I never sat down to a more comfortable or elegant breakfast in England. The linen was remarkably fine and curiously embroidered with arms and flowers, red on a white ground. Several plates of enormous strawberries perfumed the apartment, which commands a boundless extent of the Tagus.

The Judge Conservator of the English Factory[61] assisted the Marquis of Penalva[62] and his son[63] in doing everything to make the morning pass agreeably. I like this man extremely. He has risen to the highest post in the Law— *Desembargador do Paco*—by the sole strength of his own abilities, and has a nervous original turn of expression that puts me in mind of Lord Thurlow.[64] But to all this vigour of character and diction he joins the pliability and subtleness of a serpent, and those he cannot take by storm he is certain of overcoming by every soothing art of flattery and insinuation. I know not what end he has to answer in me; but whenever I appear he becomes all smiles and approbation, loads Mr.

Walpole with the bitterest invective, and declares furious war against the very Factory who have appointed him their protector. The old Marquis pressed me to stay dinner, but not being in very triumphant spirits I declined the invitation. An unaccountable oppression came over me in the evening, which all the fresh breezes blowing from the mouth of the river on the shore of Belem could not dissipate. I remained sunk in a corner of the coach during the whole drive, which we prolonged as far as Caxias. The voice of the Abbade hailing me with many a kind message from the Grand Prior and D. Pedro forced me to lift my head as I passed a Chinese-looking garden hedged round with aloes where the good old man generally spends his evenings. It belongs to Mr. Hudson,[65] agent for the Packet, who has lately lost his son, a youth of sixteen, and is now plunged in the deepest affliction.

Thursday 7 June

I could hardly sleep for the jingling of bells, beating of drums and flourishings of trumpets which struck up at daybreak in honour of that pompous festival the Corpo de Deos. I had half a mind to have stayed at home writing to you and reading Camoens; but I was told such wonders of the procession in honour of this glorious day that I could not refuse giving myself a little trouble in order to witness them. The streets in the quarter of Lisbon I inhabit, as well as those through which I passed in my way to the Patriarchal, were entirely deserted. A pestilence seemed to have swept the Great Square[66] and the busy environs of the India House and Exchange, for even vagrants, scavengers and beggars in the last stage of lousiness and decrepitude had all hobbled away to the scene of action. A few miserable curs sniffing at offals alone remained in the vacant streets, and a few palsied old women and a half dozen scabby children blubbering at being kept at home were the sole objects I could discover in the endless windows.

I heard the murmur of the crowds assembled around the Patriarchal before I discovered them. We advanced with some difficulty between rows of soldiers drawn up in battle array, and upon turning a dark angle shaded by the high buildings of the Seminary[67] adjoining the Patriarchal, discovered houses, shops and palaces all metamorphosed into tents, and hung from top to bottom with red damask, tapestry of a thousand colours, satin coverlids and fringed counterpanes glittering with gold. I thought myself in the midst of the Mogul's encampment. The front of the great church was magnificently curtained. It rises from a vast flight of steps, which being covered today with the Yeomen of the Queen's Guard in their rich parti-coloured velvet dresses and a multitude of priests bearing crosses and banners, formed one of the most theatrical perspectives I ever beheld. Flocks of sallow monks, white, brown and black, kept moving about continually like turkeys driving to market. This part of the procession lasting a tiresome while, I grew weary, left the balcony where we were most advantageously placed right opposite the great portal, and got into the church, where Mass was performing in full glory, incense ascending in clouds, thousands kneeling, and the light of innumerable tapers blazing on the diamonds and rubies of the ostensory elevated by the Patriarch with trembling devout hands to receive the mysterious wafer.

Before the close of the ceremony I regained my window to have a full view of the coming forth of the Sacrament. All was expectation and silence in the people. The Guards had ranged them on each side of the steps before the entrance of the church. At length a shower of aromatic herbs and flowers announced the approach of the Patriarch bearing the Host under a regal canopy surrounded by grandees and preceded by vast numbers of saintly mitred figures, their hands joined in prayer, their scarlet vestments sweeping the ground, their attendants bearing croziers, silver reliquaries and other insignia of pontifical grandeur. The procession, slowly descending the flights of stairs to the sound of choirs and the distant thunder of artillery, lost itself in a winding street decorated with splendid hangings, and left me with my senses in a whirl and my eyes dazzled like those of a saint just wakened from a vision of celestial splendour. My head swims at this moment and my ears tingle with a vibration of sounds—bells, voices, and the echoes of cannon prolonged by mountains and wafted over waters.

I passed my evening at Mr. Horne's very delightfully in hearing D. Luisa de Almeida and her music master, a little square friar with green eyes, <singing> Brazilian *modinhas*.[68] This is an original sort of music different from any I ever heard, the most seducing, the most voluptuous imaginable, the best calculated to throw saints off their guard and to inspire profane deliriums. I was in high spirits and danced with a parcel of young tits till two in the morning.

Friday 8 June

Soon after breakfast the old Abbade brought me a letter from the Marquis of Marialva filled with very flattering expressions of regard and affection. Our correspondence goes on at a rapid rate. The old man is in raptures at so friendly an intercourse between me and the family to which he has been a nursing father these 70 or 80 years. It was he who first pointed me out to them in the most glowing colours and who may be said to have sown the seeds of an attachment now springing up so vigorously.

The weather is cool and temperate and yet I am out of order and hang my head like a broken gillyflower. I have no comforts but in my evening drive along the sea shore. The Grand Prior accompanied me. His conversation breathes the true spirit of benevolence and humanity. He gives glory to God without ostentation and bears an unaffected goodwill towards men. I grow attached to this coast of Belem and know every hill, projecting rock or group of aloes. The hour of sunset at which I so constantly visit them diffuses a soft glow on the whole prospect and renders the most trifling objects which compose it interesting. Near the Convent of Nossa Senhora da Boa Viagem on a rude promontory is a wilderness of myrtle, oleander, broom and a thousand other shrubs in blossom. You can form no idea of their glowing tints this evening. Being situated as I have just told you on the brow of an eminence, they received the last rays of the sun and were agitated by breezes that freshened the boundless plains of ocean beyond the bar, and on that part of the Tagus which was already in shade tipped the waves with silver.

This spot was the boundary of our excursion. We turned back. The mules trotted at the rate of eight miles an hour and we soon found ourselves under the terraces of the Marialva Palace where D. Pedro and his sisters were walking to and fro in expectation of their uncle. D. Pedro looked wistfully at me as I passed by and seemed to regret my not getting out and joining him; but my heart was full of melancholy recollections and my spirits have sunk with the sun. I set down the Grand Prior after promising to call again for him tomorrow, waved my hand and drove home.

Saturday 9 June

I continue in a strange mood, feverish, impatient and good for nothing. I can hardly write a line. M. Verdeil talks of dosing me tomorrow. It is high time. D. José de Mateus, who dined here today with the Hornes, Bezerra, etc. would have made me laugh, had I been well, at a rare story he has just picked up from one of his female cousins. Two old women of quality, D. Joana de Menezes[69] and the Marchioness of Penalva[70] will have it that St. Anthony[71] has appeared to me and commanded me to raise up a wall round his convent to keep off certain lewd minstrels of the female gender who keep tinkling their guitars all night under the friars' windows and warble filthy *modinhas*. I am quite ashamed of being in such favour with old women. Don't you remember when I used to come home to Wimpole Street from the Opera at an early hour with a certain acquaintance of yours—what fame I acquired with all the dowagers in the neighbourhood, and particularly gude Lady Alva, for soberness, chastity and early hours. I was punctual to my engagement with the Grand Prior who told me D. Pedro lingered eagerly to see me again, and that he would bring him to dine with me next Tuesday, the vigil of blessed St. Anthony. This evening he could not go out with us, being engaged with <a> variety of masters. I told you before they give the poor boy no respite. I wished him in the carriage—the evening was so tranquil, the air so fragrant, and the clouds in which the sun had wrapped himself shifting into innumerable forms of towers, domes and palaces. He has a picturesque eye and would have enjoyed this scenery by no means usual in the serene atmosphere of Lisbon.

Sunday 10 June

Blessed be the salts of Epsom, they are what poor Burton,[72] that odd eccentric animal, used to call a heavenly purge; excuse the expression, I beg, it is rather inelegant, but springs from a grateful heart. I dined at Mr. Home's with the usual set—D. José de Mateus, Bezerra, etc. We went afterwards by the particular desire of D. Margarida de Brito[73] to see her daughter[74]—a lively girl of thirteen—under education at the Convent of Savoyard nuns[75] at Belem. The little thing has eyes of the most bewitching softness, and they appeared to great advantage in the twilight of a gloomy parlour, beaming from between a double row of iron bars. Diamonds you know have never more effect than when displayed by the jeweller in a dark retired shop. I passed half an hour not disagreeably in talking of music, gardens, roses and devotions with the *menina*, and had almost forgotten I was engaged to hear the Escarlate sing. She is the daughter of an old hooknosed Captain of Horse of Italian extraction.[76]

A whole posse of the young lady's kindred—brothers, cousins and uncles— stood ready at the street door to usher me upstairs into a fusty gallery hung with tapestry and tin sconces like the great room of an Italian inn, once the palace of a nobleman. To help on these posthouse ideas, there was a strong perfume of the stable, and every now and then one heard stamping and neighing, as if a party of houyhnhnms[77] were arriving to partake of the concert. There were many strange figures of both sexes assembled, a scurvy collection, I am apt to conjecture. The young lady of the house delighted me by her graceful manners and expressive countenance; but when she sung some arias composed by Perez[78] and João de Sousa[79] I was lost in amazement. Her voice modulates with unaffected carelessness into the most pathetic tones and with a tremulous sweetness steals into the heart. Though she has adopted the masterly and scientific style of Ferracuti,[80] the first singer in the Queen's service, she gives a simplicity of expression to the most difficult and laboured passages that make them appear the effusions of a young romantic girl warbling to herself in the deepest recess of a forest. I shall never forget the impression this singing had on me. I was thrown into a languor, and sat in a dark corner, unmindful of everything that passed around—the starings and whisperings and fan-tappings of the grotesque assembly. I could not utter a syllable and was vexed when Signora Escarlate proposed a dance. I walked two minuets and dragged as many country dances, to the wonder of the company who had heard much of my caperings and attributed this listlessness, I fear, to reserve and haughtiness. It was pouring with rain and the windows being open admitted a fresh current of air that dissipated the stable perfume and gave me new life, so I was sorry to go away. I wished all the kindred and their friends in the Tagus, and would have given one ear to have enjoyed a private audience of the Escarlate with the other till morning. I am to meet her, thank Heaven, at Sintra in the wild shrubberies which encircle her habitation, and we will sing like skylarks, and nobody shall hear us except a little sister of the nymph's with a fair complexion, blue eyes and long pencilled eyelashes. She may be allowed, I think, to languish away at these soft sounds at the foot of a branching citron, half lost amongst tufts of fern. I think I see her peeping from amongst them, and the old hairy *Conservador*[81] in the shape of a satyr rousing her from her concealment and coursing her over the hills.

Monday 11 June

I dined in the country today at a Mr. Street Arriaga<'s>,[82] who is of Irish extraction, six foot high, four foot broad, a ruddy countenance, swapping shoulders, Herculean legs and all the attributes of that enterprising race who so often have the luck of marrying great fortunes. About a year or two ago he bore off a wealthy Brazilian heiress, and is now master of a large estate and a fubsical, squat wife with a head like that of Holofernes in old tapestry, and shoulders that act the part of a platter with great exactitude. Poor soul! To be sure she is neither a Venus nor a Hebe, has a rough lip and a manly voice, and is rather inclined to be dropsical, but her smiles are frequent and fondling, and she cleaves to her husband with great perseverance. He is an odd character, will accept of no employment either civil or military and affects a bullying frankness that I should think must displease very much in this servile country, where independence either in fortune or sentiment is a crime seldom left unpunished.

Mr. Street likes a display, and the repast he gave us was magnificent, sixty dishes at least, eight smoking roasts and every ragout, French, English and Portuguese that could be thought of. The dessert appeared like the model of a fortification; the principal Cake Tower measured I daresay three foot perpendicular in height. The company was not equal in number or consequence to the splendour of our entertainment; a more rueful one I never saw assembled. Had not Miss Sill and Bezerra been luckily in my neighbourhood at table I should have perished with ennui. One lean damsel with portentous eyebrows and looks that reproached the male part of the assembly with inattention was the only Lady of the Palace Mr.

Street had invited. Mr. Horne and I had expected the whole troop of our Botanic Garden acquaintance—and expected to have rambled about the vineyards and citron orchards which surround this villa the whole evening in their company. Alas, I took no such gay excursion.

The tragic damsel, who I am told has been unhappy in her tender attachments, solemnly took my arm and never quitted it during a long walk through Mr. Street's ample possessions. We conversed in Italian and paid the birds that were singing many fine compliments in a sort of prose run mad, borrowed from operas, novels, the *Aminta* of Tasso and the *Adonis* of Marini. The sun was sinking behind the distant rocks of Sintra which terminated our prospect. The air was balsamic and the ground felt cool and pleasant. A thousand exotic flowers I noticed for the first time, revived by last night's rain, displayed themselves on every bank. I very politely gave up the narrow track which leads through these rural regions to the signora, and stalked by her side in a furrow well garnished with a species of prickly acanthus and spiteful aloes, stinging and scratching myself at every step. This circumstance put me a little out of humour. I regretted passing so delicious an evening in such forlorn company, and blooding my legs to so little purpose. I should have preferred wandering alone through the vineyards, which exhibit the most elegant festoons of luxuriant leaves and tendrils, climbing light canes eight or ten feet in height, not tied and fastened to stiff poles like those in France and Switzerland. Pinioned as I was, you may imagine I felt no inclination to stay tea or play at *volterete*. I made a solemn bow to the solemn damsel and got home before it was dark.

Tuesday 12 June

Some good Father of a neighbouring convent, aware of my pious disposition, sent me a mess of soup this morning, very thick, slab and oily. It seems the faithful are accustomed to swallow this penitential portion the eve of St. Anthony's festival. My reputation as a devotee spreads prodigiously and there hardly passes a day without my receiving some present of a holy nature, or edifying exhortation. The Grand Prior and D. Pedro dined here and we kept a rigorous fast. M. Verdeil adhered to meagre[83] in the first course, but was led astray by a nice roasted leveret in the second. D. Pedro looks pale and dejected. My singing affects him deeply. The Grand Prior shivers with cold and though buttoned up to the chin and stuffed out with three or four waistcoats could not bear the least breath of wind. To be sure the air is very much chilled by a constant succession of heavy showers. The hills on the opposite shore of the Tagus, which I view from my windows, begin again to robe themselves with verdure. We shall have a second Spring. The Indian corn is shooting up to an unusual height and will form shady avenues and fairy forests where like a child I shall enjoy to ramble. Unless St. Anthony lulls me to sleep by a miracle I shall have no rest tonight. There is a whizzing of rockets, blazing of bonfires, and flourishing of French horns in honour of tomorrow, the anniversary of that blessed day when my favourite saint passed by a rapturous and soft transition to the joys of Paradise. I saw his image tonight in almost every house along the shore of Belem, placed on an altar decked with a profusion of wax lights and flowers.

Wednesday 13 June

I slept better than I expected: the Saint was propitious and cooled the ardour of his votaries and the flames of their bonfires by a copious rain which pattered agreeably this morning amongst the vine-leaves of my garden. The clouds dispersed about eight o'clock, and at nine, just as I ascended the steps of the new church built over the identical house where St. Anthony was born,[84] the sun burst forth in all its splendour. I cannot say its edifice recalled to my mind the magnificent sanctuary of Padua, before which five years ago on this very day I so devoutly fell prostrate. Here are no constellations of golden lamps depending by glittering chains from a mysterious Gothic ceiling, no arcades of alabaster, no polished marbles reflecting the light of innumerable tapers. The church is supported by two rows of pillars neatly carved in stone but wretchedly proportioned. Over the High Altar, where stands the image of St. Anthony in the midst of a brilliant illumination, was stretched a canopy of flowered velvet. This drapery, richly fringed and spangled, marks out the spot formerly occupied by the chamber of the saint, and receives an amber light from a row of tall casement windows, the woodwork gleaming with burnished gold. I was placed in a chapel on the right of this splendid altar, in full view of St. Anthony's female worshippers, who I am told were much edified by my contrite and meek appearance. A great many broad English faces burst forth from amongst the crowd of profane vulgar at the portal of the church, and all their eyes were directed at me, but I was not to be stared out of a decent countenance. The ceremony was pompous enough. A Principal with a considerable detachment of priests from the Patriarchal officiated to the sound of lively jigs and ranting minuets, better calculated to set a parcel of water-drinkers a-dancing in a pump-room than to direct the motions of a pontiff and his assistants.

After much indifferent vocal and instrumental music performed full gallop in the most rapid allegro, Frei João Jacinto, a famous preacher, mounted a pulpit just by the place where I knelt, lifted up hands and eyes, foamed at the mouth, and poured forth a torrent of sounding phrases in honour of St. Anthony. What would I not give for such a voice—it would almost have reached from Dan unto Beersheba! The father has undoubtedly great powers of elocution and none of that canting nasal whine so common in the delivery of monkish sermons. He treated kings, tetrarchs and conquerors, the heroes and sages of antiquity, with ineffable contempt, reduced their palaces and fortifications to dust, their armies to pismires, their imperial vestments to cobwebs, and impressed all the audience except the heretical squinters at the door with thorough convictions of St. Anthony's superiority over these objects of an impious and erring admiration.

"Happy," exclaimed the preacher "were these Gothic ages, falsely called ages of barbarity and ignorance, when the hearts of men, uncorrupted by the delusive beverage of philosophy, were open to the words of truth falling like honey from the mouths of saints and confessors, such words as distilled from the lips of Anthony, yet a suckling hanging at the breast in this very spot. 'Twas here the spirit of the Most High descended upon him, that he conceived the sublime Intention of penetrating into savage regions, setting the inclemency of seasons and the malice of men at defiance, and sprinkling amongst lawless nations the seeds of grace <and> of repentance. There, my brethren, is the door out of which he issued: do you not see him in the habit of a *menino do coro* smiling with all the graces of innocence, dispensing with his infant hands to a group of squalid children the portion of nourishment he has just received from his mother? But Anthony from the first dawn of his existence lived for others and not for himself. He forewent even the luxury of meditation, and instead of retiring into a peaceful cell, rushed into the world, helpless and unprotected, lifting high the banner of the Cross amidst perils and uproar, appeasing wars, settling differences both public and domestic, exhorting at the risk of his life robbers and plunderers to make restitution, and armed misers guarding their coffers with bloody swords to open their hearts and their hands to the distresses of the widow and the fatherless. Anthony ever sighed after the crown of martyrdom and had long entertained an ardent desire of passing over into Morocco and exposing himself to the fury of its bigoted and cruel sovereigns. But the commands of his superior retain him on the point of embarkation. He makes a sacrifice of even this most laudable and glorious ambition. He is sent for by the Bishop of Forii, receives the last orders of priesthood, and continues to his last hour administering consolation to the dejected, fortifying their hopes of Heaven, and confirming the faith of such as were wavering or deluded by a succession of prodigies. The dead are raised, the sick are healed, the sea is calmed by a glance of St. Anthony's. Even the lowest ranks of the creation are attracted by eloquence more than human, and give marks of sensibility. Fish swim in shoals to hear the word of the Lord; and to convince the obdurate and those accursed whose hearts the false reasoning of the world has hardened, mules and animals the most perversely obstinate humble themselves to the earth when Anthony holds forth the sacrament, and acknowledge the presence of the Divinity."

The sermon ended, fiddling began anew with redoubled vigour, and I, disgusted with such unseasonable levity, retired in dudgeon. I found my table strewed over with congratulatory letters from pious souls rejoicing with <me> in this memorable day. D. José de Brito[85] who had accompanied me home from Mass, shook his fat sides heartily at the idea of the renown I began to enjoy in Portugal. We were talking on this subject when the company I had invited to dinner made their appearance. D. Margarida de Brito, D. Fernando de Almeida, and his granddaughter D. Luisa and her goggle-eyed lover. Soon after Frei Emanuel crept into the room, and a little roundabout Madeira cousin of D. Margarida's with a snug wig and a silvery waistcoat. Bezerra, D. José de Mateus, the Miss Sills, Mr. Horne, etc. All fed plentifully: we were two hours at table and had hardly finished before it was time to set off to see the procession in honour of St. Anthony pass along the Rua Augusta.

Figure to yourself a multitude of shabby lubbers walking two and two with tapers in their hands preceded by a band of scrapers in their every-day greasy cloaks, followed by negros innumerable bearing on their shoulders flat boards like dessert frames set out with flower pots and waxwork images of saints, angels and madonnas: some in armed chairs under tinsel canopies; others kneeling before crucifixes clustered with cherubims; others stretching out their lean necks to the swords of Turks and infidels in scarlet jackets trimmed with silver; two blackamoor saints one never heard of contribute their share of ridicule to the procession. I have seen many paltry shows, but none so ill-fancied as this. Our Twelfth Night cakes streaming with red rags and glittering with silvered paper carried about by four or five hundred pastrycooks would cut a grander figure. I blushed to see the well-grown, the majestic St. Anthony diminished to a prim little doll scarce three feet high in a robe of Indian taffety bedaubed with gold, and his celestial playfellow the *Menino* Jesus stuck out in a hoop petticoat with his hair in a bag, two rows of sausage curls and a toupee plastered and powdered. I made my retreat as soon as I could and returned home shrugging up my shoulders. The rest of the company soon followed and we consoled ourselves with *modinhas*.

Thursday 14 June

I hear there is no conversation in Lisbon but of my piety. Really this joke begins to have its inconveniences. I am incessantly plagued with deputations from convents, epistles and holy greetings in Latin, English and Portuguese, invitations to sacred festivals and presents of sweetmeats in cut paper from lady abbesses and young virgins supplicating me to portion them out as God's spouses in some monastery under the auspices of my much-honoured St. Anthony. But in for a penny in for a pound as the vulgar saying is. I have talked myself fairly into this scrape and must get out of it as well as I can.

The old Abbade dined here and showed me a letter of the Marquis of Marialva to him complaining grievously of his having been three days without hearing from me, that he was unhappy without my letters, did not deserve such neglect at my hands etc. This is mighty kind, is it not? So I set to writing another fine flowery epistle full of gratitude and encomiums upon yesterday's sermon, etc. etc. That I think will please at Court not a little. It rained confoundedly and the Abbade bawled louder than ever. He is a complete gossip and let out several anecdotes of the Marialvas that so zealous a friend of the family had better have concealed. I can hardly credit what he told me of the old Marquis, my friend's father's voracity, of his eating two dozen partridges, a whole ham at a meal. According to the Abbade thirty-five dishes the most exquisite that can be procured, beside the dessert, are served up every day to this prince of gluttons, who always dine<s> alone between two tubs ready to receive what he has no longer room to contain and remains three hours at table. *N.B.* I must remember never to eat ducks or sucking pig at the Marialva Palace; these are too daintily fed.

To repose ourselves a little after the vociferations of the Abbade, M. Verdeil and I went out in the post-chaise. It was charmingly cool. The rain has freshened the verdure of the vegetation on the shore of Belem, and helped innumerable flowers into bloom; the aloes have risen to the height of twenty-five or thirty feet. We drove almost as far as Paço de Arcos, a village beyond Caxias, and did not return till nine. We were drinking tea when a loud hubbub in the street and a sudden glare of light called us to the window, and there was a beastly mob of children, old hags and ragamuffins assembled, headed by half-a-dozen negros blowing French horns with unusual energy and pointing them directly at the house. I was wondering at this Jericho fashion of besieging one's door, and starting at a rocket which shot up under my nose, when Berti entered with a crucifix on a silver salver and a mighty kind message from the nuns of the Convent of the Sacrament,[86] who had sent their musicians with fireworks and timbrels to do me honour and invite me to High Mass at their church tomorrow morn, the Festival of the Heart of Jesus.

Friday 15 June

Well, I have fulfilled my engagement with the holy sisterhood and was half stifled. Their church is small, and every crevice being stopped up by thick velvet and damask hangings, every window chock-full of flower pots, and the high altar flaming with twenty ranks of wax tapers, one above the other, not a breath of air could enter. The lady abbess sent me a huge elbow-chair covered with tapestry, and there I sat three long hours yawning my soul out and dissolving at every pore whilst two or three sweating boys and half-a-score fiddles and oboes murdered some glorious music of João de Sousa. I could not get away till almost dinner-time, an old devotee of distinction and his confessor watched all my motions so narrowly. Bezerra and D. José de Mateus were waiting for me at home. They know not what to make of these fits of devotions, for I pretended not to have been in the least tired, and put on such a rueful penitential mump as almost confounded them.

During dinner the good lady abbess sent me a sugared tart and an invitation to vespers which I declined, having promised to call on the Marialvas, uncle and nephew, and take them along with me <on> my constant eternal airing. The 15 of June is a great festival in their family, being the birthday of the Marquis, Marchioness and their son D. Pedro. We drove into the principal court which was crowded by servants of all colours, sexes and ages in their holiday garments. D. Pedro and his cousins, sons of the Marquis of Tancos,[87] my friend's brother, came tripping down the great stairs to receive me. Up we ran into the apartments hand in hand like a parcel of children. My sanctity knows perfectly well how to unbend itself at times and seasons. I could not help playing with the light brown hair of the eldest Tancos, a lovely boy of thirteen, nor could the poor little stripling help finding me more youthful and condescending than he expected. We would gladly have remained a longer while together, but D. Pedro observed it was growing late and the Grand Prior gave the signal for moving by wrapping himself up in an ample cloak. The Abbade would not be left behind, so we were five in the coach, and D. Pedro sat between me and the Grand Prior. Our excursion lasted till it was dark. D. Pedro is the proudest youth that ever sat by me, but I will humble him if St. Anthony gives me health and spirits.

Saturday 16 June

I was hardly up before two monks from the Convent of St. Anthony arrived with a basket of sweetmeats and the thanks of their community for ten moidores.[88] I had sent them <on> the festival of their patron. <You> may be sure I received them with all due courtesy, and scarcely were they dismissed before Father Theodore <de> Almeida and another of his brethren were ushered in. The whites of their eyes alone were visible. Not Whitefield himself ever squinted with holier energy.[89] I was all attention to Father Almeida's orthodox and seraphic discourse. The opportunity of perfecting myself in hypocritical cant was too good to be neglected. No sooner had I conducted the Fathers to the stair's head with many endearing expressions and holy embraces than Monsignor Aguilar[90] entered. He confirmed me perfectly in the opinion I entertained of Father Theodore's hypocrisy. No person can accuse

Aguilar of being an hypocrite: he lays himself but too much open and treats the Church from which he derives so handsome a maintenance not as a patroness but an humble companion, the constant butt and object of his sarcasm. In Portugal even in the year 1787 such conduct is madness and I fear will expose him one day or other to severe persecution. <The> Miss Sills and their brother dined with us. Mr. Horne is gone to the Caldas, at this very moment perhaps over head and ears in complimentations with the Marialvas. In the evening I drove to Caxias with the Grand Prior who is to bring D. Pedro to spend the day with me tomorrow. The clouds are melting into a serene azure sky and it will soon be hotter than ever.

Sunday 17 June

A bright glowing day. I shut all my windows but opened them again for the sake of the Grand Prior who covets every ray of sunshine. He and D. Pedro came early. We had the Penalvas at dinner and the *Conservador* João Teles and were very friendly and comfortable. The young Marquis of Penalva plays upon the forte piano with infinite taste by mere force of genius, for he cannot read a note. The Portuguese fall naturally into plaintive passionate modulations that sink into my heart. Their minuets are at the same time tender and majestic. I cannot hear one without gliding about the room and throwing myself into theatrical attitudes. They seem to affect D. Pedro equally and we danced together till the Marquis was tired of playing to us. The sly old *Conservador* put on his sweetest smiles of admiration and launched forth into the warmest encomiums. I could not help thinking how certain acquaintance of mine in England would laugh could they have seen me and a young boy of the first distinction, educated with more severity than anyone in Portugal, languishing away in a minuet and never taking our eyes off each other. The Marquis' son,[91] a lad of fourteen, who was also of the party, could no longer contain himself, and seizing my hands, pressed them to his lips with a fondness of which you coldhearted northerners can form no idea. My singing, playing and capering subdues every Portuguese that approaches me, and they cannot help giving way to the most extravagant expression of their feelings. You would have thought the little Penalva bewitched had you seen how he followed me about this evening, smiling in my face and trying to dart his eyes into my very soul. No doubt every circumstance conspired to fascinate and inflame a youthful imagination—an apartment decorated with splendour and elegance; glasses rising from the ground, appearing like the portals of visionary chambers and reflecting light youthful figures swimming; the fragrance of roses, and the delightful music of Haydn, performed by Rumi, Palomino[92] and two others, the first musicians in Lisbon and perhaps in Europe. Gelati, Joaquim de Oliveira,[93] and Polycarpo who was just arrived from the Caldas sang a succession of arias with exquisite feeling. My company did not disperse till after eleven and I have reason to think they went away well satisfied with their entertainment.

Monday 18 June

Dust flies already in whirlwinds, the horizon is cloudless and the sun fierce. The Packet came in last night and I have just got a heap of letters with the confirmation of my victory at Saltash and a long-winded paragraph from Mr. Wildman about Lord Lilliput[94] consenting at length to take certain dangerous papers out of the talons of Beelzebub.[95] I dare not be too sanguine, however, in my expectations, knowing the dragon's wiliness and the Lilliputians' pusillanimity. One would think Lady Effingham and my relations were leagued together to make me appear what Walpole has represented me. All I have written cannot bring them to speak one word to Pinto[96] in my favour, so I must shift entirely for myself in this kingdom.

I have had another letter from the Marquis of Marialva in Portuguese, the most friendly, the most affectionate I ever read. I begin to more than suspect he destines me for D. Henriqueta his eldest daughter and flatters himself with prevailing on the Queen to offer me such honours and distinctions as may engage me to establish myself in Portugal. St. Anthony comes in very opportunely in his aid and is the grand machine of the drama in which if I choose to give myself the trouble I may have the honour to act. I really am inclined to believe myself on the threshold of great adventures. A new scene is disclosing itself to me, a new heaven and a new earth. The devotees say nothing is too good for so exemplary a character, that Her Majesty ought to encourage such a bright pattern of piety by a shower of gold, diamonds and titles, that my naturalizing myself in this country, and publicly casting off the scarf[97] of hereticism will once more draw down upon it the especial benevolence of St. Anthony whose favourite I am universally acknowledged to be etc., etc., etc. I should never finish were I to tell you all the nonsense trumpeted about in my favour by nuns, friars, and bigots of every rank and denomination. The plot thickens every day. The Court returns the beginning of next week and then I shall be better able to discover the point to which all these violent movements are tending.

Bezerra, Aguilar and D. José dined with me. I left them at six reading my book of *Dreams and Waking Thoughts*.[98] D. Pedro and the Abbade were waiting on the terrace of the Marialva Palace. He got into the coach with the Abbade and we proceeded on our daily drive. The Duke de Cadaval[99] passed us in a strange little curricle drawn by two furious milk-white horses with flowing tails and manes. He is continually putting himself in my way; but as he is a great partisan of Mrs. Aik[100] and other English tatterdemalions, who have prevailed on him not to return the visit Mr. Horne persuaded me to pay him ten days ago, I turn my back whenever he makes his appearance. The Countess of S. Vicente, a sister of Mme de Marialva and aunt to the Cadavals, is also I am told very far from believing in me. She has a venomous tongue and many a sting has it darted I dare say on the score of my great intimacy with the heir of the Marialvas. The families detest each other most cordially and it is impossible to be well with one branch without being abhorred by the other. I found Polycarpo at my return and sung *Tra l'horror, tra lo spavento*—a cavatina of Cicoia de Majo[101]—in no very bad style. I played too better than I have done this many a day; but singing gives me a pain in my side and sets every nerve in my frame a-vibrating.

Tuesday 19 June

Mr. Horne writes word from the Caldas that he was most triumphantly received by the whole Court, who are unanimous in sounding my praises and cursing Mr. Walpole and his colleagues. The Marquis and Marchioness of Marialva vied with each other in loading him with attentions. He thinks the Marquis perfectly sincere in his affection for me and that we shall carry everything before us with a high hand. The wind blows fresh and I am in tolerable spirits today. The thought of all these manoeuvres in the Marialva family keeps me employed. My curiosity is never off the stretch. I long to know when and in what manner Her Majesty is to give my audience. Miss Sill and I had a long conversation on the subject. She thinks the Factory in great alarm, and the Portuguese open-mouthed with surprise and expectation. The Prior-mor came into me soon after dinner and we went out together as usual. In my way back I returned the visit of a Portuguese merchant called Paul Jorge,[102] who is blessed with half a score little girls sprouting up under the tuition of a carroty-polled English governess. I know not what the deuce was the matter with me, but I spun round two or three times on my heel, and gave myself a thousand tosses, complained of heat and cold, wind and dust, and after a quarter of an hour's sidling and fidgeting left the whole family, I daresay, impressed with an idea of my being one of the proudest and most conceited puppies in the universe. It is amazing what pains people take sometimes to make themselves disagreeable. What motive could I have for treating these good folks in this manner?

Wednesday 20 June

I went broiling in the sun to the Antonine Convent at Campo <de> Santana and heard High Mass with edifying fervour. The Prior had spread a carpet for me within the rails of the High Altar and immediately under the image of St. Anthony, where I remained kneeling above an hour. Several female devotees of quality attended by their pages crept in to observe my behaviour. Not a look did I vouchsafe them. My hands were clasped and my eyes riveted to the countenance of my benign protector. Mass ended, the priests came forth in solemn procession with tapers blazing, and, kneeling before the image of St. Anthony, acknowledged his great interest with the celestial powers and implored him to work out my salvation. A solemn hymn was chanted by a full choir accompanied by the organ. I filled my imagination with the mighty deeds and miracles of the saint, and appeared so rapt and sanctified that M. Verdeil could not help staring. When all holy acts were finished, the fathers led me about their cloisters, gardens and chapels, stuffed me with sweetmeats, and summoned their whole community, sixty or seventy in number, to line the steps before the convent when I got into my carriage. Had I been Cardinal Legate they could not have paid me a higher compliment. I had some difficulty to stifle a laugh when I looked back on the group which was assembled in my honour, and saw so many boobies in hoods and cowls poking out their sturdy necks and aiming bows at me.

D. José de Brito and the Abbade came to dinner. I begin to be a person of great worship and am supposed to have so active an influence with the Marialvas and of course with Her Majesty that I am continually solicited to ask favours. D. José is amongst the number of my petitioners. He wants to be named one of the three *Mestre de Campo*[103] of the island of Madeira where he has a large property, and has taken it into his head that a hint from me would do the business. Before he preferred his request, he strewed all the approaches to it with the fairest flowers of devotion, thinking such were the most fragrant in the present disposition of my nostrils. And so I pass for a complete bigot and have received a canting sugary epistle from Father Almeida entreating me forsooth to furnish two young virgins just entering into his beloved Convent of the Visitation with shifts and sheeting. I should have enough to do indeed were I to truss out all the chickens that old fox Almeida carries into his den. But this being his first request I cannot decently refuse it. He is a dangerous rascal, confesses half the females of importance in Lisbon, and were I to treat his impertinent request as it deserves might expose the blossoms of my devout reputation to a nipping frost before they are hardened into consistence.

M. Verdeil and I went out in the chaise and met the Duke de Cadaval quite alone driving a pair of spanking mules full gallop in a gilded curricle. We had not lost sight of him a quarter of an hour before he again made his appearance in a sort of garden chair drawn by black ponies. I am half inclined to imagine the poor young man punishes himself with these solitary excursions for the sole end of exciting my envy and admiration by the variety and number of his horses and equipages.

Tomorrow the Prior-mor and D. Pedro are to accompany me to the Carthusian Convent at Caxias[104] and I am furbishing up a string of highly polished saintly speeches for the occasion. Between you and I however, I cannot help owning these eternal monkish parties become wonderfully tiresome, and unless the Court contrive to vary the scene with a few profane amusements they will never gain me over to Portugal.

Thursday 21 June

Who should pay his humble respects this morning to the worshipper of St. Anthony but Frei João Jacinto, the renowned preacher. Of all the monks I have hitherto seen, this one is the most amiable, the most eloquent and the most clearsighted. I am charmed with his conversation and the frankness with which he treats the drones of his order. He is just returned from the Caldas, where he was summoned by the Queen to preach before her on the festival of the *Coração de Jesus*, the day I was half-suffocated in the convent of the *Sacramentas*, and as far as I can conjecture from his style of addressing me I am to, ere long, expect a complete triumph over Walpole and his adherents and much solicitation to remain in Portugal.

We dined earlier than usual and at five stopped at the door of the Marialva Palace to take up the Grand Prior, D. Pedro and the Abbade. The heat would have been insupportable had not a fresh breeze from the entrance of the harbour blown full in our faces and ruffled the blinds of the coach. In half an hour we were set down before the Carthusian Church which fronts the royal gardens and were ushered into a silent, solemn quadrangle by the Abbot and his attendant friars. Several spectres of the Order were gliding about in the long cloisters which branch off from this court. In the middle is a marble fountain darkened by pyramids of clipped box. Around are seven or eight small chapels with altars richly gilt and decorated, but displaying ghastly images of our Saviour in the last horrid agonies of His passion, covered with livid bruises and streaming with blood. Whilst we were contemplating these ghastly objects, the monks, by permission of their superior, gathered around us. One of them, a tall interesting figure, attracted my attention by the deep melancholy which sat upon his features. Upon enquiry I learnt he was only two-and-twenty years of age, of illustrious parentage and lively talents; the cause of his seeking these mansions of stillness and mortification was not communicated to me. I could not help observing as this young victim stood before me, and I contemplated the calm evening light settled on the arcades of the quadrangle, how many setting suns he was likely to behold casting their gleams upon these walls, and what a long series of years in all probability he had devoted himself to consume within their precincts. The eyes of the good Grand Prior swam in tears, M. Verdeil shuddered, the Abbade shrugged up his shoulders, and I, totally forgetting the superstitious part <I> generally act in holy ground, exclaimed loudly against the toleration of human sacrifices and the folly of permitting those to quit the world whose youth incapacitates them from making any due estimate of its miseries or advantages. As for D. Pedro, his serious and melancholy disposition received additional gloom from the objects around him. The chill gust that blew from an arched hall where the fathers are interred, and whose pavement returned a hollow sound as we walked over it, froze him with horror. He had never entered a Carthusian convent before and was ignorant of the severities of the Order. Like a child afraid of hobgoblins he never stirred from my side, and when the Abbot showed us his cell and garden commanding a solitary view of the barren hills round Caxias, he lifted up his eyes with an expression I shall long remember, and leaning upon me whispered that my Abbey of Witham[105] was the only monastery in which he felt any inclination to confine himself.

I was trying to cheer his spirits by talking of the variety and magnificence of our English villas when the old Abbade called me aside to read a letter he had received this morning from the Marquis of Marialva. It confirms me in the idea I entertain of the warmth and sincerity of his friendship, but is full of mysterious expressions that seem to indicate some secret of high consequence to us both which he impatiently longs to communicate. Next Tuesday he returns. I have agreed with the Abbade to go and meet him in the Praça do Comerçio where he lands, his intentions being to come down the river from Vilanova in one of the Royal barges. My conversation with the Abbade was interrupted by the Abbot who with many excuses and monkish compliments invited us to a collation in the refectory. The tables were covered with linen perfectly white and clean. Several pyramids of excellent fruit, particularly scarlet strawberries, were presented to us on dishes of the finest Japan china by a lay brother whose high shining forehead and streaming beard reminded me of those mandarin figures our Dowagers used formerly to set a-shaking on their chimney-pieces. The same exotic figure served us with coffee, the genuine growth of Arabia, and a variety of biscuits, omelettes and conserves all excellent in their kind, but they were lost upon us. Even D. Pedro, who inherits no small portion of his grandfather's voracity, was too much dejected to pay them any attention. The sun set before we regained our carriage, and our conversation the whole way home was serious and melancholy.

I found the old Marquis of Penalva and his son waiting for me at home, and we played and sang and mutually extolled each other up to the heavens till the clock struck eleven, and I was completely jaded. They talk of giving me very soon a great entertainment and introducing me to the female part of their family, the greatest mark of attention a stranger can receive in Portugal.

Friday 22 June

The Grand Prior and D. Pedro came in unexpectedly to dinner. They had been disappointed at not meeting with one of their relations at home, and thought it best to take their chance with me. <The> Miss Sills were of the party. The heat had deprived me of appetite and I was as dull as a post. D. Pedro more dismal than ever. He swallows Burgundy as fast as you please but I doubt whether brandy itself would give him a moment's animation. The Grand Prior tried to laugh him out of his silent gloomy mood but without effect. I was too gloomily disposed myself to second these good-humoured intentions and let him pout away at a window for an hour without once interrupting his reverie.

The approaching coolness of evening reminding us it was time to drive out according to my invariable custom, we got into the coach and left General Forbes,[106] who came in after dinner, to entertain the ladies. Instead of parading along the shore of Belem, we drove all through Lisbon to Marvila, a neglected villa of the old Marquis of Marialva, which commands the broadest expanse of the Tagus. This is the very spot which a few weeks ago recalled so strongly to my mind the Lake of Geneva and all that befell me on its banks. You may imagine, then, this excursion tended much more to depress than exhilarate my spirits. I consented however to accompany the Grand Prior about the immense alleys and terraces of this shady enclosure, the scene of his childhood. The palace, of which he is peculiarly fond, courts and fountains are almost in ruins, the parterres of myrtle have shot up into wild bushes white with blossoms, and the statues are half concealed by jasmine. Here is a small theatre for operas constructed with some elegance, and a chapel not unlike a mosque in shape, and arabesque ornaments, hung around with Spanish banners, the trophies of the Battle of Elvas, gained by an ancestor of the Marialvas.[107] A long bower of vines supported by marble pillars leads from the palace to the chapel. There is something majestic in this verdant gallery, and the evening glow admitted through the foliage lighted up the wan features of several superannuated servants of the family, who crawled out of their decayed chambers and threw themselves on their knees before the Prior and D. Pedro. We rambled about this forlorn abandoned garden, whose stillness equalled that of the Carthusian Convent, till, the shadows of some tall cypress trees lengthening across the terrace, I was consumed with melancholy and so listless as to be hardly able to drag one leg after another. This wretch D. Pedro has infected me. We filled the carriage with flowery sprays of jasmine pulled from mutilated statues, and we were all half intoxicated before we reached home with the delicious but overcoming fragrance. We found tea very refreshing after our long walk up and down the terraces of Marvila and tiresome jumble through the ill-paved streets of Lisbon. Jeronimo de Lima had waited our return, and played

over a new air he had composed on purpose for me. It was late before the Grand
Prior and his nephew withdrew.

Saturday 23 June

Mr. Sill brought me a long letter Mr. Horne had just written him from the Caldas
and it has puzzled me not a little. The Queen seems still undecided when she
will give me audience, and the neglect I experience from relations in England
occasions much speculation. Melo[108] and the other Ministers know not what to
make of my being so totally abandoned. They all propose however cultivating
my acquaintance and showing me attentions. The Prince of Brazil[109] cannot help
discovering the liveliest impatience to see an animal of whom he has heard such
various and contradictory descriptions. Horne who has been kissing royal hands
with great perseverance never loses an opportunity of sounding my praises and
blowing curiosity into a blaze. In the meanwhile he is caressed and smiled upon by
the whole herd of courtiers and my name is never mentioned without a string of
complimentary epithets. These are fair blossoms and the return of the Marquis will
soon lead me to estimate what fruit I am to expect from them.

   It is hot and stifling. I took a dose of salts this morning and am very languid.
Happily I dined alone and reposed myself till the fresh gale which precedes sunset
sprang up in the Tagus and invited M. Verdeil and I to make our usual excursion
along the shore of Belem, which increases every day in picturesque beauty by the
numbers of majestic stalks shooting up from the aloes and covering themselves
with blossoms. Neither D. Pedro nor the Grand Prior appeared, but the good old
Abbade was watching our passage from behind the Chinese railing in Mr. Hudson's
garden. We stopped to take him up, and all the rest of our drive did he continue
holding forth upon the incredible affection with which I had inspired his Divinities
the Marialvas. "They talk upon no other subject," continued he, "the little ones lisp
your name and reserve their bon-bons for Monsieur Bekefor. D. Henriqueta sat
all yesterday evening on the veranda in hopes of catching a glimpse of you as you
passed by." "Pray," said I, "is not that same young lady to be married to the Duke
de Lafões? It is the current report, everybody talks of it." "You know," answered
the Abbade, with a most significant simper, "I have no secrets for you, and had
the affair been really so you would long since have heard of it; but wait patiently
the return of your affectionate friend the Marquis, and you will learn more than I
possibly can disclose to you."

   What say you to all this? Have I not cause to conjecture the mystery into which I
shall be initiated principally consists in a scheme of the Marquis for my marrying D.
Henriqueta. Unless the Abbade has lost his senses he would hardly proceed giving

so many hints of the young girl's disposition in my favour without foundation. He is forever prating about the liberty we shall enjoy at Sintra of being together and the striking conformity he has observed in our dispositions. If any idea of this sort makes its way into the gossiping world of Lisbon it will double the numbers of my enemies and arm their stings with new venom. D. Henriqueta in point of blood and connections has few equals in Europe. Her only brother D. Pedro is a sickly child and should he visit the other world, she immediately becomes heiress to the titles, estates and high privileges of the Marialvas. Of course she is an object upon which many ambitious eyes are fixed. Her own uncle D. José de Menezes[110] has placed himself in the ranks to obtain her, and till lately was much favoured by my friend the Marquis in his pretensions. I have long suspected D. José to be no friend of mine, and begin now to guess the reason. If St. Anthony or some superior being does not stretch forth his hand and lead me through the labyrinth I am about to enter, ten to one but I shall go astray and pass many a month in perplexed uncomfortable wanderings. I know not even now which way to turn myself and feel fatigued before I begin my course. Heartily do I wish the Marquis returned and our first conversation upon serious topics well over.

My conversation with the Abbade had so completely stretched my attention that I felt worn out upon my return home and went to bed earlier than usual. I was obliged to close every window in order to exclude the glare of bonfires with which the whole town and its suburbs are illuminated, tomorrow being the feast of St. John the Baptist. The Penalvas have sent word they will dine with me and I have some thoughts of going in the morning to hear Mass at the Patriarchal.

Sunday 24 June

I wish myself in some green meadow at the foot of the Alps, where fairies gambol in the twilight of midsummer and whisper in the ears of their sleeping favourites the good or evil futures which await them. It is too hot for fairies in Portugal. One must not expect their inspirations. Here is no smooth turf for them to trip about upon. I should be at a loss in this country how to entertain such visitors and could with difficulty find a bowl of cream to set before them. I have been haunted all night with rural ideas of England. The fresh smell of my pines at Fonthill seemed wafted to me in my dreams. The bleating of my sheep and lowing of herds in the deep valley of Lawn Farm faintly sounded in my ears. And shall I banish myself forever from these happy scenes of my childhood? Shall I renounce that earth where my poor Margaret is laid, that spot where her lovely infant was born? My heart beats. I am bathed in tears. I have no one into whose bosom I can pour my sorrows. If this mood continues I shall be wretched company today for the Penalvas. I can write no more at present. I am oppressed, dejected, ready to bow my head to the earth. I cannot stir out and have no inclination for the pompous rites of the Patriarchal Cathedral.

About two arrived the old Marquis of Penalva and his son, who, till a year ago when the Queen granted him the same title as his father, was called the Count de Tarouca. You must have heard frequently of that name: a grandfather of the old Marquis'[111] rendered it very illustrious by several splendid embassies; the magnificent entertainments he gave at the Congress of Utrecht are amply described in Mme du Noyer and several other books of memoirs.[112] The Penalvas brought today in their suite a famous Jesuit, Padre Duarte,[113] whom Pombal thought of sufficient consequence to be imprisoned for eighteen years, and a tall, knock-kneed rhubarb-faced physician in a gorgeous suit of glistening satins, the most ungainly, ill-favoured, conceited puppy I ever beheld. Between the Jesuit and the Doctor I had enough to do to keep my temper. They prated incessantly, pretended to have the most implicit admiration for everything that came from England either in the way of furniture or poetry, and after much commendation of the flourishing state of arts under the patronage of Sir Peter Lely, whom they believed the actual President of the Royal Academy of painting, launched forth into a panegyric of my countryman Hans Holbein. I begged leave to assure the sages that this illustrious artist was born at Basle, never saw England till he was thirty years old, and that as for Sir Peter Lely he had been dead almost a century. They stared a little at this information, and were playing off a sounding peal of compliments upon the great proficiency of the English in music, watch-making, the stocking manufactory etc. etc. when General Forbes came in and made a diversion in my favour. We had some political conversation upon the present state of Portugal and the risks it runs of being swallowed up by Spain ere many years are elapsed. I have reason to suspect from the conversation of this gentleman who has excellent sense and much experience, that like the Land of Egypt this kingdom is a broken reed upon which if a man lean he shall pierce his side. I must take care what I am about and beware of splinters. They are awkward things and when once got into the flesh, cannot be extracted without much festering and inflammation. I am more and more convinced that some great scheme of rooting me in this country is in agitation. The Marquis has spoken pretty plainly to Horne as appears by a letter Mr. Sill brought me from him just before we sat down to table.[114]

In the evening I would not be cheated of my drive and made the Penalvas go out with me. We returned to tea and there was a fiddler and a priest, humble servants and toad-eaters to the Marquis, in waiting. They fell a-thumping my poor pianofortes and playing sonatas whether I would or no. You know how I abhor sonatas, and that certain chromatic squeaking tones of a fiddle, when the player turns up the whites of his eyes, waggles a greasy chin and affects ecstasies, set my guts on edge. The purgation-like countenance of the Doctor was enough to do that already without the assistance of his fellow parasites the priest and the musician. Padre Duarte sucked his thumb in a corner. General Forbes had wisely withdrawn, and the old Marquis, inspired by a pathetic adagio, glided suddenly across the room in a sort of step I took for the beginning of a hornpipe, but it turned out a minuet <in> the Portuguese style, with all its kicks and flourishes, in which Miss Sill who had come into tea was forced to join much against her inclination. I never beheld such a fidgety performance. It was no sooner ended than the Doctor displayed his rueful length of person in such a twitchy angular minuet as I hope not to see again in a hurry. What with sonatas and minuets I passed a delectable evening. The Penalvas shan't catch me at home any more in a hurry.

Monday 25 June

Though it is very hot and my pasteboard habitation sucks up every ray of sunshine, I slept tolerably well and shall do again provided I hear no more sonatas. M. Verdeil has heard from Lady Craven, and she is as happy as I could wish at the Court of the Margrave of Anspach, and they are making gardens and reviewing regiments and amusing themselves royally.

   D. Pedro and the Grand Prior were to have dined here today, but the latter is indisposed and the Abbade has brought their excuses. I am not sorry. D. Pedro's melancholy countenance and desponding attitudes sink my spirits. The Abbade wished me to have got out as we passed the Marialva Palace this evening and seen him take his lesson of drawing; but I begged to be excused. We stopped a few minutes before the door, and the Grand Prior came down and complained bitterly of the headache. He stands in great awe of tomorrow, when sick or well he must dance attendance upon the Queen who is expected from the Caldas and instead of returning to the Palace of the Ajuda,[115] takes up her abode at the Senate House in the Praça do Comerçio.[116] There will be fine bustling and crowding and raising of dust. I shall keep out of the tumult and wait quietly at home for the Marquis.

Tuesday 26 June

Her Majesty of Portugal seems to have the same taste for piebald horses as the Caliph Motassem.[117] I have counted thirteen or fourteen sets this morning drawing coachfuls of Bedchamber women and Maids of Honour from the Ajuda to the Palace in Lisbon. I cannot say much in favour of the royal carriages. They are clumsily shaped and meanly decorated. The Queen will have a delightful row down the Tagus and be fanned by refreshing breezes. Her barge has 120 oars.

The Abbade came to dinner. He wanted me to drive at half past four to <the> Great Square to see the Queen land; but I felt unwell and preferred following my usual track along the shore of Belem. M. Verdeil and I remained in perfect solitude the remainder of the evening, walking in the veranda by moonlight.

At eleven the Marquis arrived, jaded to death with his attendance upon Her Majesty in the barge and at the card table. He caught me in his arms with parental fondness, and though he had not yet embraced his children, stayed above half an hour with me, talking over my concerns at this Court with an earnestness that showed they had become his own. I doubt much if I ever had a more zealous or affectionate friend. I only fear his excessive partiality for me will lead us both into difficulties.

Wednesday 27 June

I hear the Queen has remitted the tax upon *bacalhao*[118] and of course was received with uncommon acclamations. Above a thousand boats and barges transformed into arbours of flowers and garlands attended her progress with music and fireworks. She walked from the landing place to her Palace without guards amidst a multitude worked up to the highest pitch of grateful enthusiasm. Such genuine rejoicings were seldom seen in Portugal, and the Queen was affected by them almost to tears. I am sorry to hear that the Prince of Brazil remained sullen and motionless amidst this glorious frenzy. Though the air resounded with loud shouts calling down the blessing of Heaven upon him, he gave not the least sign of pleasure or approbation. One wave of his hand would have won him the hearts of at least a hundred thousand of his subjects. How can a human being reduce itself to the standard of a vegetable by such behaviour?

I went early to the Marialva Palace and was received by the Marquis with such tokens of affection and confidence as I believe are never shown a stranger in Portugal. He introduced me to the Marchioness and his daughters as a relation. All reserve was at end, all curtains drawn back, every apartment thrown open, the children playing about and taking their lessons as if their parents alone had been present. The Grand Prior and the good old Abbade knew not how to express their joy at seeing me thus initiated in the very bosom of their family. Even the melancholy countenance of D. Pedro received a gleam of satisfaction. D. Henriqueta was dressed in one of those baby dresses of rose-coloured silk and muslin I am so fond of, and that my lovely Margaret used to wear. The poor girl appeared in great confusion, scarce knowing what to make of this introduction. As God knows, I have no fixed plan concerning her, and should be miserable to disturb the peace of a family I so sincerely love and honour. My behaviour was not so attentive as might have been expected. I rather avoided than sought opportunities of drawing D. Henriqueta into conversation. She was often allowed to sit at a distance from her mother, and I might have said what I pleased to her; but I kept aloof and retired as often as I could contrive into the windows with the Marquis, talking of Walpole's behaviour, the cabals of the Corps Diplomatique against me, and Melo's timidity.

It is Melo who by hints and surmises has gone twisting and winding about to prevent a formal presentation, and so keep well with all sides. The Queen has irresolution enough of her own without having the stock augmented by that of her Minister. She is impatient to see <me> and has conceived a more favourable idea of me in every respect than I deserve, and yet cannot bring herself to give the word of command and order Melo to conduct me into her presence with the usual ceremonies. They would gladly have received me as it were by chance at the Caldas; but the Marquis was above smuggling an introduction, and is determined to carry the point in a decided manner and in the sight of Walpole, his colleagues and their satellites.

At two o'clock we sat down to table en famille. I was placed between the Marchioness and her husband. The dinner was served in plate, and the huge massy dishes brought up by a vast train of gentlemen and chaplains, several of them decorated with the Order of Christ. This attendance had quite a feudal air and transported my imagination to the days of chivalry when great chieftains were waited upon like kings by noble vassals. The Portuguese had need have the stomach of ostriches to digest the loads of greasy victuals with which they cram themselves. Their vegetables, their rice, their poultry are all stewed in the essence of ham, and so strongly seasoned with pepper and spices that a spoonful of pease or a quarter of an onion is sufficient to set one's mouth in a flame. With such a diet and the continual swallowing of sweetmeats I am not surprised at their complaining continually of headaches and vapours. The rain descending with violence, every window was shut, and the absence of vegetable perfumes from the garden, so delightful after a shower, supplied by a steam of burnt lavender.

My friend, being obliged to accompany the Queen to her favourite convent precisely at half past four, kept his watch on the table and communicated a share of feverish restlessness to me by continually consulting the minute hand. Said he: "I shall pass a delightful evening shut up in a close chamber with the royal family, the Lady Abbess,[119] and the Archbishop-Confessor to Her Majesty, twirling our thumbs round and round, observing how hard it rains and how unusual such weather is at this season, and then a pause, and then some such other interesting observation, and then a general yawn, and then a *merenda* or collation of preserved fruits, comfits and conserves of every sort and colour, which whether good or bad must be swallowed and commended." He continued anticipating his ennui in this style till it was time to go and swallow his dose of it. The minute hand pointed to four.

Coffee was served, and I followed him into a chaise drawn by two gigantic mules which set off full gallop to carry him to the Palace in the Praça do Comerçio, two miles I think from Belem. My house lying in the way, he set me down. I loitered half an hour talking over with M. Verdeil what I had seen at the Marialva Palace, and then returned again to Belem, and drove out by the sea shore as usual with the Grand Prior and the Abbade.

Thursday 28 June

The weather still continues overcast, with every now and then a gleam of reviving sunshine. Would to heaven I were enjoying this mild weather in the green province of Minho on the slope of flowery hills under the shade of chestnut trees.

The Marquis passed the whole day here using his utmost endeavour to draw me eternally from England. We were eleven hours together, and in the course of our conversation he expatiated so forcibly upon the neglect and coldness of my relations that I was more than once on the point of acceding to his opinion and assuring him I would never return home. We have agreed to go next Sunday to Melo and use our joint efforts to engage him to break through the sacred etiquette of the Court and present me himself to the Queen in defiance of the English Minister. "Nothing would be more certain than this event," continued the Marquis, "if you would but allow me to inform Her Majesty that you have thoughts of establishing yourself in Portugal." "That I cannot allow" was my answer; "I am not yet sufficiently acquainted with your country to form any ideas so decidedly in its favour." "At least," said the Marquis, "pass the next winter at Lisbon. We will be inseparable, and every friend or relation that values me will show you the kindest attentions. You must not think of leaving us, I could not endure the thought." I still remained on the defensive, declaring that unless the Queen admitted me into her presence immediately, and by that conduct gave public proofs of her disbelieving the calumnies of Mr. Walpole, I would scarcely continue another month in Portugal. This resolution, expressed with terms of energy and a rap on the table, called forth from the Marquis a fresh torrent of affectionate protestations and assurances of every exertion to carry the point I desired in the manner I wished. It was near twelve before we parted, the Marquis surprised and vexed at finding me so unwilling to abandon a country I have such strong reason to abhor, and I more uneasy, more agitated and more undecided than ever. I am a mere child without any plan, abandoning myself to the current of events, and letting it hurry me wherever it pleases. Whether I shall be once more safely landed in my native country or cast away in a foreign one, blind Destiny alone is acquainted. As I have just told you, I have established no fixed rule to act by, am neither one thing nor the other, neither vicious nor virtuous, and in the meanwhile lead the stupidest life imaginable.

Friday 29 June

I am become as motionless as a log, and though there were great doings at the Patriarchal in honour of the Prince of the Apostles, would not stir. Last night that simpleton the Count <of> Vila Nova,[120] whom I have seen so often dangling after the Sacrament in a scarlet mantle, opened his garden to all the rabble in Lisbon. It was lighted up with transparent paper lanterns, red, blue and purple, very dull and shabby. There was a sort of pavilion awkwardly constructed for dancing, and all the mantua-makers, milliners and abigails in the town shone off in cotillons with the Duke of Cadaval and some other young men of the first distinction who are never at ease but in low company. Two of my servants accompanied my tailor to the fete, and returned enraptured with the affability and pleasing manners of the Portuguese milliners and nobility. <The> Miss Sills, Bezerra and D. José dined with me. Melancholy as I was, I could not help laughing at the current reports in Lisbon of my giving four thousand crowns[121] to one convent, fifty moidores to another, and grovelling twelve hours by lamplight before the image of St. Anthony. Bezerra who is a mighty gossip entertained us with all the lies invented about me by the English for this last fortnight. According to their chronicle I am to be shortly hugged in the fondest embraces of Holy Mother Church, made a grandee, a Familiar of the Inquisition, and perhaps Cardinal Patriarch.

    In my way to Belem this evening I met vast crowds of carriages hurrying to the Great Square, which is to be illuminated with lanterns in the Vila Nova style I imagine. The Royal Family are expected to appear at the windows of the Senate House and there will be a firework and a line of huge bonfires surrounded by fishermen and nymphs of the Tagus, snapping their fingers and dancing fandangos. 'Tis well if the rain does not spoil their diversion, for the clouds hang low and heavy. The moon travels through them with difficulty. The Portuguese know not what to make of so moist a summer, and regard the unseasonable verdure of their hills with less pleasure than surprise.

Saturday 30 June

Pombal[122] paid me a visit. He looks worn down with gaming and lechery, but there is an ease and fashion in his address not common in Portugal. The English have been trying their best endeavours to prepossess him against me, and being conscious of having given way for some time to these insinuations, he appeared a little embarrassed. Though he has the largest fortune in Portugal, about a hundred and ten thousand crowns a year, he wished me to understand his father died in distressed circumstances, loaded with debts contracted in supporting the dignity of his post and the honour of his country. We talked a good deal about Fonthill, my father, etc. etc.

He was hardly gone when the Marquis of Marialva, the Grand Prior and D. Pedro came in. We dined together very comfortably. I was in better spirits than usual and amused the Marquis so well that he had not time to urge his favourite point of my totally abandoning England. The more I see of the Marquis, the more I have reason to like him. There never existed a more sincere attachment than that he has conceived for me. It makes him forget the duties of his office. This evening instead of accompanying Her Majesty to a convent in the very suburb I inhabit, he drove out with me to Marvila, the wild, neglected garden to which the Grand Prior is so partial. My carriage, being followed by the pages in the royal liveries who always attend the Master of the Horse, threw the whole town into a stare. Marvila has great picturesque beauties. The trees are old and fantastic, bending over ruined fountains and mutilated statues of heroes in armour, variegated by the lapse of years with innumerable tints of purple, green and yellow. In the centre of almost impenetrable thickets one finds strange pyramids of rock-work surrounded by marble lions that have a magic symbolical appearance. The Marquis has feeling enough to respect the uncouth monuments of an age when his ancestors performed so many heroic achievements, and readily promised me never to sacrifice these venerable shades to the pert, gaudy taste of modern Portuguese gardening. I laid in an ample provision of jasmine both white and yellow, the stoutest and most luxuriant I ever beheld.

We walked part of the way home by the serene light of the full moon rising from behind the mountains of Alenteija[123] on the opposite shore of the Tagus, and casting a stream of quivering brilliants across the vast expanse of waters. The Marquis exulted in the climate and repeated continually we could expect no such moonlight in England. Lisbon appeared to wonderful advantage by those soft gleams. The flights of steps, terraces, and chapels, and porticos of several convents on the banks of the river shone forth like edifices of white marble, and the rough cliffs and miserable sheds rising above them were lost in dark shadows. The Great Square through which we passed was filled with idlers of all sorts and sexes, staring up at the illuminated windows of the Palace in hopes of catching a glimpse of Her Majesty, the Prince, the Infantas, the Confessor[124] and Maids of Honour, whisking about from one apartment to the other and giving ample scope to amusing conjecture. I am told the Confessor, though somewhat advanced in his career, is far from being insensible to the allurements of beauty, and pursues the young nymphs of the Palace from window to window with great alacrity. It was after nine before we got home and drank tea in a careless indolent manner reclined on couches inhaling the perfume of jasmine. I was in a very musical mood and played and sang till after eleven. The Marquis boasted greatly of the magnificence of the King D. José II's[125] operas, when sixty horse and two hundred soldiers used to appear at once on the stage in Egiziello's and Caffarelli's triumphs. The splendid theatre on which these far-famed sopranos were wont to strut and warble was destroyed with all its velvet embroidered trappings and glittering decorations in the conflagration which followed the earthquake of '55.[126] The same dreadful commotion deprived the Marialvas of their gallery of paintings, rich jewels, and curious plate.[127] From what I learn from every person, Lisbon abounded more than any city in Europe with precious Japan wares and Indian curiosities.

Sunday 1 July

The Marquis came punctually at ten to take me to Melo's,[128] who was profuse of compliment but stingy of committing himself with Walpole or the diplomatic set. Not all my noble friend's insinuations could move him from his purpose of strictly adhering to the established etiquette. Had Melo been bribed for the purpose, he could not have conveyed a higher idea to the Marquis of my connections and consequence or enlarged more copiously on my father's merit and independence. He admitted the undoubted right I possessed of being introduced at every Court in a distinguished manner, and the ridiculous hot-brained conduct of Mr. Walpole, but urged at the same time the impropriety of overturning every received system, and of course the impossibility of having me presented by any other person than the British Minister. For above an hour and an half did he tread over and over again the same ground and try by these endless repetitions to exhaust our patience; but we were not to be starved out in this manner. The Marquis insisted upon the peculiarity of my situation; that never Minister through private pique had dared before to offer such a public insult; that my honour was deeply affected, and that I must kiss the Queen's hand immediately or quit Portugal, a step which would deprive him of the society of the friend he loved best in the world, and the country of a person whose pious and charitable dispositions served in this degenerate age as a bright example. This last part of the declamation I confess had near set me a-laughing. I resumed however a solemn gravity, and held forth on the abominable usage I had received from Mr. Walpole, in a style that alarmed Melo and obliged him to palliate the Envoy's behaviour, I am certain at the expense of truth. He assured me Walpole had never said a word to him against me, that he was convinced all might be right if I would only tranquilize myself and obtain better information, that the dispute had been fomented on both sides by officious meddlers, that he did not despair of seeing me conducted into the presence chamber by the British Minister with every demonstration of respect and kindness.

I treated this idea with such contempt and violence that the poor old Secretary wished himself a mouse to creep into some crevice of his apartment. The Marquis thought I went too far, and employed the usual set of softening courtier-like phrases to appease the tempest; but the wind was up and not so easily laid. I suffered M. de Melo to accompany me to the outward door of his ante-chamber without almost taking any notice of him, and leaving the Marquis to patch up the rents I had made in the Secretary's amour-propre as well as he was able, darted into my carriage and whisked off in a twinkling. It is amazing how I enjoy getting into scrapes. To me a scrape is like a dram. It raises my spirits and brightens my imagination. Thanks to the enthusiastic friendship with which I have inspired the Marquis of Marialva, I have had an opportunity of speaking harsh truth to the Prime Minister of Portugal, and obliging him to descend to the lowest pit of lies to avoid my reproach and indignation.

I had not been returned above half an hour before my friend arrived in a sad ferment. "This shuffling, timid old man," says he, "is enough to distract one. He detests Walpole and has confessed to me that he pointed you out to him in the blackest colours. You know, I have been hearing Mass at his chapel, and I could hardly kneel in peace for all the abuse he has been pouring out on the Envoy, and yet he would fain have persuaded you that the affair had been misrepresented, and Walpole not half so much to blame as you imagined. I am at a loss how to act," continued the Marquis. "You have frightened Melo out of his senses. For God's sake treat him with more respect and kindness, though he does not deserve it. He intends returning your visit in a day or two, and for my sake drive him not perfectly mad by your sharp taunts and menacing gestures." I promised ample reformation with all my heart. I will be as gentle as the Marquis pleases now I have had my frolic. Thank God I deal not, like Melo, in repetitions, and will behave as really becomes me by way of variety. The Marquis stayed dinner and seemed happier than can be expressed in my company. The old Abbade made the fourth at table. As he always speaks his mind without fear or disguise, he scolded the Marquis pretty roundly for neglecting his attendance upon the Queen yesterday evening, and losing his time in sauntering with me about Marvila. I suspect my zealous friend intends very shortly surprising the Envoy with a visit and demanding his reasons for using me as he has done, in a tone that will force explanations, produce peace or establish serious hostilities. The Marquis, being obliged to make up the Royal party at the interesting game of lotto on Sundays and Festivals, could not go out with me, so I took the opportunity of paying visits to the Penalvas and D. Thomaz de Almeida. Neither were within, and I continued my drive towards Marvila on the shore of the Tagus.

I got home just as it was dark, and in came Gregorio Franchi, the boy who played so delightfully on the harpsichord in the Patriarchal and does such honour to Lima, Leal, Polycarpo and all his instructors spiritual and temporal. I think his eyes are grown larger than ever, and fix themselves so inveterately upon me that I cannot help colouring. He caught my style of playing instantaneously and flourished away several overtures and sonatas at sight perfectly in my manner. These Portuguese youths are composed of more inflammable materials than other mortals. I could keep them spellbound for hours at my side, listening to the childish notes of my voice, and dissolving like snow in sunshine. It seems the poor boy's large eyes were near being scratched out by his comrades at the Patriarchal, the moment they heard from Lima and Polycarpo what a favourable opinion I entertained of his musical abilities. This cursed world is made up of nothing but envy, malice and uncharitableness in different shapes and dresses.

Monday 2 July

<The> Miss Sills and their brother dined with me. At my usual hour I drove with M. Verdeil to the shore of Belem. The Abbade joined us as we passed the Marialva Palace. I grumbled and growled the whole airing, threatened to leave Portugal unless Melo was forced by superior powers to renounce his beloved etiquette and present me in the teeth of Mr. Walpole. Under the rocks of Ribamar at the windows of a snug little mansion shaded by vines and jasmine, I spied Monsignor Aguilar in earnest discourse with two females. I beckoned to him and stopped the coach. He got in and we continued our drive. He is quite of my opinion as to the paltry shortsighted conduct of Melo, and advises me by all means to remain firm in my intention of quitting the kingdom unless presented in the manner I desire to its Sovereign. We foamed and fretted and stamped in chorus. The old Abbade was struck dumb and had not a word to say in answer to our arguments. I set down Aguilar at his haunt amongst the jasmines, and the Abbade at D. José Lobo<'s>,[129] one of the Lords of the Bedchamber, who lives near the Marialva Palace. I had given him such a dose and so roundly declared my sentiments that he had scarcely the power of wishing me goodnight, but bowed to the ground with a countenance three ells in length and a most significant shrug of the shoulders. At home I found Captain White, one of the few amongst the English who have not assisted in tearing me to pieces. The Miss Sills had remained since dinner in Mr. Collett's room, trying to keep up the good old man's spirits, which flag considerably. The unprecedented persecution I experience from my countrymen breaks his heart, and he trembles lest it should estrange me forever from England.

Tea was bringing up when the Marquis of Marialva arrived. It was a sultry night and the rising moon cast a glowing ruddy tint on the sky, which announces the setting-in of hot weather. My friend walked to and fro with me in the veranda. He took hasty strides and seemed much agitated. "Can you," said he, "think of ever returning to a country whose inhabitants pursue you to the very extremity of Europe with such bitter malevolence? I know you are neither acquainted with Mr. North or Lord Edward Fitzgerald[130] who have been here lately. Of course you have done nothing to injure them, and yet there is not a spiteful reflection they have not thrown on your conduct. Open your eyes, undeceive yourself, abandon every idea of falling once more into this nest of scorpions, and remain with us who love, pity and respect you. The Queen would in that case grant you signal favours and the whole Court unite in treating you with kind distinction." I explained as well as I was able, in answer to this vehement sally of the Marquis', the various and tender ties that bound me to England—the place of my nativity which I had rendered so eminently beautiful, the spot where my poor Margaret's remains were laid, my mother, my children! He was affected almost to tears and protested if I did return to England he should never enjoy an easy moment.

No sooner were the Miss Sills and Captain White departed, than our conversation took a most serious superstitious turn. The Marquis is convinced I was conducted by a miracle to Portugal, and that it is the will of God he should admit me into an unlimited, unreserved friendship. "In general," said he, "I am the shyest of mortals. My enemies give out that I am the proudest. I avoid strangers and particularly those of the English nation whose brutal fierceness and sullen insolence I abhor. But an unaccountable impulse drove me to you, and inspires me with the same ardent wishes for your salvation and welfare as for my own. Recommend yourself to that bright luminary of Portugal, the blessed St. Anthony, and beseech him to use his powerful intercession to conduct you in the paths of life. We may perhaps remember this conversation we now hold together in another existence. Offer up to God the sacrifice of your present sufferings. These persecutions, these black calumnies, these shafts of a rancorous and poisoned malice are tolerated at present for your final good. The ways of Providence are inscrutable, and as light follows darkness so may a never-ending triumph spring from your actual mortifications."

I received this singular sermon with all due meekness and reverence. I am grieved to find a man I honour and esteem, so far gone in the labyrinth of bigotry, so thoroughly persuaded of miraculous interpositions. If the affair of my presentation is to be given out of Melo's hands into those of St. Anthony I think I may as well pack up and take my leave of Portugal. In order more effectually to interest the celestial powers in this business and stifle every spark of etiquette in the Queen's bosom, the Marquis most solemnly entreated me to promise that in case of success I would give a considerable alms to the monks of Boa Morte.[131] "These holy men," continued he, "retain all the purity of the primitive church, and their prayers in conjunction with those of St. Anthony cannot fail of disposing the Queen to act decidedly in your favour." I readily made the vow, the Marquis lifted his eyes to heaven whilst I pronounced it, and we separated after embracing each other with devout tenderness.

Tuesday 3 July

The moon prophesied but too justly. It is furiously hot and the thermometer at 86. The Marquis came to dinner and brought his cousin-german D. Diogo de Menezes e Noronha who is colonel of the Count de la Lippe's regiment and reckoned one of the best officers in Portugal.[132] The heat rendered me feverish and languid. I lay gasping like a perch just hooked out of a rivulet. The Marquis never quitted my ear and kept pouring into it without interruption the bitterest maledictions on England. I see plainly he will never rest himself or allow me to be quiet till he has rooted out the last fibres of attachment to my native country. Again and again did I tell him that to produce so violent a change in my affairs would require more encouragement than I met with in Portugal and a very distinguished reception from Her Majesty. I talked and declared to this purpose till my mouth was parched up and my tongue as rough as those fish skins of which they make shagreen cases. My friend assumed a doleful air, turned up his eyes and fetching a deep sigh told me he feared my attachment to England was unconquerable, and that even the Queen's efforts, supposing her ready to shew the most flattering distinctions, would prove ineffectual. I had little to say to the contrary. I cannot yet bring myself to dash to the ground every hope of reestablishing myself at home, and enjoying in honour and tranquility the lawns I have formed and the woods I have planted.

Happily the arrival of the Grand Prior put an end to our conversation. The Marquis went to the Palace and his uncle accompanied me and M. Verdeil in our usual no drive. We took the great street which leads through the square all along the riverside towards Marvila. We passed the Palace. All the windows were open, and the rich yellow damask curtains of the royal apartments blown about by a fresh wind which ruffled the bosom of the river and tempered the warmth of the atmosphere. I returned home exactly at eight and passed the remainder of the evening pleasantly enough in hearing Gregorio Franchi, who takes me to be not much older than himself, and imagines I shall soon lose the high clear notes of my voice. I could not help smiling at this notion, but I am not surprised at it. My movements, gestures, attitudes become, whenever I please, as careless, sportive and supple as those of a child.

Wednesday 4 July

The Marialvas are all gone to Belas, a villa of the Count de Pombeiro[133] who gives a grand entertainment to the Corps Diplomatique tonight with ball, supper and fireworks. I expect my friend will attack Mr. Walpole upon the frantic abuse with which he has loaded me and make him pass half an hour not very agreeably. Bezerra, D. José de Mateus, the Miss Sills, their brother and the Abbade dined here. The Abbade has not yet recovered <from> the hail-shower of execration I poured down t'other evening on Melo and the supporters of etiquette. I felt extremely happy to see Bezerra, whose unprejudiced mind and disinterested heart renders <him> a much better judge of any merit I may chance to possess than the rest of his countrymen.

In the evening I sallied forth to pay Mme Arriaga,[134] the Queen's favourite attendant, a visit. She was gone out with her royal mistress to some garden in the neighbourhood. The Maids of Honour were leaning over their balconies waggling their hands and giving me great encouragement to run upstairs to them; but I was lazy and would not move. The Archbishop-Confessor displayed his goodly person at one of the windows. From a clown he became a corporal, from a corporal a monk and so on till it pleased the great Marquis of Pombal to appoint him Confessor to Her Majesty, then Princess of Brazil. Since her accession he is become Archbishop *in partibus*, Grand Inquisitor and the first spring in the present bungling government of Portugal. I never saw a sturdier fellow. He seems to anoint himself with the oil of gladness, to laugh and grow fat in spite of the wretched situation of political affairs in this kingdom and the risks it runs of relapsing once more into a Spanish province.

From the Palace I drove to the Marquis of Lavradio's,[135] who came to see me a night or two ago with his son, the Count de Avintes.[136] They were both of the party at Belas. I am sorry to have missed the old Marquis. Everybody tells me his talents for Court intrigue and manoeuvre are so considerable that Pombal thought him of sufficient importance to be banished to the Viceroyship of the Portuguese West Indies, in which post he remained until her present Majesty's accession. He is now risen again upon this horizon and is President of the Tribunal of the *Desembargadores do Paço*, a post of the highest dignity and importance. The Lavradio Palace is situated on an eminence near the Patriarchal Cathedral and overlooks that glorious expanse of the Tagus which never fails putting me in mind of the Lake of Geneva. A thousand glowing tints reflected from a variegated sky were cast this evening on the river and the distant mountains. I continued my drive along the water's edge beyond Marvila, breathing the fresh noontide air impregnated with the fragrance of broom.

Thursday 5 July

It is so sultry that I hardly know what to do with myself. I hope the Marquis of Marialva will grant me a truce today, and not enter upon holy subjects. If he does I greatly fear giving in to his opinions, through mere laziness. The sun deprives me of all force of argument. I could recover tolerably well in the shade; but there is no shade in my habitation, which though tolerably neat and fair to the eye is composed of planks and came ready made from America soon after the earthquake. If destiny impels me to spend many months longer in Portugal I must look out for a more substantial dwelling.

I had the pleasure of the Grand Prior's company at dinner, who returned at six this morning from Belas. By the description he gave me of the entertainment it must have been highly romantic and magnificent. The villa and its flowery ornamented gardens is wrapped up in a wild forest of timber trees and. boundless shrubberies of orange and myrtle. Choirs of musicians were stationed in the thickets, and glittering illuminated pavilions appeared emerging like fairy edifices from the gloom of impervious foliage. The Portuguese take their swill of amusement whenever an opportunity offers, and the Count de Pombeiro's company which assembled yesterday several hours before sunset did not abandon him till this morning at six o'clock.

General Forbes and the *Conservador* João Teles came in just before my hour of taking the sea breezes. The *Conservador* could not help letting me know the English cabal raged against me with more virulence than ever. I expressed my contempt and indifference in a lofty style, got into the carriage with the old Abbade and rattled over the cracked pavement on the shore of Belem. My mules are growing fat and sleek. They trot at a vigorous rate and their paces are even and agreeable. I wish they were drawing me along the smooth roads on the banks of the Lake of Geneva. I am sick to death of sandy hills and leaden-coloured aloes, and sigh after waterfalls and verdure. My imagination having taken its flight to <the> hanging woods and rocks of Meillerie, I hardly opened my lips to the Abbade during our excursion. He fancied, I believe, I was meditating my escape from Portugal, and dropped his chin in a piteous manner.

The Marquis did not fail making his appearance about ten o'clock after he had danced his usual attendance upon Her Majesty. The conversation between him and Mr. Walpole took place at Belas in the style I expected—much anger and indignation on one side, much alarm and reddening on the other. My friend forced the Envoy to come to one point at least, and allow he had no authority from the Court of England for behaving in the manner he had done. I am heartily tired of all these cabals and manoeuvres and wish myself most heartily under the canopy of my favourite chestnuts at Evian.

Friday 6 July

The Packet which sailed in last night has brought me a letter from Pinto to Secretary Melo; but it is far from being written in a style that will do me much service. I am not at all pleased with it. Bezerra and D. José who have been with me the chief part of the day think the arrival of this epistle a mighty event in my favour. Poor Mr. Sill is of the same opinion. I fear they are all mistaken. My being humbly recommended to the protection and *benevolenza* of Melo will flatter his vanity much more than I could wish, and set him a-crowing. I learn from Foxhall[137] that painting and furnishing goes on briskly at Fonthill, that Bacon and Banks are making chimneypieces for me and that Loutherbourg has just finished two capital views of Wales to be placed in the Great Apartment.[138] Alas, when shall I enjoy these fair ornaments and improvements in tranquility. When shall I cease acting the part of the Wandering Jew and being stared and wondered at as if I bore the mark of God's malediction on my countenance. I am almost ready to give up the contest and build my nest in the first country whose inhabitants will promise to keep the English at a distance. Could the Marquis of Marialva look into the depths of my heart, he would see its blood boil with indignation and rage against England. How gladly would he seize the moment of effervescence (?)[139] to lead me to the Queen and make me abjure in Her presence my religion and my country. I trust the gust of passion will never drive me into such desperate measures. What would become of me, poor childish animal, accustomed to mild temperate climates and rural landscapes, in this dusty sunburnt capital. Supposing Her Majesty was to honour me with a gold key[140] and a pompous title, how ill am I suited to the confinement and etiquette of a drawing-room. I should make a wretched courtier and should grumble myself into total disgrace the first evening I was forced to dangle after the Queen to a convent or sit down to a card table.

Bezerra accompanied me this evening to Marvila. We were both in a romantic mood peculiarly calculated to enjoy the melancholy scenery of this ruined garden. The sun was just sinking when we arrived there, and the thick shrubbery of myrtle looked black and dismal in the twilight. The whole atmosphere was perfumed with the subtle odour of the jasmine. I gave way to enervating languid sensations, and found myself imperceptibly declaiming some of the most tender and passionate recitatives in my beloved opera *Quinto Fabio*.[141] Night drew on before we left Marvila, and a cool wind having risen, waved the cypresses and scattered the white jasmine flowers over the parterres of myrtle like flakes of snow. Soon after I came home, the Marquis arrived and I showed him the letter for Melo. We both agree in disapproving the greatest part of the expressions, and my friend is determined to write to Pinto upon the subject. He went so far even as to desire I would dictate whatever I thought most likely to sound well for me at home and assured me he was ready to subscribe to any philippic I chose to compose against Walpole. You must allow this is a proof of boundless attachment.

Saturday 7 July

I went to Melo's in the morning but he was out overlooking the works in the Botanic Garden. So I left my letter in the hands of his old crabbed porter. In my way back, who should I meet but my adversary Walpole driving ding-dong to the Secretary's, and swelling with malice [like a venomous reptile. His countenance appeared boiling hot, and his nose a coal of fire]. I conjecture the report of my having received recommendations has thrown his brains into a dreadful ferment and called up new fire into his purply countenance. If the first grandees begin receiving me into the interior of their families and distinguishing me by pompous entertainments, the toad will burst and the Factory be floated with venom.

M. Verdeil and I dined alone for a wonder and drove at sunset as far as Caxias. We caught a glimpse of the Abbade, but being in the chaise had no room for him. I was in fine spirits, expecting Gregorio Franchi, whose genius and style of playing delights me beyond measure. I found him and Polycarpo waiting my return. The Count de Obidos[142] had been to make me a visit. My party strengthens every day. The Marquis, who came in as usual from the Palace at ten o'clock, bids me be assured we shall tread down the mobility[143] and crush their stings out. "All the grandees," said he, "are resolved to support you, and from me you shall receive the most public marks of confidence. I will even bring my wife and D. Henriqueta to dine with you at Sintra. According to the etiquettes of the Portuguese nobility I could pay you no higher compliment. Would to heaven you would send for your children. I would answer for their forming the first alliances in Portugal."

Sunday 8 July

The Marquis and D. Pedro who dined here today accompanied me in the evening to the bull feast.[144] Twelve of these devoted animals were standing with all the dullness and resignation of oxen, in the middle of an open amphitheatre about the size and diameter of Ranelagh, capable of holding two or three thousand people. The poor beasts gave no signs of courage or ferocity, no furious pawings, no tearing up of the ground. I never saw a quieter party in one of the cow yards of Tottenham Court Road. After we had waited a quarter of an hour in our box, there tumbled into the amphitheatre about a dozen hideous negros grotesquely dressed in a sort of Indian-Chinese fashion, who after several awkward leaps and vaultings drove the herd of bulls into an enclosure fastened up with painted boards. Then entered a procession of blackamoors in laced jackets, preceding the principal combatant and his aide-de-camp mounted on fine managed horses prancing and curvetting. Having paraded round the amphitheatre and saluted the company in the boxes, the door of the enclosure was thrown open and a bull forced out much against his inclination. He stood stock still for a moment or two till the horseman whisking round him, darted his lance into his shoulder. Though stung with pain, he made no violent efforts to defend or revenge himself, and was lanced with lances till he dropped down dead, his joints slackening and his whole frame quivering with agony. Eleven more were slaughtered pretty nearly in the same stupid manner, and though scared with fireworks, pricked with swords, worried by dogs, and provoked by the grinning negros, never ventured to attack the horseman. It requires little courage to attack such patient animals. I was highly disgusted with the spectacle. It set my nerves on edge, and I seemed to feel cuts and slashes the rest of the evening. Gregorio Franchi and Lima came in and I tried to compose myself with music.

Monday 9 July

I was at the Marialva Palace by nine o'clock and set off from thence with the Marquis for Sintra. Having the command of the Queen's stables in which are four thousand mules and two thousand horses, he orders as many relays as he pleases, and we changed mules four times in the space of an hour. A few minutes after ten we were landed at Ramalhão,[145] the villa Mr. Street Arriaga has lent me, about twelve or thirteen miles from Lisbon, on an eminence under the pyramidical rocks of Sintra, an exposed situation overlooking a vast stretch of country bounded by the ocean. I was struck with the suite of apartments, which are spacious and airy. Unless the heat becomes more violent, I shall be frozen in them as there is not a chimney except in the kitchen. Mr. Collett has reason to praise the air of the heaths and mountains with which Ramalhão is surrounded; it has set him up again and he was stout enough to accompany us all over the house and the terraces. I found the garden in excellent order and flourishing crops of vegetables sown by my gardener springing up between rows of orange and citron trees.

  After I had passed half an hour in looking about me, the Marquis and I got into our chaise and drove to his own villa,[146] a new creation which has cost him above ten thousand pounds sterling. Five years ago it was a wild hill strewed over with stones and fragments; at present you find a gay pavilion designed by Pillement[147] and elegantly decorated; a parterre with statues and fountains, thick alleys of laurel, bay and laurustine; cascades, arbours, clipped box trees and every ornament the false taste of Portuguese gardening renders desirable. We dined at a clean snug

inn situated towards the middle of the village of Sintra.[148] The Queen has lately
bestowed this house and a large tract of ground adjoining it on the Marquis. I like
the situation much better than that of his villa, which as well as Ramalhão is placed
on the bleak naked side of the Sintra mountains. From the inn you look down
shady ravines and bold slopes of woods and copses, variegated with mossy stones
and ancient, decayed chestnuts.

As soon as we had dined, we went to Colares and walked to and fro <on> a
terrace belonging to one La Roche, a French merchant, who has shewn some
glimmerings of taste in the laying out of his villa. The groves of pine and chestnut
starting from the crevices of rock and rising one above the other to a considerable
elevation give Colares the air of a Savoyard village. Several fountains of clear water,
overhung by cork trees and branching lemons, burst out of ruined walls by the
wayside, and are received in marble basins round which in general are assembled
groups of loathsome beggars.

A servant of the late King's who has a very large property in these environs invited
us with many bows and cringes into his garden.[149] I thought myself entering the
orchards of Alcinous. The boughs literally bent under loads of fruits, the slightest
shake strewed the ground with plums, oranges and apricots. This villa boasts a
grand artificial cascade with tritons and dolphins vomiting torrents of water, but I
paid it not half the attention its proprietor expected, and retiring under the shade
of the fruit trees feasted on the golden apples and purple plums that were rolling in
such profusion about me. The Marquis, aware of my predilection for flowers, filled
his carriage with carnations and jasmine; I never saw plants more remarkable for
size and vigour than those which have the luck of being sown in this fortunate soil.
The exposition likewise is singularly happy, screened by sloping hills and defended
from the sea airs by four or five miles of thickets and orchards. I was unwilling to
quit this woody, sheltered spot and the Marquis flatters himself I shall be tempted
to purchase it.

The wind grew troublesome when we got back to the Marquis' pavilion. The sky
was clear and sunset fiery. The distant convent of Mafra[150] looked like the palace of
a giant, and the whole country around it as if the monster had eat it desolate. To
repose ourselves a little after our rapid jumble, we sat in the pavilion I told you just
now Pillement had designed. It represents a bower of fantastic trees mingling their
branches, and discovering between them peeps of a summer sky. From the mouth of
a flying dragon depends a magnificent lustre with fifty branches hung with festoons
of brilliant cut-glass that twinkle like strings of diamonds. We loitered in this saloon
till it was pitch dark.

The pages riding full speed before us with flaming torches, and the wind driving
back the sparks in volleys and smoke full in our faces, I was stunned and dazzled
and felt like a novice in sorcery mounted for the first time behind a witch on a

broomstick.[151] In less than an hour we had rattled over twelve miles of the rough pavement, going up and down the steepest hills in a convulsive gallop, which, if not dangerous, is extremely disagreeable. I expected every instant to be thrown flat on my nose, but happily the mules were picked from perhaps a hundred, and never stumbled. I found the air on the heights above the Ajuda very keen and piercing. The climate must be strangely altered, or I could never complain of cold at Lisbon on the 9th of July.

Tuesday 10 July

Yesterday's exercise has done me a deal of good. I slept undisturbed by the howl of dogs or the sputtering of rockets continually letting off by some fool or other. Scarce a night without them. The old diamond dealer Gildemeester[152] celebrates his son's nuptials in a day or two and then I imagine there will be rare whizzing. Gregorio was with me from ten till twelve and I sung seven arias. He accompanies tolerably well but is often hurried out of time by the impetuosity of his singer. Aguilar and Bezerra dined here. Aguilar went out with me in the chaise to Belem and continued painting all the way in brilliant colours the advantages I might reap from an establishment in Portugal. We returned and drank tea together and he sat till past eleven advising me by all means to take advantage of the tide now setting in so decidedly in my favour, and connect myself solidly with the Marialvas. I stared to hear him declaim on this side of the question, well knowing his antipathy to Portugal.

Wednesday 11 July

I took it into my head to plunge over head and ears in cold water this morning and I feel myself greatly revived. It is very odd I should have so long neglected this simple method of bracing my nerves and strengthening my spirits. The Marquis brought a posse of the young nobility to dine with me today, his brother D. José, the Count de Assumar,[153] D. Bernardo de Lorena,[154] the Count de Obidos, and D. Diogo de Noronha.[155] Assumar is a smart, hook-nosed young fellow, mighty jaunty and conceited. The Marquis has them all in a string and plays them off like so many puppets. The manner in which he made them dance attendance on me today is proof of his influence. D. José is a jovial companion, fond of boxing, badgering, wenching, and bull-fighting, tosses off his glass with the true English smack, and is pure hearty and vulgar.[156] D. Bernardo I liked the best of the party and should not have much objection to cultivate his acquaintance; but he sails in a month for a government in the Brazils to which he has been lately appointed. My company all left me at half past seven, and I took a solitary drive along the shore of Belem. The aloes are bursting into full yellow bloom, and <a> variety of enormous moths buzzing about them.

Thursday 12 July

Feeling dull and spiritless I had recourse to the cold bath. I write such stupid stuff that if it were winter and I had the happiness of sitting by a crackling wood fire, my papers should increase the blaze. Bezerra came to dinner with his brain in a whirl, raging and foaming against the English. He hates them worse than I do, and does his utmost to rouse my indignation.[157]

Friday 13 July

The Grand Prior dined with me and soon after coffee arrived the Marquis. We went out to pay visits together and upon our return found Polycarpo and Franchi, who sung and played away the rest of the evening.

Saturday 14 July

The Marquis has written to Pinto a long energetic letter full of encomiums upon my conduct in this country. I think it will show my stupid relations that I merit some attention. Verdeil likewise is plying my mother and Mrs. Hervey with epistles. I have just heard from Wildman that Lord Courtenay has been once more overawed by old Beelzebub, and like a contemptible coward suffers the most obnoxious papers to remain in old Beelzebub's clutches. I cannot yet discover any decisive method of smoothing my way home to England.

Sunday 15 July

The sailing of the Packet is put off till this day sennight. I am sick of writing home to so little purpose. We had the old Abbade at dinner giving broad hints, half joke, half earnest, of what a delightful spouse my Margaret[158] would make for the heir of the Marialvas. That would never do. The little spirited thing has too much of her father and mother's taste for beauty and elegance not to spurn away such a stiff, dismal, pigtailed sapling as D. Pedro. The Marquis of Minas paid me a visit.[159] His manner is frank and easy without any mixture of puppyism. I made my daily excursion towards Marvila. The Great Square was full of people staring up at the Palace windows. Amongst the crowd I remarked several strings of French Navy officers, arm in arm, with slouched hats and short postillion-like jackets. They belong to a fleet of observation (?) commanded by the Count de Neuilly[160] and are entertained very splendidly every day by their ambassador the Marquis de Bombelles. This dash of French figures gives a new air to Lisbon. Wind and dust rendered my drive not very agreeable, and I was glad to get home and pour some tea down my parched throat. Franchi came in looking silly and sheepish.[161] I fear the boy takes more pleasure than he ought in hearing me sing J. de Sousa's compositions. <The> Miss Sills, who drank tea with us, stared him completely out of countenance.

Monday 16 July

'Tis a wonder I do not expire with ennui, the life I lead is so stupid and uniform. My habitation is close and confined. I have no suite of apartments to decorate, no galleries to stretch my legs in, no rural spots to resort to of an evening like the little lawn in the Bois de Blonay on the banks of the Lake of Geneva. I was much happier at Evian, translating Arabian tales, rambling over the rocks of Meillerie with young Caron, and talking of India and the Brahmins with black Pigott.[162] Here every night my good friend the Marquis bores me with zealous perseverance, and repeats the same professions of regard for my person, and zeal for the salvation of my soul. How I long after the verdure and tranquillity of my beloved haunts in Savoy in Switzerland. M. Verdeil and I dined alone today, and walked at sunset under the rustling plane trees of the Botanic Garden. In our way there we called upon the Marchioness of Marialva, but she was gone out. The evening hymn of the workmen finishing the balustrades at the Botanic Garden and the ringing of their tools on the marble formed so drowsy a sound that I was half lulled asleep, and dozed all the way home in my carriage. We were roused from supper at half past eleven by a glare of torches under my windows. It was the Marquis and his attendants who happily for me, finding the door barred and porter gone to roost, drove off again.

Tuesday 17 July

I cannot say *Les jours se suivent et ne se ressemblent pas.* Every day in my Lisbon existence is tinted with the same dull colours. I rise, gape about me, wipe the dust off my books, receive begging epistles and sweetmeats from convents, dash into my tub of cold water, talk over Franchi, St. Anthony, the Marquis, and Evian with M. Verdeil, who to do him justice exerts his powers of speech to persuade me into some more consistent agreeable way of life. He thinks me in the way to seize Fortune by those flowing locks she so invitingly holds forth to me at this moment, and make something of my peculiar position in Portugal. I might certainly climb up on the shoulders of the Marialvas to lofty dignities, but I have not sufficient strength of nerves and spirits to run the risk of tumbles.

Tonight the Marquis came earlier than usual and held forth upon the delights of wild-boar hunting at Salvaterra, a shabby village to which the Court resorts in the winter season. I expressed my indifference to field sports with an energy that convinced him the Salvaterra party was not likely to contribute much towards my conversion. He left me much out of spirits.[163] About an hour after his departure, just as I was going to bed, the fire bell of the Necessidades rung a furious alarm, and was answered by an universal jingle. Troops of horse passed by full gallop and drums beat far and near. The cause of this commotion was a fire at the Ajuda Palace; I saw the blaze from my windows. Towards two in the morning the racket subsided and I fell asleep.

Wednesday 18 July

Little damage done by the fire, I hear, and no lives lost. The shabby buildings fronting the Botanic Garden are levelled with the ground. So much the better. They were a mere lousery, the receptacle of every species of filthiness. Mr. Horne is arrived from the Caldas. He came early and was at breakfast when I went to see him. We had a long conversation upon the dirt, dullness and despotism of Portugal, and the little such a government had to offer worth my acceptance. Our opinions perfectly coincide. General Forbes, the Marquis, and D. José de Mateus dined with me. One of the Marquis' horses tied under the window kept me in a perpetual worry by his stampings and neighings.[164] D. Bernardo de Lorena, nicely perfumed and bespangled, glided into the room after dinner. He was going to a fête at the French Ambassador's. I have been telling my dearly beloved friend that it would be as well for him to present me to M. de Bombelles, the only person in this stagnated capital who has any idea of society; but he seems determined to keep me to himself, and very little desirous of extending my acquaintance by his exertions. This is wretched policy and must end in the total discomforture of his expectations. He goes to Sintra tomorrow for a week, and wished much I would accompany him; but the winds are so cold and violent that I feel no inclination for naked, unsheltered mountains. I went in my chaise to set him down at the

Palace, where he was obliged to go to take leave of Her Majesty. In our way, we met the Sacrament marching in state to pay some sick person a farewell visit. Out we tumbled with great precipitation and followed it as fast as our legs would carry us. There was that idiot the Count de Vila Nova trotting along in a scarlet mantle with a huge wax taper in his hand. He is always in close attendance upon the Host, and passes the flower of his days in dangling after it. Whilst we were most piously for the moment following his example and dusting ourselves up to the ankles, I could not help casting a longing eye at the French Ambassador's hotel, hard by the house into which the Sacrament had entered. The apartments were gaily illuminated and a vast number of smart hats and feathered *têtes* glancing along them.

Having dropped the Marquis at the Palace, I returned home to tea, and found M. Verdeil and Franchi walking to and fro my apartment, and talking an almost unintelligible gibberish, half Italian, half Portuguese.[165] I know not what demon inspired me, but I felt in a wild lively mood as if I could have danced on the slack rope, or vaulted over three horses like Astley.[166] Franchi had brought me a glorious aria of Cimarosa;[167] but I had neither voice nor power to sing it; all my talents lay this night in my heels, and I kept cutting *entrechats à huit* and leaping over chairs and tables without intermission. In the midst of my exertions, the Marquis came back from the Palace, stopped at the door a moment, cried "Bravo," and thought me bewitched. However, the same frenzy soon seized him. The glass at the upper end of my saloon reaching from the floor to the cornice shews the whole figure from top to toe, and he could not resist the temptation of exhibiting some steps before it. He has been an excellent dancer, firm and graceful in all his motions. I believe the thoughts of going to Sintra tomorrow and enjoying a few days truce from Court dangling in the bosom of his family, gave his spirits an unusual flow, and recalled the vivacity of his youthful hours.

Thursday 19 July

Mr. Horne and his family dined with me. In the evening I went with Horne to see the Lacerdas[168]—two young handsome sisters, Maids of Honour to Her Majesty, who lodge at the Palace in a shabby plastered apartment up the Lord knows how many pair of stairs. The room was full of nephews cuddling and cackling like poultry in windy weather. Amongst the rest Mrs. Street Arriaga, who lends me Ramalhão. We should never have found our way to this cage had not an aide-de-camp of the Duke de Lafões, who was waiting to give out the parole, very civilly directed us. The heat and lustiness of the apartment affected me very disagreeably, and a raw carroty-pated youth, *perfusus liquidis odoribus*, putting me completely out of humour, I am afraid <I> appeared to the ladies extremely reserved, stupid and indifferent. Had it not been for Mr. Horne my visit would not have lasted ten minutes. It was prolonged however by his means till half after eight. The corridors and staircases of the Palace, formed upon a magnificent scale, were illuminated with vast numbers of wax lights in handsome lanterns. Having no aide-de-camp to conduct us, we lost our way like a couple of geese, and strayed about several arched passages and galleries, stretching out our necks for information and looking simple and helpless. A yeoman of the guard set us right. We descended into the Great Square by a grand flight of steps and were almost blown into our carriage by a violent blast of wind that filled Mr. Horne with all the terrors of rheumatism. <The> Miss Sills had not had the patience to wait for us. We drank tea alone, and sat talking over my affairs in Portugal till after eleven.

Friday 20 July

Whenever I am out of humour, I fall on the old Abbade, whom like the scapegoat in the wilderness I never fail loading with all the sins of my adversaries. Today he came to dinner and was severely trimmed because his nephew Manique, the Intendant of Police,[169] would not deliver up some cases of books etc. that are arrived for me at the Custom House, without an *aviso* from the Queen. I whined and stormed alternately, declared there was no living in Portugal, and that the Marquis was benumbed, and that one might as well choose for one's bosom friend a torpedo. The Abbade let me run on till, like a Billingsgate scold, I had exhausted my torrent of obloquy. He then attempted pouring oil into the wounds and vindicating with great reason the conduct of Manique. Horne, who was sitting by during the altercation, chuckled heartily; as an honest Englishman he always rejoices when any little event takes place to disgust me with Portugal. I am extremely impatient to rummage the contents of the cases in question. They contain I believe some very valuable prints, and the last monthly reviews in which I expect to read a critique on *Vathek*.

Though the wind raged furiously in the evening, M. Verdeil and I confronted its violence on the shore of Belem. We drove beyond the Convent of Bom Sucesso. The postillions could hardly keep their hats on. I wonder the Marquis' habitation at Sintra, perched on the summit of a bleak hill, is not blown away by these hurricanes. Ramalhão and its woody *quintas* are somewhat more sheltered, but still so much exposed that I shall seldom walk unblowsed about them. Mr. Collett is just returned from this airy residence, and its keen blasts have done him considerable service. I believe he would be as well as ever were it not for the continual terror he suffers lest I should sacrifice my country and give way to the Marquis' solicitations. The Packet sails next Sunday and I must prepare my letters. Marialva's epistle to

Pinto takes its departure with them. He has put it into the Secretary of State's parcel for greater security. Saturday 21 July

I have written myself muzzy. Last night the wind howled dismally and I heard it in my dreams accompanied with piteous wailings. In spite however of its turbulence, I will set off for Sintra tomorrow. I owe my friend this attention, and indeed every other I can pay: his regard for me is truly parental. Manique has been solicited again about my cases; but there is no prevailing upon him to release them till a formal order is given out by Her Majesty, and to obtain this favour he hints at an application to Melo. The devil burn me if I make one. The Marquis shall speak to the Queen without any circumbendibus, and I have little fear his request will be complied with, without any Secretary of State's interference. I send neither cooks nor scullions this time to Ramalhão, intending to feed constantly at my friend's. Berti has despatched the cabinet-maker to paper my bedchamber; the glare of white plastered walls makes my eyes ache. Rumi the violin player and Franchi passed the evening with me but I was far from being musically disposed and played and sung very indifferently.

Undated jotting

Lisbon feels hot and fusty. Manique has released my pianoforte from the Custom House, but still detains four or five cases in spite of the Marquis' solicitations. I must obtain a special order from the Queen, or shall never get peaceful possession of my books and candlesticks.

Sunday 22 July

[Went to Sintra.] The gust having blown its fill, nothing could be milder or more pleasant than the morning. Light showers had refreshed the thickets of orange and citron, and the hills above the Ajuda were enamelled with newborn flowers. We dined at the Marquis', in a low stuccoed apartment under the great pavilion better calculated for the climate of Bengal than that of the Sintra mountains. The Marchioness is comfortably fat and no friend to exercise: her spouse could not prevail upon her to go out with us in the evening. We drove to Colares and walked about M. La Roche's terrace; M. Verdeil was not so much pleased with it as I expected, nor do I like it so well a second time. We returned to tea, and I played about the pavilion with the little girls, D. Maria and D. Joaquina. D. Henriqueta looked on with longing eyes. D. Pedro is the dismallest child I ever saw, <and> seemed undecided whether to retain his usual stateliness or follow our example. We supped late, and it was one before I got back to

Ramalhão. The coach with Berti and Mr. Collett was not arrived, and I was obliged for want of my bed to sleep upon mattresses full of fleas. I hardly closed my eyes.

Monday 23 July

The Marquis was walking about the garden before I was up. He is sadly nervous and low spirited; his Court attendance sits heavily upon him. I feel warmly attached to him. He took me home to breakfast, which was served uncomfortably upon a dusty table without a cloth. The Marchioness and D. Henriqueta sat with us all the morning. I am worn to a skeleton with doing nothing. Not a book to be seen at the Marialvas'. They never read. I took to drawing through pure ennui. Verdeil followed my example. It is strange weather, more like spring than summer. The vegetation looks green and flourishing. Stout bushes of laurustine, the flowers much larger than in England, cover the rough declivities of the hill, which the Marquis has enclosed for his garden. I am fond of rambling about this shrubbery. The fresh mountain air gave me a violent appetite, and I fed hoggishly on a variety of Portuguese ragouts. We went out all together in the evening to José Dias' garden at Colares—M. Verdeil and I in a low garden chaise drawn by a vigorous mule, the Marchioness and D. Henriqueta in their gilded cabriole, and the Marquis and D. Pedro on horseback. Towards night a thick damp fog overspread these hilly regions; the pointed rocks staring out of the vapours looked so bleak and comfortless that I thought myself in the Apennines, and felt happy to take shelter under the hospitable roof of my friend, and warm myself by running about with the children in the pavilion. The little ones hang fondly about me and press my hands to their lips, and take inexpressible joy in my leaps and capers.

Horne arrived this morning. I stopped at his house a moment in my return from Colares.[170] He has a small square terrace overhung by a fantastic cork tree, which commands the most romantic point of view in Sintra: vast sweeps of varied foliage, banks with twisted roots and < > trunks of ancient chestnuts mingled with weeping willows of the tenderest freshest green, and citrons clustered with fruits. Above this sylvan scene tower three shattered pinnacles of rock, the middle one diversified by the turret and walls of Nossa Senhora da Pena,[171] a Convent of Hieronymites[172] frequently concealed in clouds.

Tuesday 24 July

I slept comfortably in my own bed. Five or six wenches are scrubbing the floors of my long suite of apartments and I hope will soon wash the fleas out. Aguilar,

Bezerra, and D. José are all at Sintra, and they came to see me this morning. We sallied forth together on horseback; but I stopped short at the Marquis', where I dined as usual, drew caricatures, and went to see a hideous garden belonging to D. José Lobo in the evening. I am half crippled with a cursed corn and was obliged to take off my boots. The waters of Sintra disagree with me. I am a good deal out of order, and yet am able to skip about with the children, which I wonder at. I believe the Marquis expects every instant I should make up seriously to D. Henriqueta, whose graceful modest carriage would win from every male mortal but myself the tenderest assiduities. Horne came in to us whilst we were at tea. He had been at Ramalhão with old Gildemeester the Dutch Consul to pay me a visit, and they had squabbled all the way. I have been persuading the Marquis to accompany me tomorrow to Gildemeester's. It is the old man's birthday and he opens his new house[173] with dancing and suppering. There will be a pretty sample of the Factory misses, clerks and apprentices, some underlings of the Corps Diplomatique, and eight or nine hundred pounds weight of Dutch and Hamburg merchants.

Wednesday 25 July

Grand gala at Court, and the Marquis gone to attend it, for this blessed day not only gave birth to Gildemeester but to the Princess of Brazil. I felt aguish shiverings after breakfast, and basked in the sun. M. Verdeil has had the kindness to uncripple me by paring away my cursed corn in a workmanlike manner. We went to dine with the Marchioness. I never saw D. Pedro appear to such advantage. He begins to grow childish and engaging. A band of regimental music on their march to Gildemeester's began playing in the court, and drew forth a swarm of servants. D. Henriqueta and I sat on the steps which lead up to the great pavilion. She bent gracefully forwards talking to one of her favourite attendants. The children sat at our feet playing with some flowers I had gathered for them, and often looking up at my countenance with an engaging fondness that recalled to my mind the sweet smiles of my own little ones, and brought tears into my eyes. I should have sunk into deep melancholy had not an old Irish woman, first and foremost in the group of maids which had gathered around us, diverted my attention by her noisy tittle-tattle and shrewd observations.

Just as D. Pedro and I were preparing to set off together for the ball, we were agreeably surprised by the arrival of the Marquis, who had escaped from the Palace much earlier than he expected. I carried him in my chaise to Horne's, where we drank tea. Verdeil followed with D. Pedro. The lofty crags, crowned by the Convent of Hieronimites, was still glowing with rosy red, but the broad mass <of> the woods beneath were already in shadow. I leaned against a branch of the cork tree, staring idly at the queer figures passing along to Gildemeester's in the dusk. My friend grew impatient and uneasy, the Count de São Vicente, to whom he has a mortal aversion, having made his appearance.[174] I never saw the blackness of revenge and murder stronger marked in any countenance, and I fear it is not without reason he has been accused of assassination. We moved off the first opportunity, and were near being jerked into a ditch as we drove up to the old Consul's door.

The space before his new building is in sad disorder. The house has little more than bare walls, and was wretchedly lighted up. In several of the apartments—you will hardly believe me—one woeful candle depended from the ceiling in a solitary lantern. I leave you to represent to yourself the effect of this stable-like decoration. As for the company, it turned out just what I expected. The English part of it [looked blank] seemed to shrink into their native insignificance <at> every look I cast upon them. Their confusion was not decreased by the stern eye of the Marquis, and the contemptuous sneers of Mrs. Gildemeester. She presented me to her daughter-in-law, and continued during the whole night paying me the most studied attentions. I handed her in to supper. This part of the entertainment was splendid and magnificent. There was a bright illumination, a profusion of plate, a striking breadth of table, every delicacy that could be procured, and a dessert frame fifty or sixty feet in length, gleaming with burnished figures and vases of silver flowers of the most exquisite workmanship. The Marquis sat on the left of Mrs. Gildemeester, and the old Consul stood behind our chairs the chief part of the supper, handing us the choicest fruits of his extensive gardens, and the best Cape Vine I ever tasted.[175] Opposite to us sat Mrs. Aik, one of the most lively and flippant of the Factorial ladies, and close to her side, like a limpet to a rock, stuck Mr. Burn the *bacalhao* merchant, her constant admirer.[176] This fond couple, I am told, have been amongst the most active in spitting their venom at me ever since my arrival. I saw more tameness than malice in their looks this evening, and I fancied even the lady was only waiting for some encouragement to wriggle up to me with her softest smiles and graces.

I felt no inclination to dance after supper. The music was not inspiring, and the company thrown into the utmost confusion by the freaks of a Frenchman called Marcel, on whom Mme Gildemeester is supposed for two or three years past to have placed her affections. A *coup de soleil* and a quarrel with M. de Bombelles it seems had turned the poor fellow's brain. There was no preventing him rushing from room to room with all the sputter and eccentricity of a firework, now abusing one person and now another, confessing publicly the innumerable kindnesses he had received from good Mrs. Gildemeester, and the many marks of tender affection a certain Miss Warden had bestowed on him. "Why," said he to the two ladies, who I am told are not upon the best terms imaginable, "should you squabble and scratch? You are both equally indulgent and have both equally made me happy."

Whilst the light of truth was casting its rays upon the bystanders in this very singular manner, I leave you to imagine the surprise of the worthy old Consul and the angry blushes of his spouse and her fair associate. I never beheld a more capital scene. In some of our pantomimes, if I recollect right, harlequin applies a touchstone <to> his adversaries and by its magic influence draws truth from their mouths in spite of propriety or interest. The lawyer confesses having fingered a bribe, the soldier his flight in the day of battle, and the whining methodistical dowager her frequent recourse to the bottle of inspiration etc. etc. This wondrous effect seemed to have been here realized and some malicious demon to have possessed the talkative Frenchman and obliged him to disclose the mysteries to which he owes his subsistence. Amongst other harsh truths hurried out by this flow of sincerity was a most vehement apostrophe to the English canaille upon their behaviour to me. Mrs. Gildemeester, who was become dauntless through despair, took up the cudgels in my cause most vigorously and compared her guests to a swarm of venomous insects, unworthy to crawl upon the hem of her garment, and whom she would shake off with a vengeance the first opportunity. The Marquis, D. Pedro and I enjoyed the scene so much that we stayed later than we intended.

Thursday 26 July

As soon as the Marquis was up, he came to Ramalhão, and we talked over the very original pranks of Mme Gildemeester's favourite. We returned both together to his villa, and I fell drawing the strange phizzes I had seen the proceeding evening. After dinner we scrambled about the *quinta* with Monsignor Acciaoli, a good natured, [round,] laughing prelate, for ever playing at whist or reciting his breviary.[177] The cascades and fountains were set a-playing; the children were driving about the fragrant alleys of citron and myrtle in their gay little cabriole, D. Pedro and I running after them; the Marchioness and my friend leaning over the margin of a tank and feeding a shoal of goggle-eyed gold and silver fishes.

Friday 27 July

I was at the Marquis' by nine, and we rode over wild heathy hills which overlook a vast extent of sunburnt country and a boundless expanse of ocean. The fresh morning air was impregnated with the perfume of innumerable aromatic shrubs and flowers. The sky was of the purest softest azure. We followed a winding goat's path which leads over the brow of the eminences to the Cork Convent,[178] which looked at a distance like the settlement of Robinson Crusoe. Before the entrance, which is formed by two ledges of ponderous rock, is a little smooth spot of greensward browsed by cattle. Their tinkling bells filled me with rural ideas. The hermitage is lined with cork; its cells, chapel and refectory are all scooped out of the rock. Several of the little passages which lead about are not only roofed but paved with cork, soft and pleasant to the feet. The monks offered us a collation of wine, sweetmeats and excellent oranges. Their shrubbery and paths amongst the rocks are delightful. Bushes of lavender start out of the crevices, and rosemary of a tender green. D. Pedro and I scampered madly home over the rough craggy pavement. 'Twas a mercy we escaped unmaimed. We had made such haste that, finding it was still very early, we mounted up to Nossa Senhora da Pena, from whence the view is boundless. Several hovering clouds of a dazzling whiteness, suspended low over the sea, had a magic effect. They looked like the cars of marine divinities just risen from the bosom of their element and going in solemn procession to the annual festival of the Ethiopians at the farthest extremities of the earth.

Saturday 28 July

I walked about the *quinta* of Ramalhão. It is a walled park full of Goa cedars and Portugal laurels grown to timber, surrounded by shrubby hills covered with fern. There is a little vine arbour with a trickling fountain.

Undated entry [179]

… regions of chalk and pasture, where I may sleep upon new mown hay, and breathe the fresh mountain air uncontaminated by the breath of slaves and bigots wallowing in the slough thrown up by some choleric volcano ten thousand years ago in the spot now called Sintra. Contemptible as these hills appear when the Alps are brought into comparison with them, I shall not be sorry to avail myself of their coolness. I hope next Thursday to be fixed at Ramalhão and that the winds will fan me once more into existence. At present I lie gasping in a piteous condition, Dr. Verdeil having forbid me to bathe whilst I have any remains of cold hanging about me. D. José de Mateus dined with us. I like him extremely; he has real taste and discernment, a cool head and a glowing heart, a proper sense of the capabilities of his country, but no blind ignorance of its abject state and numerous deficiencies. I felt my spirits cheered and put into motion by his conversation. We agreed to go together to the Portuguese play or opera, or whatever it is. But first I went to the Palace, and passed half an hour with Marialva, who complains of his confinement. I learnt from him that Her Majesty's Confessor is desirous I should pay him a visit, and wishes I would name a morning.

Next Tuesday, then, at eleven o'clock the interview shall take place. I must speak a sort of lingua franca, for I hear the good Archbishop's knowledge of languages is very slender, and strictly confined to the Portuguese.

The play afforded me much more disgust than amusement. The theatre[180] is low and narrow, the stage a mere gallery, and the actors, for there are no actresses, below criticism. Her Majesty, who to be sure is all prudence and piety, has swept females off the stage and commanded their places to be supplied <by> calvish young fellows. Judge what a pleasing effect this metamorphosis must produce in the dances, where one sees a stout shepherdess in virgin white with a soft blue beard and a prominent collar bone, [with a little hat stuck on one side and a garland of roses,] clenching a nosegay in a fist that would almost have knocked down Goliath, and a train of milkmaids attending her enormous footsteps, tossing their petticoats over their head at every caper. Such flouncing, sprawling, jerking and ogling I never saw before and hope never to see again.

Thursday 2 August

No paladin who drank at the fountains of Merlin was ever more suddenly disenchanted.

Friday 3 August

I rose somewhat refreshed, not having been scared with visions of portentous northern lights and quaking houses. One of the females over the way, who imagines no doubt from the tender compliments she probably received from me last night, that I am sighing away my soul for her, had the goodness to let fall a flow of jetty ringlets over a panting bosom, to lean pensively on her arm, and to steal several looks at me full of pity and encouragement. She remained at this sport the whole morning.

Sunday 5 August

I went to the new Church of St. Peter of Alcantara,[181] and heard Lima's mass. All my musical acquaintance were employed—Rumi, Palomino, Ferracuti, Totti[182] etc. Totti sang delightfully, he happened to be in voice, a blessing he seldom enjoys. I was placed to great advantage in the music gallery. The sprite had got in, I know not how; but he appeared divested of all those beams my imagination had cast around him. In the procession of the Sacrament from its tabernacle to the High Altar, the Count de São Lourenço,[183] an uncle of Marialva, carried over it a little pert umbrella. This piece of pious gallantry took off much more than added to the solemnity of the spectacle.

In the evening I went late to the Palace. The Marquis was with the Queen, but desired permission to quit her the moment he heard I was waiting for him. The happiness of his life seems to consist in being with me. I fancy J. Lima will get a fat addition to his income upon the strength of my recommendation. I have been settling with him how much I am to pay a band of musicians I wish to have at Ramalhão. The dogs had the impudence to ask first twenty moidores a month, then fifteen, then ten. They shall come down to eight, or I will have nothing to say to them. To be sure, they are excellent; the first bassoon who played at F. José<'s> mass this morning is of the number, and a capital musician. Walked by moonlight in the Terreiro do Paço; soft light on the sea; happy groups under the statue.

Monday 6 August

I have received a letter from Mrs. Hervey by land conveyance, and I read to my great joy that Mercier's (?)[184] edition of my *Vathek* is at length published. D. José dined with me. In the evening went to the Palace. Walked at night on the platform before the Necessidades.

Tuesday 7 August

The Marquis accompanied <me> to the Archbishop who is lodged in a mean house adjoining the Palace. His apartment however is clean, neatly matted, and hung with beautiful tapestry. Those who expect to see the Grand Inquisitor of Portugal a doleful meagre figure with eyes of reproof and malediction would be disappointed. I never saw a pleasanter or more honest countenance than that of the Archbishop. He received in the most open cordial manner. We sat conversing about half an hour. He told me that he had left the Queen on purpose to see me, and that when he had a moment to spare he would <be> happy to give it me. This man has no ambition, knowing the value of ease and tranquillity; he has refused being Prime Minister, Cardinal and Patriarch. I dined with my friend, with D. Thomaz[185] and two or three other Noronhas, Assumar, Lorena. They have almost persuaded me to go to a grand bull feast next Friday in an amphitheatre on the opposite shore of the Tagus, where they are to combat themselves. In the evening Franchi and I walked and on the platform etc.

Wednesday 8 August

Intense heat; but having got rid of my cold I bathed and was much refreshed. The Packet is arrived and I have a heap of letters. M. Verdeil and D. José went to see the Prince of Brazil's apartment over the Ajuda, and returned home to dine with me. In the evening went to the Palace for a < > and then (?) Franchi.

Thursday 9 August

I bathed. The Abbade at dinner. The sprite has been playing over its monkey tricks at the window, and I, like a fool, cannot help wasting my time in looking at them. Oh that it were decent and proper for me to lay this spirit, not in the Red Sea, but on a bed <of> rose leaves, defended from mosquitoes by awnings of gauze, and cooled by an almost imperceptible rain of iced perfumed water. I went to the Palace as usual, and as usual was pestered by a variety of petitioners most clamorously instructing me to use my influence at Court to obtain their respective demands. An old dapper Frenchman, brother to the celebrated natural historian the Abbé Nollet, skipped after me up the < > staircase with an agility I should not have expected at his advanced time of life, for he has been near fifty years in Portugal and was no chicken when he came there. I know not what he wants, but he is extremely importunate and has taken <it> into his head that one word from me in his favour would instantly operate with the Marquis and procure the pension he solicits. He was a favourite attendant of the Infant D. Manoel,[186] so celebrated for his romantic travels and adventures. My friend was much hurried tonight by innumerable applications. My books, owing to the negligence of one of the Custom House officers, have <not> yet been delivered up to me. The Queen's orders were positive. I shall take care that the officer be well trounced. Before supper I went in hopes of catching some fresh air to the obelisk and fountain in front of the Necessidades. There did I meet the sprite who most faithfully delivered me many kind messages from the signoras. One of them had got severely scolded by her brother for a-leaning a little too far out of the window and expressing herself in my favour with rather too much vivacity. I could have fondled and caressed the sprite, but a certain black pig wrapped up in an ample capote that stood aloof, kept me within bounds of the strictest decorum. Franchi's mother and her spouse were walking about. I entered into conversation with them etc.

Friday 10 August

The Tagus is covered with boats crossing over to the bull feast. I bathed. General Forbes and D. José dined with me and went to the bull feast. I had a *scalera* or barge with eight oars. Never did I behold such doughty bargemen as the natives of Algarve. We crossed the river with astonishing rapidity, and passed <the> old Marquis of Marialva in his galley with fifty oars. He hardly ever misses a bull feast. We were landed in a pleasant hilly country shaded by pines and overgrown with a wild shrubbery of low aromatic bushes. We drove directly up to a Convent where D. José, Assumar and the principal combatants lodged. We found them accoutring themselves in their fantastic Spanish dresses. D. Bernardo complained of a fever and swilled porter. The amphitheatre was decorated in the same paltry style as that at Lisbon. To my great surprise my dear friends D. Bernardo and D. José, instead of seating me commodiously in the principal box with the Countess of Assumar and several other ladies, left me to shift for myself and get a box as well as I was able. General Forbes who is truly polite and attentive took care I should be well placed. Fifteen or sixteen wretched bulls were massacred. The band of negros tumbled about the amphitheatre in the dress of monkeys, and waggled their tails to the woeful sound of some wretched bassoons and fiddles. Another party of the same colour were sewed into sacks, falling and rolling about in the bull's way, and putting him out of all patience. D. Bernardo, notwithstanding his fever, displayed courage and activity, D. José the most consummate address, and Assumar nothing but his smart jacket and puppyish attitudes.

I walked about the fair after the dismal sport was ended, and was half choked with dust. D. José came up to let me know there was to be dancing in a tent, and hoped I would be of the party. The tent had no promising appearance; it was lined with dingy red damask, felt very hot, and smelt very fusty, and I took care to keep out of it. That impudent buffoon nicknamed the Duke of Parma found me out and began pestering me. The negros too advanced in a body, playing on all their confounded instruments, and begging for drink money. A band of prize-fighters and fencing masters began also to gather around us, stamping and letting fly such volleys of < > for monies as turned my stomach. I lost all patience, and finding General Forbes, D. José and M. Verdeil were as sick as myself of the entertainment, we took our departure about nine o'clock, regained our *scalera*, and rowed back to Lisbon with great expedition. The night was delightfully mild, serene and tranquil; a gentle breeze rippled the waters, which upon being struck by the oars sparkle and gleam with a clear bluish light, like that produced by those Chinese fireworks in which camphor is a principle ingredient. I was heartily glad to get home.

Saturday 11 August

The nymphs over the way are so perfectly convinced of my devotion for their beauties, that carts and carriages loading and other tokens of departure have played them into sorrow, and they are crying their eyes out. I feel quite compassionate and should be extremely happy to afford every little consolation in my power. I wish Bezerra was here. He should < > for me, and show me the way to the ladies' apartment with which he pretends to be so well acquainted. Berti, who, I hear, fancies his allurements have won him the affection of a young tit of sixteen with a tolerable (?) future, knows no longer whether he walks on his head or his heels; all his actions are topsiturvical. He sends blankets with charcoal, by which means they are dyed of a russet hue, <and> pianofortes with tuning hammers and keys lying loose and entangling themselves in the wires, etc. etc. My household is in sad confusion and a parcel of knaves playing into each others' hands. Half my baggage will be left behind for want of mules to transport it.

I went to the Palace in the morning, and brought back my long < > for case of books which I don't believe were ever spread on the Censorial Table,[187] and might just as well have been delivered me ten days ago when the *aviso* was issued, but the demon of confusion and disorder reigns triumphantly in the Lisbon Custom House. I would not dine at the Palace, being in fear of their greasy messes. I did nothing but fret and bustle the evening; Berti having taken his arrangements for my departure so wretchedly, I was obliged to load my light carriage with my bed, and send it off with four mules at seven in the evening, so I was forced to borrow Mr. Horne's curricle to carry me to the Palace. The Marquis, who was just released from his Court attendance, had been waiting for me half an hour, and met me a hundred paces from the Palace; I got into his carriage and off we drove full gallop to Sintra. Half way we encountered a violent whirlwind that covered us with dust and extinguished our torches. We had an uncomfortable jolting expedition. We found the Marchioness, D. Henriqueta and all the family upon their knees before their chapel door reciting the litanies. Gabble, gabble, gabble—never heard such a jabbering in all my life.

One of the Marquis' servants arrived soon after us with a little negro imp, a present from the Governor of Angola. All the children gabbled <to> the newcomer, who skipped and jumped about the room, chattering his teeth like a monkey, and showing a strong propensity towards biting the tips of my fingers, <and> promises to become a mighty favourite. Another African was called in to speak to him. This tarry young gentleman and D. Pedro seem upon very familiar terms; D. Pedro leaned on his shoulder and kept whispering to him with great perseverance.

Sunday 12 August

The vine arbour is garnished with jasmines and periwinkles and looks very pleasant. Poor old Collett is in agonies with the rheumatism. This air no longer agrees with him, and back to England must he go or perish. He complained to me grievously of Berti's indolence, and even dropped hints of a knavish association into which he suspected him to have entered with the cook and purveyor. I dined at the Marquis', who went with me to Horne's in the evening, where we drank tea. The Escarlate were there, attended by a set of gawky young fellows their relations. We sat in the veranda under an awning. The walls of the house are lined with jasmine white and yellow. Mr. Sill busied himself the whole evening in trimming and setting to rights a pair of patent lamps just come from England. But there was no making them burn; they stunk and sputtered worse than any lamps I ever knew, and soon left us in darkness. Horne has taken it into his head that I had neglected him of late and looked cool at me; but I exerted myself to prove the contrary, and succeeded so well that we are as good friends again as ever, and I invited myself to dine with him tomorrow. I returned home with my friend to his house, which is exposed to every blast that comes blustering over the ocean. Much do I envy Horne his veranda so snugly sheltered by woody hills. I passed a sad yawning evening. We did not sup till midnight. I never spent my time so dully and unprofitably as at present.

Monday 13 August

All night did the winds roar and the fleas leap about me. I heard the dry cough of poor old Collett resounding in the long lonesome passages of this ill-contrived villa. It was morning before I could close my eyes. I dined at Horne's and strolled about Penha Verde[188] in the evening by the serene light of a calm sunset with Bezerra. They are repairing the apartments for the Visconde Vila Nova da Cerveira,[189] who is to occupy the villa during the Queen's residence at Sintra. The whole fabric has an Italian, classic air that delights me, and the boughs of pines and cork trees have forced their way between the marble balustrades of the windows. Most of the apartments have fireplaces. There is a little square parterre before one of the fronts of the villa with a fountain in the middle and niches in the walls with antique busts. Above these walls a variety of trees and shrubs rise to a gallant elevation and compose a mass of the richest foliage. We returned to tea at Horne's with Mme Gildemeester and one or two of her humble companions. At nine I went to my friend's, where I supped and coursed the children about the pavilion till I was heartily tired.

Tuesday 14 August

No wind this morning. For the first time I can walk about my loggias enjoying the view of the distant sea without being blown at and blustered by rude gales that have no mercy nor moderation. The Marquis and D. Pedro spent the whole day with me. Berti having neglected everything, we had a miserable dinner and no dessert. Both my dear friend and his son are the greatest loungers in Europe. They absolutely know not what to do with themselves, but gape and tramp about in the most listless uncomfortable manner, striking a spanking new repeater, finely chased, he has just received from Paris,[190] humming an opera tune or a *Gloria Patri* or a *Kyrie eleison*. They wear me to a mere bone. Such society is enough to impair one's faculties. I am perfectly sure I sink deeper and deeper in the slough of idleness and stupidity. Even to write this wretched diary of my present wearisome existence costs me trouble, for I do nothing but yawn with facility. The torpor of my mind communicates itself to my body. I can no longer leap, dance or run with any spirit, and when we got back to Sintra after sipping tea with our elbows in the table, the children were obliged to use their united efforts to drag me into the pavilion.

Wednesday 15 August

Old Collett is gone to Lisbon to take his passage on board the Packet which sails in a week or ten days. How I envy him the delight of turning his back on Portugal! When will the hour of my deliverance arrive? We had a better dinner today, the joint performance of Messrs. du Noyer and Degramont, and my friend and D. Pedro failed not to partake of it.

M. Verdeil, tired of sauntering about the verandas, proposed a ride to a neighbouring village[191] where there was a fair. He and D. Pedro mounted their horses and preceded the Marquis and me in a garden-chair drawn by a most resolute mule. The roads were abominable and lay partly along the sloping base of the Sintra mountains, which in the spring perhaps are clothed with a tolerable verdure, but at present every blade of grass is parched and withered. Our carriage-wheels as we drove sidling along these slippery acclivities pressed forth the odour of innumerable aromatic herbs, half pulverised. Mr. Thicknesse[192] would have said perhaps in his original quaint style that Nature was treating us with a pinch of her best cephalic. No snuff ever threw me into a more violent fit of sneezing. I could hardly hold my head up when we arrived at the fair, which is held on a pleasant green lawn, bounded on one side by the picturesque buildings of an ancient convent of Hieronymites,[193] and on the other by rocky hills shattered into a variety of uncouth romantic forms. One cliff in particular, called the Penedo dos

Ovos, terminated by a cross, crowns the assemblage and exhibits a very grotesque appearance. Behind the convent a thick shrubbery of olive, ilex and citron fills up a small valley refreshed by fountains whose clear waters are conducted through several cloisters and gardens, surrounded by low marble columns supporting fretted arches in the morisco style. The peasants assembled at the fair were scattered over the lawn, some conversing with the monks, others half-drunk sliding off their asses and sprawling upon the ground, others bargaining for silken nets and spangled rings to bestow on their mistresses. We rambled about the convent and its gardens in perfect incognito; the monks not having discovered the Marquis, we escaped being stuffed with sweetmeats and worried with compliments.

We returned to Ramalhão and drank tea in its lanternlike saloon in which are no less than eleven glazed doors and windows of large dimensions. The winds were still, the air balsamic, and the sky of so soft an azure that we could not remain within doors, but got again into our carrinho and drove as far as the Dutch Consul's new building about a league from my villa, by the mingled light of innumerable stars. It was after ten before we got back to my friend's. The cascades were set a-playing and the Marchioness waddled forth to enjoy their murmurs. I thought supper would never be served up, not that I was hungry, but ennuied and tired to a degree I despair of describing. D. Henriqueta, instead of turning out the lively girl I expected, appears to be the prey of a green and yellow melancholy, scarcely ever lifting up her eyes or opening her lips. I could not get home till one o'clock.

Thursday 16 August

Mr. Collett returned to breakfast much fatigued and very feverish. He expects to sail the day after tomorrow. We had a great deal of conversation. M. Verdeil and I dined alone. Ramalhão begins to assume a furnished appearance. My apartments are neatly papered and matted. The beds and sofas are spread with coverlets of most beautiful chintz, and almost every table has its Japan coffer or cabinet. The new cook—M. d'Aigremont as he calls himself—proves a very indifferent acquisition, and shall be packed off next Saturday with the gardener. I hope they will not strangle old Collett on the passage for finding out their light-fingered dispositions. After sunset I drove to Horne's, and perching myself in his veranda, contemplated the deep woods and spires of rock discovered from it. <The> Miss Sills were alone. I ought to have paid Mrs. Gildemeester a visit, but was lazy and would not stir. I supped at the Marquis' and went away early.

Friday 17 August

I am getting into excellent order at Ramalhão, and shall soon be tolerably comfortable. Lima came from Lisbon to ask my pleasure concerning the band of musicians he is to bring down to me. I have settled to have six, and appointed them for the first of September. Music will sound delightfully in the echoing galleries and spacious terraces of Ramalhão. The Marquis sent to beg I would dine with him, but I excused myself, having invited Horne and his family. They came with Bezerra. We were very cheerful and congratulated Mr. Collett on his approaching departure from this land of ignorance and awkwardness. The poor old man is fondly attached to me and would sacrifice his life to do me a benefit. He flatters himself the accounts he will bring over of the influence I have acquired here will facilitate my reestablishment in England. Alas poor man, I fear he is sadly mistaken, but I let him depart uninformed of the abject sentiments and mean abilities of those he has to deal with.

Saturday 18 August

All the winds are combined, I believe, to blow my villa off its terraces. They howled and whistled without intermission from the hour I went to bed to that when I rose from it. The Spanish courier has brought me a letter from Brandoin,[194] very puling and unsatisfactory; he sends me no intelligence of Evian, but fills half his epistle with pressing enquiries after certain cheeses he sent me last November, and of which I have never heard a syllable. The Marquis came to dinner and I prevailed on him to escort me to Mrs. Gildemeester's in the evening, whom we found in a dingy apartment, her toads squatting round her. She gave us some vile tea and a huge loaf smoking hot and swimming in rank butter. D. Genuefa, the toad passive in waiting, is a little jossish old woman with a head as round as a humming top, and a large placid lip, very smiling and good-natured. Miss Coster or Cotter, the toad active, has been rather pretty some twenty or thirty years ago, makes tea with decorum, shuts doors and opens windows with judgment, and has a good deal to say for herself when allowed to sit still on her chair. I amused myself tolerably well with her tittle-tattle, and have asked her and her patroness to dine with me tomorrow. I set down the Marquis at his villa, excused myself from the ennui of supping there, and drove home. M. Verdeil was drinking a solitary dish of tea in the lantern to the piping of wintry breezes. Never did I hear a more dismal, hollow sound. I rushed into the garden to experience the full power of the wind, and to observe the faint crescent of a new-born moon struggling to emerge from angry clouds. Pears, apples, olives and citrons shaken down by the fury of the blasts rolled along the alleys.

The air was so keen and piercing that I felt glad to retreat into the house, where I found Franchi just arrived, looking as pale as a phantom, shivering with cold, and making sad complaints of the long time he had been on the road. My brute of a coachman thought fit to be five hours and a half going twelve miles. No wonder the poor boy, who was very impatient to see me, thought himself embarked on an endless expedition.

Sunday 19 August

No abatement as yet in the violence of the winds. All the windows in my lantern apartment shake and clatter. The pianofortes are gone out of tune and Franchi can make little of them. I have been trying to sing but seem to have lost my powers. Mme Gildemeester and her spouse, the Marquis and the Abbade—who came last night—dined here. M. du Noyer had exerted himself and gave us an excellent repast, of which the old Consul partook plentifully. Miss Cotter was left in her hole, for want of conveyance, to deplore the unhappy state of toadism. When I ask her another time she shall certainly have my carriage. Mme Gildemeester is very superior indeed to the generality of females of this country and has a dry manner of expressing herself full of spirit and discernment. She is not of the merciful tribe and spares nobody. We had a great deal of slashing conversation and joined forces in cutting up the Factory. The Consul being obliged to go to town on particular business, the thread of our discourse was snapped off sooner than we wished. My friend too went home early and the old Abbade could not rest till he had paid a visit to Horne, so I was left alone with M. Verdeil and Franchi. We wrapped ourselves up in our greatcoats, and descending the flights of steps which lead from the terraces, walked in a sheltered alley of the *quinta* half a mile in length. After sunset the wind fell and the citron flowers began to exhale their fragrance. The blossoms of the azareiras or Portuguese laurels dangled over our heads, and their shadows cast by the gleams of the moon played before us. I loaded Franchi with childish caresses[195] and <he> gambolled along with an awkward calvish vivacity. At supper he told several wonderful stories of the late Queen's pounding a pearl of inestimable value to swallow in medical portions, and would fain make us believe that a woman very fair and plump to the eye with an overflowing breast of milk, who took in sucklings cheaper than anybody else, regularly made away with them, and was now in the prisons of the Inquisition, accused of having massacred several hundred innocents. This tale, exaggerated as it is, has probably some foundation, and I will remember to ask the Archbishop about it. Verdeil and I laughed heartily at the booby's simplicity and sat listening to his marvellous narrations till midnight.

Monday 20 August

The weather continues windy and comfortless. I wander about the spacious range of apartments like a ghost on the confines of the infernal regions whilst Franchi plays adagios of Haydn in the most mournful melancholy keys. Just before dinner we rambled into the citron orchards and gathered fantastic branches studded with buds of a reddish purple, but were driven home by cold blasts scattering clouds of leaves over the terraces. Who could have expected such wintry blusterings in the height of summer and in the soft climate of Portugal? Bezerra and Aguilar dined with me. The Marquis and the Abbade came to tea. The lamps and lustres being lighted, the long suite of rooms wore a cheerful appearance, and the lantern-like apartment hung round with curtains of beautiful English chintz, and furnished with ample sofas, begins to look like the tent of an *omrah*.[196]

I sat snug amongst the folds of the drapery. The Marquis and Verdeil were tumbling over two folios of Hogarth's, purchased for me at Sir John Elliott's sale,[197] and Franchi flourishing away with all his might on the pianoforte. Notwithstanding these loud musical sounds, and the murmur of M. Verdeil<'s> explanation of Hogarth, the Abbade fell into a gentle slumber and I into a sort of doze. The recollection of poor old Cozens[198] took possession of my fancy. I seemed to hear him commending the oriental scenery of my apartment and the lulling whispers of the winds. I seemed to behold him seated at my feet, examining the sprigs of citron I had gathered, and saying with a smile: "Shall I give them to Lady Margaret?" I woke from my trance in tears, and to dissipate the impression it left upon me, began dancing and coursing along the galleries. Marialva, who is never behindhand in any sort of exercise, followed my example. We hopped upon one leg, leaped over handkerchiefs held four feet from the floor, and amused ourselves like schoolboys with these fooleries. Franchi must have thought it rare sport to be playing about so familiarly with the *Marquez Estribeiro-mor* and the *Fidalgo Rico*![199] I often think what pleasure he will take in recounting our exploits at the Patriarchal.

Tuesday 21 August

Though the winds are at length hushed, and the ardour of the sun tempered by floating clouds, I remained lazily at home the whole morning, stretched on my sofas reading Cowper's poems and hearing Franchi play my favourite adagio of Haydn. The Abbade, who was the only one of the Marialva party we had at dinner today, swilled claret till he got tipsy and talked nonsense without intermission. To get out of his way, I retreated into my interior apartments with Franchi, and passed an hour and a half in looking over my cameos.

At six I sent my young musicians back to Lisbon, and went to Horne's, where I found a fussocky[200] Presbyterian merchantess and her young—a pert Miss and a gawky Master. No sooner had I made my appearance than the old one, after sitting on thorns a few minutes, unclung her broad bottom from her chair, and moved off with her brood in great trepidation. Mrs. Gildemeester, who happened to be of the party, enjoyed the confusion I occasioned, and to help it forwards offered both hen and chickens a lift in her carriage which waited at the door. This gave me an opportunity of handing her out, and in so doing to brush by the Lady Merchantess, who in her alarm scarcely knew how to waddle. <The> Miss Sills contemplated the scene from their veranda. I drank tea with them and closed the evening at the Marialvas. Verdeil and the Marquis sat down to draughts. D. Pedro, the children and I gambolled in the pavilion. We supped very late and I did not get to bed till after one. Mr. Collett was off the bar yesterday morning at five o'clock.

Wednesday 22 August

I know not how it happens, but I never find a moment to explore the wild shrubberies at the base of the neighbouring hills. From my windows I view several winding paths that lead to their summits, bordered by bushes of rosemary and coronilla[201] beautifully green in defiance of wind and sunshine. Herds of goats browse on the declivities; but here are no smooth lawns and fields of clover pastured by sheep. My friend and D. Pedro dined with me. Towards evening a thick fog overspread the crags of Sintra. It did not prevent us however from going to Mr. Horne's. The lofty elms and chestnuts which arch over the road, moistened by the mist, exhaled a fresh woody odour. High above the vapours appeared the turret of the Convent of Pena, faintly tinted by the last rays of the sun. This edifice, so strangely perched on the very pinnacle of the rock, reminded me of those prints one sees of the Ark on Mount Ararat, looking down on a sea of undulating clouds.

At Horne's, Aguilar, Bezerra and the usual set were assembled. The Marquis and D. Pedro, as soon as they had drunk tea, returned to their villa, and I took Mr. Horne in my chaise to Mrs. Staits'[202]—a little slender-waisted, wild-eyed woman, by no means unpleasing or flinty-hearted. It was her birthday and she had assembled all the Scrubs and Scrubesses of the English nation at Sintra, in a damp garden about fifty feet long by twenty-two, illuminated by twenty or thirty dingy lanterns. My good friend Mme Fussock and her brood, who wriggle away whenever they catch sight of me, were here; likewise Mr. Burn and his sultana, an old toothless Mr. Connolly[203] and five or six other counting house beaux with whose names I am unacquainted. Mrs. Gildemeester, sparkling with diamonds, shone like a star in the midst of this murky atmosphere. 'Twas a rueful party, and I called myself fool ten times over for coming to it. My sole amusement consisted in observing the uneasiness of Mrs. Fussock, who being pinned down to a card table could not effect her escape, and the bridlings of that sweet Miss her daughter. We had a cold funereal supper under a low tent in imitation of a grotto lined with that identical sort of brown < > tapestry called *point d'Hongrie* one sees so often in French post-houses, and to which bugs and fleas have a peculiar attachment.

   Mrs. Staits' well-disposed, easy-tempered husband placed me next Mme Gildemeester, who amused herself tolerably well at the expense of the entertainment. The dingy, subterraneous appearance of the booth, the wan light of the lanterns sparingly scattered along it, and the cadaverous smell of the dish of rotten prawns just under our nose seized me with the idea of being dead and buried. "Alas!" said I to Mrs. Gildemeester, "it is all over with us now, this is our first banquet in the infernal regions, we are all equal and jumbled together. There sits the pious Presbyterian Mrs. Fussock and close to her those adulterous doves Mr. Burn and his sultana. Here am I, miserable sinner, right opposite your righteous and much-enduring spouse, a little lower our kind host, that pattern of conjugal meekness and resignation. Hark! Don't you hear a thumping noise? They are letting down a cargo of fat souls into a neighbouring tomb." In this strain did we continue till the subject was exhausted and it was time to depart.

Thursday 23 August

I have received some letters from England, but they contain nothing material, except accounts of the preparations which were making in Jamaica for my reception, and which will cost me a swingeing sum. Mr. James Wildman pretends my not proceeding on my voyage was felt by the whole Island as a severe disappointment.[204] Verdeil and I dined alone. Polycarpo and Luis Antonio, D. Pedro's preceptor, came in whilst we were drinking coffee. I sat down to the pianoforte and played far better than I have done this long while. The misty dampness of the evening did not keep me at home. I drove out with M. Verdeil in my open Portuguese chaise to Penha Verde. Just before the gate of the villa, we met a caravan of *burras*—in plain English, asses—mounted by <the> Miss Sills, Bezerra, a Monsignor Gomes,[205] and his cousin, a young officer with a most engaging countenance.[206] The caravan stopped a few minutes to speak to me, and then proceeded its way and I mine. I did not enter the villa, but traversed the square parterre before it, and mounted the rude mossy stairs which lead up to a small chapel built by the far-famed João de Castro to whom this villa belonged, and whose heart still reposes in the midst of a small platform which forms the summit of his beloved rock. A crooked cork tree, coeval with the edifice I have just mentioned, bends over it. Whilst leaning against its trunk, you survey on one side the green shrubby slopes of innumerable hills and the thickets of chestnut and orange in which the village of Colares is embosomed; on the other, a vast extent of parched up, blasted country, bounded by the ocean and diversified by the gigantic buildings of Mafra.

The prospect being partially veiled in mist, and the sun deposed, I felt chilled and dejected. Hurrying down the steps and across the groves of pine, I regained my carriage and drove to Mr. Horne's; from thence to Mrs. Gildemeester's, where Mrs. Fussock and her young, Mrs. Steets, the toads in waiting etc. were seated in solemn circle. Mrs. Gildemeester and I soon began levelling our conversations at Goody Fussock, and talked of waddling and twaddling, of the amiable simplicity of geese, and the lively talkativeness of turkeys, till the old lady, perceiving the drift of the allegory, called her chickens together and abandoned the field of battle. She amply deserves this persecution at my hands, having never ceased loading me with all the abusive cant of a starch presbyterian since my arrival. No sooner was her broad back turned than a fiddler was sent for, and a dance proposed. We continued to make up a cotillion and to continue in motion till near eleven, when I went away to sup with the Marquis.

Friday 24 August

Wind and sun cooling and broiling alternately. I remained at home all the morning reading a new History of Mexico translated from the Italian of the Abbade Clavigero by Cullen, and full of very curious information. The author stands up resolutely for the splendour and magnificence of Montezuma, the immense size of his palace and the admirable construction of his aviaries. Robertson and M. de Pauw are made very free with for treating the Americans with contempt, and Solis accused, not without reason I believe, of a strong partiality for Cortes, who, according to this history, appears to have been guilty of the most wanton and unwarrantable acts of cruelty and oppression.[207]

We were eight at dinner—Horne, the Miss Sills and their brother, Bezerra and Aguilar. The wind, which in spite of all my curtains still finds a thousand ways of entering the lantern apartment, gave me an uncomfortable feel in my head very like the headache. I was prevailed on however to walk out, but grumbled all the way at finding every alley in the *quinta* thick strewn with fallen leaves. Had I but a large chimney like that in the great hall at Evian, I should have no objection to these signs of approaching winter, and I would soon make a cheerful blaze and warm myself with good humour. At Ramalhão, except in the kitchen, there are no chimneys, and I shiver already at the idea of being fireless. Whilst we were straying about the thickets of bay and laurel, the Marquis arrived and entered into close conversation with Bezerra. I am in hopes I have prejudiced him in his favour, and that he will do him essential service by explaining to the Queen a law affair in which he is deeply concerned. Monsignor Gomes Freire and his young cousin paid me a visit. They stayed but a short time, being on their way to Lisbon. In a few days they return, and I have invited them to come often to see me. Horne and his family went away at nine. The Marquis and I sat talking together upon the affairs of Portugal for two hours. The Archbishop has suffered himself to be pressed into the Cabinet, and may perhaps consent ere long to be declared Prime Minister, though his natural laziness and monkish love of ease makes him heartily averse to so tempestuous a situation.

Saturday 25 August

If I am sick of writing about the wind, how much more tired must I be of feeling it. I cannot put my nose out of my lantern without having its tip snapped off and reddened by a keen blast right worthy of the month of November. And yet the trees are in leaf, the flowers in blow, and the sun in splendour, and we are in the month of August, under the boasted sky of Portugal. Were there ever such contradictions? M. Verdeil persuaded me to get on horseback and try whether the climate on the other side of the peaks of Sintra would not prove more tolerable. He was in the right. I had no sooner turned the corner of the rock than we entered snug shady lanes, and rode unmolested by the wind almost the whole way to Colares. It was a clear transparent day like those I have enjoyed in Italy.

Lima, who came from Lisbon to ask me some further questions about my musicians, dined with us. In the evening came the Duke de Lafões and the Marquis. This is the identical personage so well known in every part of Europe by the name, style and title of Duke of Braganza. He is no business however to be called Duke of Braganza: nobody can be Duke of Braganza but the Sovereign. If he was called Duchess Dowager of Braganza I should think nobody would have any objection. He is so like an old Lady of the Bedchamber, so fiddle-faddle, and so coquettish and so gossiping. He had got on rouge and patches and a solitaire, and though he is seventy years old, contrived to turn on his heel and glide about with juvenile agility. I was much surprised at the ease of his motions, having been told he was almost crippled with the gout. After lisping French with a most refined accent, complaining of the wind and the roads and the state of our architecture etc., he departed—thank God!—to mark out a spot for the encampment of the Cavalry, who are to guard the Queen's person during her residence amongst these mountains. The Marquis was in duty bound to accompany him, but soon returned. I made him write out an order to expedite Lima's *aviso*. We passed the evening in earnest conversation and agreed to go to Mafra the day after tomorrow. To avoid the importunities of the monks we shall lodge at the *Capitão-mor's*,[208] an old servant of the Marialva's and the companion of my friend's infancy.

Sunday 26 August

No care being taken to fasten my windows, they rattled all night and kept me awake an hour or two. I cannot complain of the air of Sintra; it may be sharp, but it is very wholesome, and enables me to eat my breakfast with appetite. I walked in the *quinta*, and visited my vases of flowers. Vegetation is so rapid in this climate that the oleanders, heliotropes, and geraniums, which in their way here from Lisbon were almost stripped naked, are again covered with leaves and blossoms. I went to dine at Horne's with D. José de Brito and his homely spouse. Bezerra, who was also of the party, took a ramble with me in the evening up lofty crags and slopes of slippery greensward, from whence you look down upon the villa of Penha Verde and its groves. The rocks are covered with Latin inscriptions in honour of Pombal, not unclassically imagined. Upon our return to Horne's we found the Marquis waiting for me. He got into my carriage and we drove to his villa. Who should I find there but the Grand Prior just arrived, wrapped up in an ample capote and execrating the cool breezes of Sintra. In these maledictions I heartily joined, and being fatigued with rock climbing, retired to Ramalhão and reposed till supper time on my sofas.

Monday 27 August

We set off for Mafra at nine in spite of the wind which blew full in our faces, the Marquis and I in a chaise, D. Pedro and Verdeil in the *carrinho*. The distance from Sintra to this stupendous convent is about fourteen English miles, and the road, which has been lately mended, conducted across a parched open country thinly scattered with windmills and villages. The look backwards on the woody hills and pointed rocks is pleasant enough, but when you look forwards nothing can be more bleak or barren than the prospect. Three relays of mules being stationed on the road, we advanced full speed, and in less than an hour and a quarter found ourselves under a strong wall which winds boldly across the hills and encloses the park of Mafra. We now caught a picturesque glimpse of the marble towers and dome of the convent, rising above the brow of healthy eminences, diversified here and there by the green heads of Italian pines and the tall spires of cypress. The roofs of the edifice were not yet visible and we continued for some time winding about the swells in the park before we discovered them. A detachment of lay brothers were waiting to open the gates of the royal enclosure, which is sadly blackened by a fire which about a month ago consumed a great part of its wood and verdure. Our approach spread a terrible alarm amongst the herds of deer; off they scudded and took refuge in a thicket of half-burnt pines.

After coasting the wall of the great garden, we turned suddenly and discovered one of the vast fronts of the convent, appearing like a street of palaces. I cannot pretend that the style of the building is such as a Roman or English architect would approve; the windows and doors are fantastically shaped, but though wretchedly designed are well proportioned. I was admiring their ample range as we drove rapidly along, when upon wheeling round the lofty square pavilion which flanks the edifice, the grand façade extending above a thousand feet opened to my view. The middle is formed by the porticos of the church, richly adorned with columns, niches and bas-reliefs of marble. On each side two towers, somewhat resembling those of St. Paul's in London, rise to the height of three hundred feet. They are light and clustered with pillars remarkably elegant, but their shape borders too much on a gothic or what is still worse, a pagoda-ish style, and wants solemnity. These towers contain several bells of the largest dimensions and a famous chime which cost several hundred thousand crusados, and which was set a-playing the moment our arrival was notified. The platform and flight of steps before the principal entrances of the church is grand beyond anything of which I had conceived an idea in Portugal. Looking up to the dome which lifts itself up so proudly above the pediment of the portico, I was struck with pleasure and surprise.

My eyes ranged along the vast extent of palace on each side till they were tired, and I was glad to turn them from the glare of marble and confusion of sculptured ornaments to the blue expanse of the distant ocean. A vast level space extends before the front of this colossal edifice, at the extremities of which several white houses lie dispersed. Though these buildings are by no means inconsiderable, they appear when contrasted with the immense pile in their neighbourhood like the booths of workmen. For such I took them upon taking my first survey, and upon a nearer approach was quite surprised at their real dimensions. Few objects render the prospect from the platform of Mafra interesting. You look over the roofs of an indifferent village and the summits of sandy acclivities. On the left your view is terminated by the craggy mountains of Sintra; to the right a forest of pines in the Viscount of Ponte de Lima's extensive garden affords the eye a refreshment.

To screen ourselves from the sun, which shone on the flight of steps leading up to the great entrance, we entered the church, passing through its magnificent portico, which reminded me of the entrance to St. Peter's, and is adorned by colossal statues of saints and martyrs carved with infinite delicacy out of blocks of the purest white marble. The first coup d'oeil of the church is very striking. The chief altar, supported by two majestic columns of reddish variegated marble, each a single block above thirty feet in height, immediately fixes the attention. Trevisani has painted the altar-piece in a masterly manner. It represents St. Anthony in the ecstasy of beholding the infant Jesus descending into his cell amidst an effulgence of glory. Tomorrow being the festival of St. Augustine, whose followers now possess this monastery, all the golden candelabras were displayed and tapers lighted. We knelt a few minutes in the midst of this bright illumination.

The monks came forth bowing and cringing with their usual courtesy, and led us round the collateral chapels, each adorned with highly finished bas-relief and stately portals of black and yellow marble richly veined and so highly polished as to reflect objects like a mirror. Never did I behold such a profusion of beautiful marble as gleamed above, below and around me. The pavement, the roof, the dome, even the topmost lantern is encrusted with the same materials. Roses of white marble and wreaths of palm branches most exquisitely sculptured enriched every part of the edifice. I have seen Corinthian capitals far better designed, but none executed with so much precision and sharpness. D. Pedro and I having satisfied our curiosity by examining the various ornaments of the chapels, followed our conductors through a coved gallery into the sacristy, a magnificent vaulted hall panelled with marble and spread, as well as a chapel adjoining it, with Persian carpets. We traversed several more halls and chapels adorned in the same style, till we were fatigued and bewildered like errant knights in the mazes of an enchanted palace. I began to think there was no end to these spacious apartments. The monk who preceded us, taking for granted I could not understand a syllable of Portuguese, attempted to explain the objects which presented themselves by signs, and would hardly believe his ears when I asked him in good Portuguese when we should have done with chapels and sacristy. The old fellow seemed vastly delighted with the *meninos*, as he called me and D. Pedro, and to give our young legs an opportunity of stretching themselves, trotted along with such expedition that the Marquis and M. Verdeil wished him in purgatory. To be sure, we advanced at a most expeditious rate, striding from one end to the other of a dormitory six hundred feet in length in a minute or two. These vast corridors and the cells with which they communicate are all arched in the most sumptuous and solid manner. Every cell, or rather chamber—for they are sufficiently lofty, spacious, and well-lighted to merit that appellation—is furnished with tables and cabinets of Brazil wood.

Just as we entered the library, the Abbot of the Convent, dressed in his ceremonial habit, with the episcopal cross dangling on his bosom, advanced to bid us welcome and invite us to dine with him tomorrow, St. Augustine's Day, in the refectory, which it seems is a mighty compliment, guests in general being entertained in private apartments. We thought proper, however, to decline the honours, being aware that to enjoy it we must sacrifice at least two hours of our time and be half parboiled by the steam of huge roasted calves, turkeys and gruntlings, long fattening no doubt for this solemn occasion. The library is of a prodigious length, not much less than three hundred feet; the arched roof of a pleasing form, beautifully stuccoed, and the pavement of red and white marble. Much cannot be said in commendation of the cases in which the books are to be arranged. They bulge forth in a heavy lumbering manner and are darkened to boot by a gallery running round like a shelf and projecting into the room in a very awkward manner. The collection of books, which consists of at least sixty thousand volumes, is lodged at present in a suite of apartments which opens into the library. Several curious first editions of the Greek and Roman classics were handed to me by the Father Librarian. My nimble conductor would not allow me much time to examine them.

He set off full speed, and ascending a winding staircase, led us out upon the roofs of the convent and palace, which form a broad, smooth terrace guarded by a magnificent balustrade unencumbered by chimneys and commanding a bird's-eye-view of the courts and gardens. From this elevation the whole plan of the edifice is comprehended at a glance. In the middle rises the dome like a beautiful temple from the spacious walks of a royal garden. It is infinitely superior in point of design to the rest of the edifice, and may certainly be reckoned amongst the lightest and best proportioned in Europe. D. Pedro and M. Verdeil proposed scaling a ladder which leads up to the lantern, but I begged to be excused accompanying of them, and amused myself during their absence with ranging about the extensive loggias, now and then venturing a look down on the court and parterres below; but oftener enjoying the prospect of the towers shining bright in the sunbeams, and the azure bloom of the distant sea. A fresh balsamic air wafted from the orchards of citron and orange fanned me as I rested a moment on the steps of the dome, and tempered the warmth of the glowing ether. But I was soon driven from this peaceful situation by a confounded jingle of the bells; then followed a most complicated sonata, banged off on the chimes by a great proficient. The Marquis would have me approach to examine the mechanism, and I was half stunned. I know nothing of chimes and clocks and am quite at a loss for amusement in a belfry. My friend, who inherits a mechanical turn from his father, investigated every wheel with the most minute attention. I, poor ignorant soul, who can only judge from exteriors in these matters, have little to observe upon the piece of clock I had been surveying, except that the brasswork is admirably polished, ornamented with sculpture, and like everything else at Mafra most highly finished.

Descending the stairs and escaping from our conductor, we repaired to the *Capitão-mor's*, whose jurisdiction extends over the park and district of Mafra. He has seven or eight thousand crowns a year, and his habitation wears every appearance of ease and opulence. The floors are covered with neat mats, the doors hung with red damask curtains, and our beds quite new for the occasion and spread with satin coverlids richly embroidered. We had an excellent dinner prepared by the

Marquis' cooks and confectioners, and a much better dessert than even the monks could have given us. The *Capitão-mor* waited behind our chairs, taking the dishes from his servants and placing them on the table. Whilst coffee was serving up, we heard the sound of a carriage, and behold the Grand Prior entered the room, to our great joy and surprise; for I had tried in vain last night to persuade him to be of our party.

We left him with M. Verdeil to take some refreshment, and hurried to Vespers in the great church of the Convent. Advancing between the range of illuminated chapels, we fell down before the High Altar with a devout and dignified composure. Two shabby-looking Englishmen[209] confounded amongst the rabble at the entrance of the choir watched all my motions and followed me with their eyes till I was seated between the Marquis and D. Pedro in the royal tribune. We had not been long in our places before the monks entered in procession, preceding their Abbot, who ascended his throne, having a row of sacristans at his feet and canons on his right hand in their cloth-of-gold embroidered vestments. The service was chanted with a most imposing solemnity to the sound of organs, for there are no less than six in the church, all of an enormous size.

When it was ended, we joined the *Prior-mor* and M. Verdeil who were just come in, and being once more seized hold of by the nimble lay brother, were conducted up a magnificent staircase into the Palace. The suite extends seven or eight hundred feet, and the succession of lofty doors seen in perspective strikes with astonishment; but we were soon weary of wandering about forlorn unfurnished apartments, the dullest and most comfortless I ever beheld. There is no variety in their shape and little in the dimensions: a naked sameness universally prevails; not a niche, not a cornice, not a carved moulding breaks the tedious uniformity of dead-white walls. I was glad to return to the Convent and refresh my eyes with the sight of marble pillars and my feet by treading on Persian carpets. We were followed wherever we moved by a strange medley of inquisitive monks, sacristans, lay brothers, *corregedors*, village curates and country beaux with long rapiers and pigtails. Whenever I asked a question half-a-dozen poked their necks out to answer it, like turkey poults when addressed in their hobble-gobble dialect. The Marquis was quite sick at being trotted after in this tumultuous manner and tried several times to leave the crowd behind him; but it kept close to our heels and increased to such degree that we seemed to have swept the whole Convent and village of its inhabitants and to draw them after us like the rolling Giaour in my story of *Vathek*. At length perceiving a large door open into the garden, we bolted out and striking into a labyrinth of myrtle and laurels, got rid of our pursuers. The garden, which is about a mile and a half in circumference, contains, besides a wild thicket of pine and bay trees, several orchards of lemon and orange, and two or three parterres, more filled with weeds than flowers. I was much disgusted at finding this beautiful enclosure so wretchedly neglected and its luxuriant plants withering away for want of being properly watered. You may suppose that after adding a walk in the principal alleys of the gardens to our other peregrinations, we began to find ourselves somewhat fatigued and were not sorry to repose ourselves in the Abbot's apartment till we were summoned once more to our tribune to hear Matins performed.

It was growing dark, and the innumerable tapers burning before the altars and in every part of the church, began to diffuse a mysterious light. The organs again played and the Abbot resumed his throne with the same pomp as at Vespers. The Marquis began muttering his orisons, the Grand Prior to recite his breviary, and I to fall into a profound reverie which lasted as long as the service—near three hours. Verdeil, ready to expire with ennui, could not help leaving the tribune and the cloud of incense which filled the choir, to breathe a freer air in the body of the church and its adjoining chapels. My orthodox companions seemed as much scandalised by these heretical fidgetings as edified by the pious air and strict silence I maintained. It was almost nine when the monks, after chanting a hymn in praise of their venerable father, St. Augustine, quitted the choir. We followed their procession through lofty chapels and arched cloisters which by glimmering light appeared to have neither roof nor termination, till it entered an octagon forty feet in diameter with fountains in the four principal angles, and the monks, after dispersing to wash their hands at the several fountains, again resumed their order and passed two and two under a portal thirty foot high into a vast hall communicating with their refectory by another portal of the same lofty dimensions. Here the procession made a pause, for this chamber is consecrated to the remembrance of the departed, and styled the Hall De Profundis. Before every repast the monks, standing around it in solemn ranks, meditate in silence on the precariousness of our frail existence, and offer up their prayers for the salvation of their predecessors. I could not help being struck with awe when I beheld by the glow of flaming lamps so many venerable figures in their black and white habits bending their eyes on the pavement and absorbed in gloomy meditations. The moment allotted to this solemn supplication being past, everyone took his place at the long tables in the refectory, which are made of Brazil wood covered with the whitest linen. Each monk had his glass carafe of water and wine, his plate of apples and salad set before him. Neither fish nor flesh were served up, the vigil of St. Augustine's Day being observed as a fast with the utmost strictness. To enjoy at one glance this singular and majestic spectacle, we retreated to a vestibule preceding the octagon, and from thence looked through the portals down the long row of lamps into the refectory, which owing to its vast length of full two hundred feet seemed ending in a point.

After remaining a few minutes enjoying this perspective, four monks advanced with torches to light us out of the Convent and bid us good night with many bows and genuflexions. Our supper at the *Capitão-mor's* was very cheerful. D. Pedro, in high spirits, delighted with what he had seen, gave way to a childish vivacity. We sat up late notwithstanding our fatigue, talking over the variety of objects which had passed before our eyes in so short a space of time, the crowd of grotesque figures which had stuck to our heels so long and so closely, and the awkward activity of the lay brother. The Abbade told me he remembered the wooden Convent on the sandy plain where now stands the magnificent buildings of Mafra.[210]

Tuesday 28 August

I was half asleep, half awake when the sonorous bells of the Convent struck my ears. The Marquis' and D. Pedro's voices in earnest conversation with the *Capitão-mor* in the adjoining chamber completely roused me. We swallowed our coffee in haste. The Grand Prior reluctantly left his pillow and accompanied us to high Mass. The monks once more exerted their efforts to prevail on us to dine with them; but we remained inflexible, and to avoid their importunities hastened away as soon as mass was ended to the Viscount Ponte de Lima's garden. The deep shades screened us from the meridian sun. The Marquis and I, seating ourselves on the edge of a marble basin of clear water, entered into serious conversation about my stay in Portugal. He entreated me not to think of abandoning him, and begged me to be assured that the Queen, who had warmly espoused my interests, was very desirous of my marrying and forming an establishment in Portugal. "I myself," continued my friend with the utmost earnestness, "will answer for your forming the first alliance in the Kingdom, and connecting yourself by such a match with all the crowned heads in Europe. A formal renunciation of the Protestant religion is not at all necessary; we can procure a dispensation from Rome. The Queen, when she finds you married to perhaps the most distinguished lady of her Court, will employ all her power and influence to procure your re-establishment at home by soliciting your King to give you the peerage we know you were promised,[211] and which the vile plots of your enemies alone prevented your receiving three years ago." I was not more surprised than pleased at all ideas of abjuration being laid aside and struck, I must confess, with the apparent liberality of the proposition. I dared not enquire what person he meant to bestow on me in marriage lest I should have heard the name of D. Henriqueta de Menezes and his daughter. Such a declaration would have thrown me into the utmost embarrassment. I continued therefore soothing him by professions of my regard and grateful thanks for the Queen'<s> favourable opinion, enlarging at the same <time> upon the difficulties of bringing my relations to approve a foreign alliance however splendid, and the deep-rooted affection I bore to Fonthill, the happy scene of my childhood

PORTUGUESE JOURNAL 125

and place of my nativity. How could I persuade myself to make such long and frequent absences as he would undoubtedly expect from this beloved spot. What hopes could I have that the lady would imbibe a similar attachment, and consent to pass several years away from her parents and country. Sea voyages, I observed, were so repugnant to my constitution that I never could undertake them, and to be often performing the journey from hence to England by land would be exposing myself and the lady to endless harassment. These arguments, though vigorously supported, had little effect in cooling the ardour of his projects. He seemed to flatter himself every difficulty in England might be surmounted by employing Pinto in the negotiation, and that once married to the person he had in his eye, her superior merit would win me entirely over to Portugal.

I was happy when the return of D. Pedro and his uncle, who had been walking to the end of a long avenue of pines, broke the thread of a conversation that pressed too hard upon me. We returned to the *Capitão-mor* all together and found dinner ready. At four we set off for Sintra. Both D. Pedro and myself were sorry to leave Mafra, and should have had no objection to another race along the cloisters and dormitories with the lay brother. The evening was bright and clear and the azure tints of the distant sea inexpressibly lovely. We drove so rapidly over the rough paved roads that the Marquis and I could hardly hear a word we said to each other. D. Pedro had mounted his horse. M. Verdeil, who preceded us in the *carrinho*, seemed to outstrip the winds. His mule, one of the most fiery and gigantic of her species, excited by repeated floggings and shouts of a hulking Portuguese postillion perched up behind the carriage, galloped at an ungovernable rate, and about a league from the rocks of Sintra took a sudden turn and jerked out its drivers in the midst of some bushes at the foot of a lofty bank nearly perpendicular. There did they still lay sprawling when we passed by. Verdeil hobbled up to us and pointed to the *carrinho* in the ditch below. Except a slight contusion in the knee, he escaped without any hurt. I exclaimed immediately his escape was miraculous and that perhaps St. Anthony had had a hand in it. My friend, who has always the horrors of heresy before his eyes, whispered me that the Devil had saved him this time, but might not be so moderately disposed another. It was not quite half past five when we reached Sintra. The Marchioness, the Abbade and the children were waiting our arrival in the pavilion.

Feeling a good deal fatigued, I returned home soon after it fell dark, and was agreeably surprised to find the metamorphosis of my lantern room into a magnificent tent completed. The drapery falling in ample folds over the large sofas and glasses produces a great effect and forms the snuggest recesses imaginable. Four tripod stands of burnished gold, supporting lustres of brilliant glass half concealed by chintz curtains, add greatly to the richness of the scenery. The mat smoothly lain down and woven of the finest straw assumes by candlelight the softest and most agreeable colour, quite in harmony with the other objects. It looked so cool and glistening that I could not refrain from stretching myself upon it. There did I lie supine, contemplating the serene summer sky and the moon rising slowly from behind the brow of a shrubby hill. The curtains blown aside by a gentle wind discovered the summits of the woods in the garden, and beyond a wide expanse of country terminated by plains of sea and hazy promontories.

Wednesday 29 August

I trifled away the whole morning in my tent amusing myself with the different views reflected in the glasses. Aguilar dined with us. The Abbade came in at the dessert in full cry with a rare story of the miraculous conversion of an old consumptive Englishwoman, who finding herself on the eve of departure had called out for a priest to whom she might make confession and abjure her errors. Happening to lodge at the Sintra Inn kept by a most flaming Irish Catholic, her pious desires were speedily complied with, and Acciaoli, Mascarenhas,[212] and two or three priests and monsignors summoned to further the good work. To work they went, baptism was administered, all sins remitted, and the feeble old creature despatched to Paradise in the very nick of time, without having a moment to conceive a sinful thought or merit the least singeing from the flames of purgatory. "Great," said the Abbade, "are the rejoicings of the faithful upon this occasion. This evening the aged innocent is to be buried in triumph. Your friend, the Count of S. Lourenço, the Viscount de Asseca,[213] and several more of the principal nobility are already assembled to grace the festival. Supposing you were to come with me and join the procession?" "With all my heart," said I, "though I have no great taste for funerals, so gay a one as this you talk of may form an exception."

Off we set, driving as fast as the mules would carry us, lest we should come too late for the entertainment. A great mob was assembled before the Inn door. At one of its windows stood the Grand Prior, looking as if he wished himself a thousand leagues away, and reciting his breviary. I went upstairs and was immediately caught in the embraces of my friend, and surrounded by the old Count of S. Lourenço and other believers, overflowing with congratulations, turning up the whites of their eyes, and praising God for delivering this strayed sheep from the jaws of eternal perdition. Mascarenhas, one of the soundest limbs of the Patriarchal, a most capital devotee and seraphic doctor, was introduced to me. Acciaoli skipped about the room, rubbing his hands for joy, with a cunning leer on his broad jovial countenance, and snapping his fingers at Satan as much as to say, "I don't care a damn for you. We have got one at least safe out of your clutches and clear at this very moment of the smoke of your cauldron." There was such a bustle in the interior apartments, where the wretched corpse was laid, such chanting and praying, for not a tongue was idle, that my head swam round and I took refuge by the Grand Prior. He by no means relished the party and kept shrugging up his shoulders and saying that to be sure it was very wonderful, very wonderful indeed, and that Acciaoli had been very active, very alert, and deserved great commendation, but that so much fuss might have been spared.

By some hints that dropped, I won't say from whom, I discovered the innocent, now on the high road to eternal felicity, by no means to have suffered the cup of joy to pass by her untasted in this existence, and to have long lived on a very easy footing with a stout English merchant. However, she had taken a sudden turn upon finding herself driving apace down the steep of a galloping consumption, and had been fairly towed into port by the joint efforts of the Irish hostess and the Monsignors Acciaoli and Mascarenhas. All her peccadilloes, according to their firm persuasion, were remitted, and as she expired with the cross of baptism still wet on her forehead, the Devil and all his imps could not prevent her marching straight to the gates of Paradise and gaining immediate admittance. "Blessed soul!" said the Marquis, "how much is thy fate to be envied! No ante-chambering in Purgatory; immediate access will be granted thee to the Supreme Presence, and in this world thy body will have the honour of being borne to its grave by persons of the first distinction, followed by men of the most exalted piety, the favourites of the most illustrious saints, by you my dear friend, by my uncle, Mascarenhas and Acciaoli."

The arrival of a band of priests and sacristans with tapers lighted and cross erected called us to the scene of action. The procession was marshalled in due form, the corpse dressed in virgin white, laying snug in a sort of rose-coloured bandbox with six handles, strewed with flowers, brought forth. My friend, who abhors the sight of a dead body, reddened up to his ears and would have given a good sum to have made an honourable retreat. But no retreat could now be made, consistent with piety. He was obliged to conquer his disgust and take a handle of the bier. Another was grasped hold of by the murderous hand of that scoundrel the Count de São Vicente; a third fell to the share of the poor old snuffling Count of S. Lourenço; a fourth to the Viscount de Asseca, a mighty simple looking young gentleman; the fifth and sixth were allotted to the *Capitão-mor* of Sintra and the village Judge, a gaunt fellow with a hang-dog countenance. No sooner did the Grand Prior and I catch sight of the ghastly visage of the dead body as it was conveying downstairs in the manner I have recited, than we made an attempt to move on and precede instead of following the procession. But Acciaoli who acted as Master of the Ceremonies would not let us off so easily. He allotted us the post of honour immediately at the head of the corpse, and placed himself on our left hand, giving the right to Mascarenhas.

All the bells of Sintra struck up a loud peal, and to their merry jinglings we trudged along up to the knees in dust, a rabble of children prancing after us, and their old grandmothers hobbling after, telling their beads, and grinning from ear to ear at this triumph over the Prince of Darkness. Thank heaven the way to the Church was not long, or the dust would have choked me. The Grand Prior kept his mouth close not to admit a particle of it, but Acciaoli and his colleague were too full of their notable exploit not to chatter incessantly. Poor old S. Lourenço, who is fat, squat and pursy, gasping for breath, his eyes as red and as watery as those of a stewed carp, stopped several times to rest on his journey. My friend whom disgust rendered heartily fatigued with his burden, and whose piety had much ado to keep his stomach from turning, was very glad likewise to make a pause or two. Happily, as I said before, the distance from the inn to the church was trifling. We found all the altars blazing with lights, the grave gaping for its immaculate inhabitant, and a band of priest<s> and friars waiting to receive us. The moment we entered, the very same hymn which is chanted at the obsequies of babes and sucklings was bellowed, incense diffused in clouds, and joy and gladness shining in the eyes of the whole congregation. A murmur of applause and congratulation went round anew, Acciaoli and Masearenhas receiving with much affability and meekness the compliments of the occasion. Old S. Lourenço, waddling up to me, hugged me in his arms, said he knew how holily disposed I was, and strewing me all over with snuff, set me violently a-sneezing.

São Vicente, as soon as the innocent was safely deposited, sneaked away, being never rightly at ease in the presence of his brother-in-law Marialva. As for Marialva, exaltation and triumph carried him beyond all bounds of decorum. He scoffed bitterly at Satan and heretics, represented in glowing colours the actual felicity of the convert, and just as we went out of church cried out loud enough for all those who were near, had they understood French, to have heard him: *Elle se fou<t> de nous touts à présent.* Our pious toil being ended, we walked to the heights of Penha Verde to breathe fresh air untainted by dust. Then returning soberly to Ramalhão, drank tea and concluded the evening with much rapturous discourse on the happiness of the sheep now in the arms of the Shepherd.

Thursday 30 August

The holy party who had so notably distinguished themselves yesterday dined here— Mascarenhas, Acciaoli, the Count de S. Lourenço, the Grand Prior, and the Marquis. Old S. Lourenço has a prodigious memory and a warm imagination, heightened by a slight touch of madness. He seems not ill acquainted with the general politics of Europe, and I can easily conceive must have acted no trifling part at the Congress at Aix-la-Chapelle at which he assisted. Notwithstanding the high favour he enjoyed

William Beckford, aged twenty-one, by George Romney
© NTPL / John Hammond

Belem Monastery and the Marialva Palace, from an engraving by H. L'Evéque, 1816
By permission of The British Library, Maps K.Top.74.67.g

The Marquis of Marialva on horseback, from Andrade's *Luz da Cavallaria*, 1790
By permission of The British Library, 1812.a.21

Two pages of Beckford's manuscript
© The Bodleian Library, University of Oxford, MS Beckford e. 2, pp. 52 & 53

Martedi 9 Luglio
1811

Andrebbe a vivere nel Kings bench o
dove si vuole — colla Farfalla __non di__
__altra forma__ — Robison (di cui penso sempre
tanto bene che lei) ha fatto alfine qualche
cosa colli maledetti Mercanti — Detesto quelle
segnature di __acceptances at six weeks__ ec
— Ho descritto tutto, fuor della 1ma
persona nominata in questa jeremiada L
gli Cabinets di Wilkinson, che ho pregato Lenox
di esser divisi — Non dubito, credo nel
suo Eye tanto che nel mio — Corona
è tornato ieri di Wilkinson con qualche frutto
— ecco un __Specimen__, ten pounds, per evitar il suo
viaggio — Se un'ora miserabile, non mandrebbe
miserie — Già le storie di battaglie si hanno
Spinose a Salisbury — Per l'amor del senso
commune non aspettate troppo gran maraviglie —
— poveri Epicurei — Non mi seduivo della sua
Catastrophe, ma dubito della franchezza delle sue
vendite — il 9 aura toujour un petit coin de reserve
..... Dammi pezzo meglio cura — Soffro bastante
molto più che lei crede o ch'io gusto — Farò bene
di venire con Nicholas 9 si manderò gli Cavalli
a Salisbury — sotto il giorno che finisce — L'idea di
questa funesta mio compagno così Mercato mi fa bollire il
sangue 9 mi distrugge — Che vergogna ec ec.

Royal palace and monastery of Mafra
© Conway Library, Courtauld Institute of Art

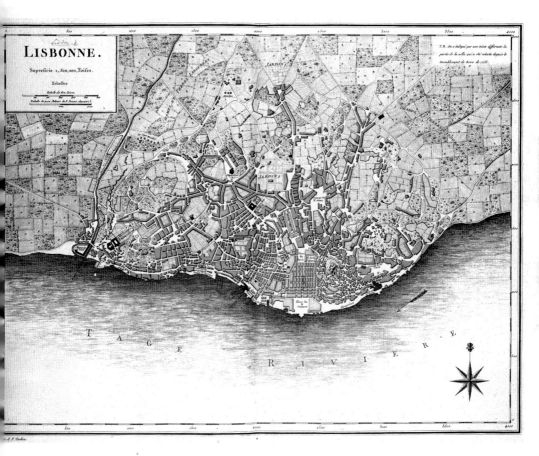

Map of Lisbon
By permission of The British Library, 457.f.5

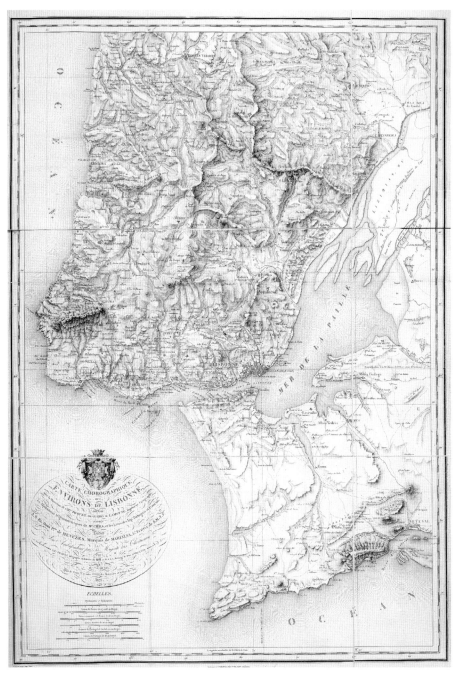

Map of the environs of Lisbon
By permission of The British Library, Maps 20425.(4)

with the Infant D. Pedro,[214] Pombal cast him into a dungeon with the other victims of the Aveiro conspiracy,[215] and for eighteen years was his active mind reduced to prey upon itself for sustenance. Upon the Queen's accession, he was released, and found his intimate friend D. Pedro sharing the throne. But thinking himself coldly received and neglected, he threw the key of Chamberlain which was sent him into no very savoury place, and retired to the Convent of the Necessidades. No means, I have been assured, were left untried by the King to soothe and flatter him; but they all proved fruitless. Since this period, though he has quitted the convent after a short residence, he has never appeared at Court and has refused all employment. Devotion seems at present to gain ground upon him and take up his whole attentions. Except when the chord of imprisonment and Pombal is touched upon, he is calm and reasonable. I found him extremely so today, full of amusing anecdotes.

After dinner I sat down to the pianoforte and played almost without interruption. Mascarenhas, who is passionately fond of music, never quitted his chair by the side of my instrument. I cannot help flattering myself that my compositions resembled those of my dear Lady Hamilton,[216] those pastoral movements full of childish bewitching melody I have heard her so frequently compose during the autumn I passed at Caserta. The reflection of her being for ever lost to me, and the thought too that my lovely Margaret was fled to the same dark cold regions from whence there is no return, and had left me desolate and abandoned, steeped my mind in profound melancholy. I yielded up my soul to its influence, and scarce moving my fingers over the keys, drew forth modulations so plaintive and pathetic that every person in the apartment was affected. My friend sighed bitterly, the Grand Prior hung his head, Mascarenhas seemed beside himself, Acciaoli had no spirits for joking, and D. Pedro, leaning over my chair, breathed short with frequent sobbings. He begins to be conscious of existence since he grew acquainted with me. When first I knew him, no boy I ever beheld was so dull or inanimate. The full moon, rising like a globe of fire from behind the wild hillocks which skirt the garden, cast a yellow gleam on the verandas level with the saloon. I hastened out to inhale the perfumed evening air and view the wide extended landscape by this serene and mellow light. D. Pedro followed me, and as we sat fondly leaning on each other, admiring the beauty of the scene, gave me a lesson of Portuguese. I shall soon acquire the genuine accent.

Friday 31 August

We are no longer vexed with howling winds. The flowers on the edge of the verandas blow in peace without having their seed scattered prematurely. I take great delight in the saloon I have so comfortably curtained, and lay listlessly on the mat hour after hour reading Tibullus and composing tales. This is the first time since my arrival in this land that I begin to enjoy myself. An agreeable variety prevails in the apartment I am so fond of: half its curtains admit no light and display the richest folds, the other half are transparent and cast a mild glow on the mat and sofas, where I lay and read. The glasses multiply this profusion of drapery, and like a child I am not yet tired of running from corner to corner to view the different groups of objects reflected in them, and fancying myself admitted by enchantment into a series of magic saloons.

Nobody interrupted my day-dreams this morning. M. Verdeil and I dined alone. In the evening he drew me reluctantly from my mat to take some exercise, and rumble over rough pavement to Mr. Horne's, where we drank tea. There is a sad bustle of preparation in Sintra for Her Majesty's arrival. Houses are taken by force from their proprietors to accommodate her train, and a row of sheds intended for kitchens and stables starting up on the flat space before the Dutch Consul's new building. I am in high luck to have got roosted at Ramalhão out of the way of racket and defended from the dust and stir of a constant thoroughfare by lofty walls and woody *quintas*. I went from Horne's to Mrs. Gildemeester's in hopes of unkenneling <and> giving chase to Goody Fussock, but she was not there. The party was more than usually dull. I gaped and ennuied myself sadly and could not get away so soon as I wished, Verdeil having been allured into a party of *volterete* by <the> Miss Sills and a scrubby female companion of Mrs. Staits. We supped at my friend's. D. Pedro and I took a run in the garden by our beloved moonlight. One of the little ones, D. Joaquina, in attempting to follow us, fell down on the flat stones before the pavilion and set up a rueful squall, not without reason, for she had given herself a severe thump. The Marchioness and José Antonio, an ingenious young surgeon in great favour with the Marialvas, came forth to her assistance, and administered poultices with due solemnity.

Saturday 1 September

Miss Cotter, one of the toads in waiting on the Consuless Mme Gildemeester, plucked up resolution to dine with me today, though her patroness declare I shall spoil her by civilities, and to be sure I never was more attentive in my life than I have been to this neglected nymph, and she repays my attentions with the warmest encomiums. She came with Horne and his family. Bezerra and Aguilar escorted them on horseback. The Marquis, Grand Prior and Abbade were likewise at dinner. I was in a very musical humour and felt loath to quit my pianoforte upon the Marquis calling me out on the veranda to consult with him on a fête he is persuading me to give the Queen. I have no great wish to have this honour. It will cost me a great sum and a vast deal of trouble into the bargain. Besides, I am at a loss how to decorate the garden and terraces. We are too much at the mercy of the wind here to trust to external illuminations. One moment he proposed a masked ball, and another a French play. He knows not what he would be at, nor I neither.

Sunday 2 September

Packet sailed with letters dated the 2nd. Soon after we had breakfast, Lima and six musicians arrived in one of the royal lumbering coaches with eight mules, which the Marquis lent me for the occasion. D. José de Sousa[217] came also from Lisbon to pass a day or two with me. I was delighted to see him, and vexed to have engaged myself to dine at the Marquis'. Whilst I was there early in the evening a packet of English letters was brought me. I tore them open in haste and find my mother, sister and relations all scared out of their senses by accounts sent them from Portugal of my going to abjure the Protestant religion and accept titles and employments at the expense of my honour, future and liberty. Mr. Wildman too appears by these furious epistle<s> to be also the prey of bugbears. He thinks, as men would throw a cucumber, that I shall throw myself away. The Marquis looked blank upon my explaining the cause of my agitation. The Marchioness and D. Henriqueta were dressed out to go to Sintra and sit dully in their carriage in the midst of the street, staring at the people assembled at a wretched fair. The Marquis and I followed them in my chaise. D. Pedro and his uncle brought up the rear. It was horribly dusty. The roads are bedevilled with loose sand strewn thick all over them. Whilst the ladies stopped to look about them, my friend and I went to the Palace and took a survey of the preparations going on in the Royal Apartments. The Alhambra itself cannot well be more morisco in point of architecture than this confused pile which crowns the summit of a rocky eminence and is broken into a variety of picturesque recesses and projections. 'Tis a thousand pities that <they> have whitened its venerable walls, stopped up a range <of> bold arcades and sliced out the great hall into four or five mean apartments that look like the dressing rooms belonging to a theatre. From the windows, which are all of an oriental fantastic shape, crinkled and crankled, and supported by twisted pillars of smooth marble, various striking views of the cliffs of Sintra are commanded. Several irregular courts and loggias are formed by the angles of square towers enlivened by fountains of marble and gilt bronze. The flat summit of one of the loftiest terraces is laid out in a neat parterre, which, like an embroidered carpet, is spread before the entrance of a huge square tower, almost entirely occupied by a hall encrusted with bright tiles and crowned by a dome most singularly shaped and glittering with mosaic ornaments—red, blue and gold. Amidst the scrolls of arabesque foliage appear the arms of the chief Portuguese nobility gaudily emblazoned. The achievements of the unfortunate House of Tavora are blotted out and the panels which they occupied left bare.[218] We had climbed up to this terrace and tower by one of those steep corkscrew staircases, of which there are numbers in the Palace. Almost every apartment has its vaulted passage and staircase winding up to it in a secret and suspicious manner. The Marquis made me observe a small chamber whose mosaic pavement was fretted and worn away in several places by the steps of Alfonso the Sixth, who was confined to its narrow space above twenty years.[219] I followed the Marquis into the rooms preparing for the Queen and the Infantas. They are awkward and ill-proportioned, with low narrow doors and wooden ceilings which a swarm of signpost painters were employed In daubing. Instead of hanging these antique saloons with rich arras and tapestry, representing the battles and adventures of knights and worthies, Her Majesty's upholsterers are hard at work covering the stout wall with light silks and satins of the softest colours. No furniture as yet has been put up in the palace, neither beds, glasses nor tables.

After my friend had given some orders with which the Queen had charged him, we rejoined the Marchioness, bought toys for the children, and drove out of the bustle and dust of the fair. The Marchioness, Acciaoli and Mascarenhas drank tea with me at Ramalhão, D. Henriqueta having been prudently dropped by the way. The old Abbade cried out "A miracle, a miracle!" when he saw me handing the Marchioness into my apartments. She seldom consents to move anywhere, not even to the houses of her nearest relation<s>, and according to Portuguese etiquette her visit to me might be looked upon as a prodigy. The night was serene and delightful, the folding doors which communicate with the veranda thrown wide open, and the harmonious notes of French horns and oboes issuing from thickets of citron and orange; not a breath of wind disturbed the clear flame of the lights in the lustres, and they cast a soft gleam on the shrubs shooting up above the terraces. In the course of the evening D. Pedro and I danced several minuets. We are growing much attached to each other. The scenery of my apartment, the music I select, the prints and books which lie scattered about it, have led his imagination into a new world <of> ideas, and if I am not mistaken he will long remember the period of my stay in Portugal.

Monday 3 September

Verdeil went to my friend's in the morning and enlarged copiously on the innumerable difficulties which would attend my marriage and establishment in this kingdom. All his eloquence however could not convince the Marquis, who still flatters himself, by the assistance of Pinto's negotiations, to surmount all obstacles in England, obtain my peerage, and give my hand to D. Henriqueta with the full approbation of all my relations. Whilst the Marquis was exhausting Verdeil's attention by calling it continually to the contemplation of fairy castles, I remained indolently reclined on my sofas conversing with D. José and Bezerra.

Verdeil brought the Marquis to dine with us, and in the evening arrived Horne and his family, Acciaoli, Mrs. Steets, her fat confidante, husband and lover. The last mentioned pair, in defiance <of> common prejudices, are upon the most peaceful amicable footing, and never give each other the least disturbance. Both are equally dull and equally insipid; both portion out their attentions to the lady in a sober phlegmatic manner, and I should almost imagine from the style of their appearance and conversation keep a balance of debit and credit with commercial regularity. Notwithstanding the wildness of the lady's glances and the slenderness of her waist, she found little favour in my eyes this evening. If the belonging to <a> heavy husband excited my pity, the selection of so dull a lover roused my disgust. I felt out of humour, and kept parading up and down the long suite of apartments with the Marquis, paying my company little or no attention. Verdeil, who had invited them in the morning, contrived likewise they should stay supper. Just before it was brought in, I walked two or three minuets. The violins and French horns played so enchantingly that I was inspired with musical ideas, called for Lima and sung the *Serene tornate pupille vezzose* of Sacchini[220] in its native key, with so clear a voice that I half believe Mrs. Staits suspects me to border at least upon a soprano, and blesses God for the deep tones of her spouse and his coadjutor.

Tuesday 4 September

I am ashamed to say that I passed my whole morning without reading a sentence, writing a line, or entering into any conversation, lulled by the plaintive harmony of the wind instruments, softened by distance. These notes steal into my soul and swell my heart with tender and melancholy recollections. It was in vain I attempted several times to retire out of the sound and compose myself. I was as often drawn back as I attempted to snatch myself away. Did I consult the health of my mind, I ought to dismiss these musicians. The harmony they produce awakens a thousand enervating and voluptuous ideas in my bosom. Extended on my mat, I look wistfully round me in search of an object to share my affection. I find a silent melancholy void. I stretch out my arms in vain. I form confused and dangerous projects, and as they successively rise and wither in my imagination, am depressed or elated. The general result of these conflicts is a deep and chilling dejection which renders me incapable of any exertion, and forces me to consume my time and trifle away my precious youthful hours.

D. José [221] took leave of me after dinner. He is going to his estate in the province of Tras-os-Montes, and has been pressing <me> in the kindest manner to make an excursion that way, offering to be my conductor. Verdeil wishes much I would accept this proposition, and promises me great amusement. Really t'would be no bad scheme. I should take the Convents of Batalha and Alcobaça in my way, pass a few days at Coimbra, and after meeting D. José at Oporto, ramble into the interior of the green shady province of Minho under his auspices. M. Verdeil forced me out after D. José had left us. We went as usual to Horne's and supped with the Marquis.

Wednesday 5 September

The Marquis, Grand Prior and D. Pedro dined with me. The Grand Prior every wit as indolent, as lounging and as fond of music as myself. Not one of Boileau's *chanoines* ever sunk into a sofa more voluptuously. It was with difficulty either of us could be persuaded to stir after dinner. D. Pedro made me dance a minuet with him, and after having been once set going I consented to walk in the alleys of the *quinta*. The Marquis is fallen a little lame and hobbles. D. Pedro and I, having the full use of our limbs, coursed each other like greyhounds.

Thursday 6 September

Music has once more taken full possession of me. I bow under its influence, and imbibe thirstily those enervating sounds that impair the force of my understanding. My voice is returned with all its powers and I execute the most difficult passages with facility. Bezerra who dined with us today could scarce draw from me one reasonable idea. The Marquis and the Grand Prior came in the evening. Their presence roused me at intervals from my musical delirium. M. Verdeil began describing Fonthill, and I seconded him with an energy that alarmed my friend and convinced him it would be no easy matter to allure me from England.

Friday 7 September

Whilst I was walking amongst the orange trees in the *quinta* after breakfast, the Grand Prior made his appearance on the veranda, and I hastened up to him. I perceived plainly that the fondness with which I had spoken of Fonthill last night had made a strong impression on him, and that he feared I should be soon persuaded to leave Portugal. I waived this topic of conversation, which I saw cast a gloom over his good-natured countenance, and summoning Lima to the pianoforte, sung one of his best compositions—*Ah! non turbi quae fiero sembiante.* The Marquis joined us at dinner and at six drove me out towards Colares in the *carrinho.* The weather proved misty and uncomfortable. We stopped in our way home at Horne's and drank tea. The woody scene discovered from his veranda had assumed this evening a dingy hue and the cliffs were lost in clouds. It was pitch dark when we returned to Ramalhão. I threw myself on my sofa shuddering at the gloomy aspect of the night. A whistling wind inspired me with sadness; but after all I believe it was the absence of D. Pedro that rendered me so disconsolate.

Saturday 8 September

I sent M. Verdeil to my friend's and they had a long conversation upon the usual topics. The Marquis still continues indulging himself in the hopes of levelling all obstacles by the Archbishop's assistance, who I have indeed every reason to believe is strongly prepossessed in my favour. But what talents have I for Court intrigue? None. I am too indolent, too listless, to give myself any trouble. Bezerra passed the morning with me in expatiating upon the friendship with which I had inspired Marialva, and the effects which might, if I please, result from it. Whilst we were seated on the sofa, in earnest consultation, the Marquis entered and was soon followed by D. Pedro and the Grand Prior. D. Pedro looked confused, as if he had been too often thinking of me since we last parted. Lima sat down to the pianoforte and I sung till dinner. Never in my life did I sing with more expression. There is a scene in one of Lima's operas in which the ghost of Polydorus calls upon Aeneas, just arrived on the Thracian shore, to revenge his death on Polynestor.[222] The music is melancholy and pathetic to a striking degree, and I gave the bitter cry of *Vendica i torti miei,* which often recurs in the air, its full energy. I was so possessed by these affecting sounds that I could hardly eat. Lima was enchanted with the attention I paid his compositions. The evening turning out mild and pleasant, we rambled about the *quinta* till dark. The waters, flowing in rills round the roots of the lemon trees, formed a rippling murmur. Not a leaf rustled, the most profound calm reigned amongst the thickets. D. Pedro and I, who become every day more and more attached to each other, run hand in hand along the alleys, bounding like deer and leaping up to catch at the *azareiro*[223] blossoms which dangled over our heads. No child of thirteen ever felt a stronger impulse to race and gambol than I do. My limbs are as supple and elastic as those of a stripling, and it gives me no pain to turn and twist them into the most playful attitudes.

Sunday 9 September: Cork Convent

Clouds and vapours hanging over the plain, sun frequently concealed. After Mass, D. Pedro went with Verdeil to sketch a view of the Convent. I straggled about the shrubberies which clothe the rocky sides of a shelving hill. Ivies clustered with berries, and periwinkle with purple blossoms. We had a greasy dinner, but a noble dessert: large baskets of the finest fruit. The Abbade seemed animated after dinner by the spirit of contradiction. I was cross and uneasy. D. Pedro paid me little attentions,[224] and I felt ready to burst into tears. How unhappy, how vexed I felt, wandering about, dragging one foot after another. All the hopes I had yesterday conceived are vanished. I climbed up in the evening sun amongst the mossy rocks to a little platform overgrown with lavender. There I sat, lulled by the murmur of the waves rushing over a broken shore. The clouds came slowly sailing over the hills. The Marquis pounded the cones of the pine and gave me the kernels. They have an agreeable almond taste.[225]

The Prior of the Cork Convent is appointed by the Marialvas, so we all set forth this morning—the Marquis, Grand Prior, D. Pedro, and the old Abbade—to dine with him and be present at his installation. He is a sturdy, clownish-looking fellow, very jovial and openhearted. After Mass, D. Pedro and M. Verdeil posted themselves on a mossy stone and began sketching something which they imagined to be a view of the Convent with the surrounding rocks and thickets. Though the sun broiled them unmercifully and lighted up the verdure of the citron and laurel shrubberies with his liveliest rays, the vast plains of land and ocean which are discovered from these eminences were lost in clouds. The effect was singular and I sat on the shelving acclivity of the mountain to enjoy it. The hanging shrubberies of arbutus, bay and myrtle, and the bushy pines which bend over the crags reminded me of the scenery of Mount Edgecumbe. Between the crevices of the rude rocks which lie tumbled about in the wildest confusion, you find luxuriant tufts of herbage which on the least pressure exhale a fresh aromatic perfume. I delight in exploring these nooks and corners. The Marquis was too lame to accompany my rambles, and sat with the monks and Luis de Miranda,[226] the Colonel of the Cascais regiment, at the entrance of the cells, so I remained, till dinner was announced, in total solitude. We had a greasy repast and abundance of high-flavoured cabbage stewed in the essence of ham and partridge, four sucking pigs, as many larded turkeys, and two pyramids of rice, as yellow as saffron could tinge them. Three of the principle monks were of our party. The Grand Prior made wry faces at the copper forks and spoons which were set before us. We could hardly persuade him to make use of them. For my part I am always glad of an excuse to eat in the oriental style with my fingers. For never mortal handled a knife so awkwardly. Our dessert both in point of fruit and sweetmeats was truly luxurious. Pomona herself need not have been ashamed of carrying in her lap such peaches and nectarines as rolled by dozens about the table.

* The Abbade seemed animated after dinner by the spirit of contradiction, and would not allow the Marquis or Luis de Miranda to know more of King John the Fifth and his Court than of that of Pharaoh King of Egypt. D. Pedro and I ran out of the sound of the dispute in which the monks began to join, and climbed up amongst the mossy rocks to a little platform overgrown with lavender. There we sat, lulled by the murmur of distant waves rushing over a broken shore. The clouds came slowly sailing over the hills. My companion pounded the cones of the pine and gave me the kernels which have an agreeable almond taste. The sun set before we abandoned our peaceful retired situation, and joined the Marquis who had not yet been able to appease the Abbade. The vociferous old man made so many appeals to the Father Guardian of the Convent in defence of his opinions that I thought we should never have got away. At length we departed, and after wandering about in clouds and darkness for two hours, reached Sintra exactly at ten. The Marchioness and the children had been much alarmed at our long absence, and rated the Abbade severely for having occasioned it.

Friday 21 September

How different the weather this morning from that with which it pleased Heaven to favour us yesterday: the winds blustering, the clouds touching the ground, and heavy drops of rain trickling down the windows. I got up late. Franchi and Polycarpo were gone. The apartments wore a silent deserted appearance. I felt however in better spirits than I could have expected. Mr. Sill and his clerk Wilson breakfasted with me.[227] As soon as they were gone, I propped myself up with cushions in a corner of the sofa, and, whilst the music was playing a slow and melancholy strain, folded my arms, closed my eyes, and fancied I beheld Franchi in a gloomy chamber of the Patriarchal, totally abandoned and counting the drops of rain as they fell on a discoloured, mouldering cornice. We had nobody at dinner but Lima. The whole evening it continued pouring. I thought night would never arrive. Verdeil lay gaping at one end of the couch, and I yawning and dozing on the other. Lima occupied himself in sorting the vast load of music I have lately received from England. The illumination of the apartment gave me a momentary animation. Lima accompanied me three or four arias, and I sung till I was fatigued and extenuated. It was one before I went to bed, Verdeil and I having had a long conversation concerning the last letters I received from England.

Saturday 22 September

When I got up, the mists were stealing off the hills, and the distant sea discovering itself in all its azure bloom. The sheep I brought from England were feeding under my windows. I could not resist riding out after breakfast with M. Verdeil. We took the road to Colares, and found the air delightfully soft and fragrant. The late rains have refreshed the whole face of the country and tinged the steeps beyond Penha Verde with purple and green, for the numerous tribe of heaths has started into blossom, and the wild mossy spots overhung by crooked cork trees now bloom with large white lilies streaked with pink. We met Bezerra, who arrived this morning from Lisbon, and brought him home with us to dinner. He was standing at D. José's window with Aguilar when my chaise passed by yesterday. The livery caught their eye immediately, down they ran thinking it might be me and Verdeil, but behold it turned out <to be> Franchi, lolling at his ease and looking gay and triumphant. Bezerra added that my good friend Walpole frequently enquired how I went on at the Patriarchal. I am in for a pound at present, and must expect the circulation of many a pleasing story. As I passed by the Marquis' on my way home, I stopped a moment to see him. He appeared much dejected on account of D. Henriqueta, who is threatened with a fever. Notwithstanding the weight which oppressed his mind, he talked to me a good deal concerning my intimacy with the Archbishop, and desired me to press home the point of my introduction to Her Majesty. I am tired of hearing of this same introduction and care not a farthing about it. Like people who wait for their dinner three or four hours beyond their usual time, I have lost my appetite. Not so the Marquis. His eagerness for my gaining an entrance into the presence chamber seems rather to have increased than diminished. Whilst Bezerra and I were walking in my favourite alley at sunset, Horne, his nephew and Miss Sills, all mounted on *burras,* trotted by. They were going to pay the Countess of Galveas a visit, and, having performed this duty, returned and closed the evening with me. Verdeil went to see D. Henriqueta and found her somewhat recovered.

Sunday 23 September

I heard Mass in the chapel of my villa, and prayed fervently to St. Anthony, whose image, finely bedizened, is placed on the High Altar. A raw-boned housemaid squinted through the keyhole at my idolatrous proceedings. We dined at one o'clock by particular desire of the Marquis, who is obliged, in his capacity of Master of the Horse, to accompany the Queen whenever she makes her sally. Assumar came today with the Marquis. I thought him less puppyish than usual. The prints, the music, the scenery of my saloon afforded him great amusement and he expressed his feelings with openness. In general the Portuguese, especially those of the higher class, appear ashamed of admiring anything. Besides the Abbade, who seldom misses, we were illuminated at dinner by the radiant presence of the Father Guardian of the Cork Convent. The flaming nose and juicy forehead of this worthy eremite beggars description. He contrived to toss off the better half of three bottles of port in a twinkling, and soon gulped down an equal quantity of claret and madeira. 'Tis true, Assumar plied him well and a little waggishly, but he was nothing loath. I soon saw by the Marquis' countenance that D. Henriqueta was better. In the evening I drove to Horne's, where I found Bezerra, whose fidgeting, restless disposition readily prompted him to leave the Miss Sills with whom he was sitting and accompany me to Mrs. Gildemeester's. That good lady was gaping her soul out in the society of Mme Fussock, João Antonio Pinto,[228] and Bandeira,[229] the Palace *corregedor,* and his son and heir, a goggle-eyed boy with a head like a pumpkin. I flattered myself Goody Fussock would have moved off upon my entrance, but she stood her ground with great sweetness and resolution. Growing soon tired of the party, I returned to Horne's, drank tea, read newspapers, scratched my head, which I suspect has lately received a Portuguese colony, and after enduring a long recital of a commercial scrape into which Horne has lately fallen, got into my carriage and drove home. Lima was exercising his musical troops. They continued playing till supper whilst I ranged disconsolately through the apartments.

Monday 24 September

Miracles have not yet ceased. Franchi, whom I believed safely entombed in the Seminary, entered the room just as we were sitting down to breakfast. J. Antonio had forgot to issue an *aviso* to the Rector of the Seminary for his restoration. The poor boy, finding he could not be received without this ceremonial, had hurried back to tell me so. I felt no inclination to part with him, and the *aviso* shall take its chance. I will not apply for it this day or two. The weather continues to lower, and the blackness of the clouds which hang over the sea threatens a deluge of rain. I have need of some young sweet-breathed animal to enliven my spirits, to run into the citron thickets and bring me flowery branches, to arrange my prints, transpose my songs, and write down the musical ideas which rush into my mind in happy moments. I was agreeably surprised in the course of the morning by the arrival of General Forbes and Captain White, who are come to settle some regimental affairs with the Viscount Ponte de Lima, and mean to pass a day or two at Sintra. They dined with me, and so did the Abbade and Bezerra, which last mentioned personage arrived in a dripping condition. Our conversation at table turned chiefly upon the lovely province of Minho. Both Forbes and White exerted themselves to persuade me to make an excursion into that quarter, and offered to be my conductors. I have a great mind to accept their proposal and meet them and D. José de Sousa at Oporto. Bezerra begs I will take him in my suite and has already arranged the order of our march. After the two officers left me, I let down all the curtains, for the winds blew and the storms descended with redoubled violence; a wintry gloom was diffused throughout the apartment. I sat cross-legged on the mat, reclining my head on the sofa, in a pensive melancholy mood. At tea the Marquis came in and behaved very graciously to Franchi. The heaviness of the atmosphere had affected my nerves and thrown me into a feverish weary state which lasted the whole evening.

Tuesday 25 September

I took advantage of a short interval of sunshine to ride with Verdeil as far as Horne's. It rains every day and all day long, and I begin to lose patience. Amongst other evils of this particular period of my existence, I reckon that of dining at one o'clock, out of complacence for the Marquis. My mornings are by this custom totally disjointed. I have neither time to write or read before dinner, and am good for nothing after it. Oh that Her Majesty would change her hours of riding out, or go to Mafra or to the devil. She little thinks what woes she occasions both me, M. Verdeil, and the cook M. du Noyer.

I agreed with the Marquis to give him a meeting this evening at Padre Rocha's,[230] the Archbishop's prime favourite and confessor, and speak my mind decidedly concerning this nonsense of my introduction to the Queen. I hate going out and quitting my sofa and my music. However I was tolerably punctual to my engagement, and, at seven of a cloudy night with fits of moonshine, drove to the Palace [231] and made directly to Father Rocha's quarters. The Marquis was there and had been half an hour waiting my arrival. I found Rocha perfectly well disposed and ready primed to act in my favour. We shall carry our point such as it is, I daresay; but what care I! I told Rocha that whether the Archbishop would or would not take my presentation upon him, he would ever hold a conspicuous place in my affection and esteem, but that unless I was immediately introduced to the Royal Family I would quit Portugal, and instead of personally cultivating the Archbishop's acquaintance, must coldly content myself with admiring and esteeming him at a distance. Rocha entered into all my ideas with a most cheerful vivacity, and I have no doubt will convey them improved and augmented to the ear of his patron. This Rocha, though an Inquisitor and a Dominican Friar, has nothing flinty or scarecrowish about him. His address bespeaks a knowledge of men and manners seldom gained within the walls of a convent, and his eloquence, of which he possesses a copious flow, appeared to me nervous and unaffected.

Our conversation ended, my friend went to play at lotto in the Royal apartment, and I returned to Ramalhão. I stopped to take up Verdeil, whom I had[232] left by the way at[233] the Marquis'. D. Pedro came running out the moment he heard the sound of my carriage. His sister's illness confines him at home, but as she is now recovering apace, I hope he will be soon at liberty. Verdeil told me he had left old Tancos,[234] the *Camareiramor*, and two or three other hideous cats of the same species feeding like cormorants upon ham, fricassees and partridges. It was only half past eight when I got home. Not having yet acquired a Portuguese stomach, I contented myself with drinking tea and nibbling biscuits. As I have renounced dogs this long while, I enjoyed being welcomed home by the gambols of Franchi, whom I have reason to think a very faithful animal strenuously attached to me.

Wednesday 26 September

No chance yet of its clearing up. I look in vain for the sea, and discover nothing but dismal clouds rolling along in heavy volumes. The verandas are flooded. There is no moving out. I tried twenty times to get on horseback but was as often repulsed by a driving shower, each drop sufficient to drown a beetle. Neither Lima nor the Abbade appeared at dinner. The Marquis I knew was engaged, so we dined at three. Being at a total loss for occupation in the evening, and tired with confinement, M. Verdeil and I, though it still continued to pour, drove out in the chaise as far as Rio de Mouro. The thick vapours clouding the hills, and the dark troubled sky which hung low over the barren plains, gave a Northern air to the prospect, which reminded me of Cornwall. I thought myself once more traversing the heaths near Truro on the high road to Falmouth or some other cursed place of embarkation.

Just as we were returned home and candles were lighting, the Marquis arrived with the Prior of S. Julião,[235] a mighty friend of Rocha's and a person of great worship. My great Dutch bible[236] lying open upon a table, they began tumbling over the prints in the most awkward manner. I, who abhor having my books thumbed, snapped at the Marquis and cast an evil look on the Prior, who was leaning over the volume and creasing its corners. Pedro Grua[237] played on the violoncello a solo of his own composition with infinite taste; but the Marquis was too much employed in lamenting the Massacre of the Innocents to pay any attention, and his reverend companion had entered into a long-winded dissertation upon parables, miracles and martyrdoms, from which I prayed in vain the Lord to deliver me. Verdeil, scenting from afar the saintly flavour of our discourse, stole off. I cannot say much in favour of the Prior's erudition even in holy matters; for he positively affirmed that it was Henry the Eighth who knocked Thomas à Becket's brains out, and that by the Beast in the Apocalypse Luther was plainly indicated. I hate wrangles, and had it not been for the soiling of my prints should never have contradicted him. But as I was a little out of humour, I lowered him somewhat in the Marquis' opinion by stating the true period of Thomas à Becket's murder, and by specious arguments shoving the Beast's horns off Luther and clapping them tight on Calvin. The Marquis and I took at least a hundred turns in my long suite of apartments, talking round and round in a desultory manner and ending where we began, whilst the Prior remained in the saloon hearing Franchi play. A little before eleven they departed and left me to sup in peace.

Thursday 27 September

I took a hard trot this morning on the rough road to Rio de Mouro. In cloudy weather the heaths at the foot of the Sintra mountains form a scene which in point of blackness and desolation yields not to the saddest regions in Cornwall or the Devil's D<yke> of the Peak. We were eleven at dinner today—the Marquis, Frei José do Rosario[238]—a Dominican friar,—Luis Texeira, the Abbade, Horne, Bezerra, Lima, Forbes, White etc. I cannot launch out too warmly in praise of Forbes. He speaks his mind with a manly openness that comforts my heart, and gives me the soundest disinterested advice I receive in this cursed country. In the course of the evening we had much conversation. He is clear of opinion that the sooner I leave this land of lice, cheats, and beggars, the happier I shall find myself.

Friday 28 September

The sky being serene and the sun enlivening, I rode with Bezerra and Verdeil through the shady lanes and pleasant orchards which fill the rich, well-cultivated valley of Colares. Riding is of infinite service to my health, and enables me to bear up against the ennuis of Portugal. Bezerra returned home with us to dinner. We found the Abbade as usual seated in a snug comer of the saloon ramming his nose with snuff and fancying himself very busy in reading my Arabian Stories.[239]

At tea-time the Marquis came in, looking so dismal, so woe-begone that I started. He took me aside and with heavy sighs informed me that Walpole, through the counsel of Melo, had had the audacity to make representations in the name of the Court of England against my being introduced to Her Portuguese Majesty, and that the Archbishop was thrown into the utmost consternation at so violent and unexpected a measure. "The Queen knows not how to act," continued my friend. "She is highly disposed in your favour and convinced that you are the innocent victim of the blackest machination, but her good inclinations are frustrated by this attack. She dares not receive you." "Oh pray," answered I, "let her cease giving herself the least trouble. I am perfectly ready to acquiesce in keeping out of her presence. My resolution is taken. I shall pack up and depart. Nothing will now detain me." I never saw a more doleful expression of countenance than that which the Marquis assumed upon hearing this firm determination. The tears were ready to start in his eyes, his voice faltered, and he walked two or three times the length of the apartment before he could compose himself.

Saturday 29 September

I continue firm in my resolution of leaving Portugal and have given orders to prepare for my journey. Mass was performed in my chapel this morning in honour of the valiant St. Michael. I assisted with apparent devotion, but could not help feeling all the while more sympathy for the old Dragon than became a pious Catholic. Alas, we are both fallen angels! Six years ago how triumphantly did I pass this festival at Fonthill,[240] seated at the foot of my father's statue, receiving the congratulations of the first personages in my nation, universally esteemed, looked up to, and admired. The loss of Lady Margaret has harrowed up my feelings, or else the contrast between my present and past situation would have rushed this day into my mind with all its bitter circumstance, and almost have driven me distracted; but I remained unmoved. I even dined with appetite and cheerfulness. General Forbes, White, and the Abbade partook of our goose. I told Forbes what had passed between Melo and Walpole concerning my introduction at this Court. He believes not a word of it, and is convinced that the Archbishop himself, prompted by Rocha, has invented this story to avoid scrapes and perplexities. For my part I care not; all I desire is a safe and happy deliverance from this region of poverty and ignorance.

Sunday 30 September

After Mass, I got on horseback and rode with Verdeil to Colares. The Abbade, whom I have not yet made acquainted with my intentions of visiting Spain, occupied his usual place at table. We had hardly rose from it before Berti came in to tell me that Mme Arriaga and a bevy of the Palace damsels were prancing about the alleys of the *quinta* on palfreys and *burras*. I hastened to join them. There was

D. Maria do Carmo and D. Maria de Penha[241], with her hair flowing about her shoulders, mounted on a pert little *burra,* and her large eyes looking as wild and roving as those of a stag. I called for my horse and galloped with them through canes and citron bushes, brushing off leaves, fruit and blossoms. The sound of the wind instruments wafted across the thickets enlivened all our motions. The evening, though cloudy, was not unpleasant. The ladies seemed to enjoy their excursion and to regret the short time it was doomed to continue, for at seven they are obliged to return to strict attendance in the Queen's apartment. A collation was served up in a sort of grotto adjoining one of the terraces, whilst the music continued playing. The ladies would fain have danced, but the fatal hour of seven arriving, they were compelled to hurry away—I flatter myself, much against their inclination.

Monday 1 October

All the morning was I obliged to pass in writing home to England the blessed news of my having at length determined to leave Portugal. I wished much to have rode out and unmuzzed myself; but Aguilar coming in at two o'clock prevented me. He stayed only half an hour and then whisked back to Lisbon. At night the Marquis, who arrived as it fell dark, renewed all his offers and most earnestly solicited me to pronounce the magic words "I will remain in Portugal" and enjoy the effect they would produce. "Only assure me you will not abandon us," continued my zealous friend, "and the Queen will set Walpole and his Court at defiance, receive you with unprecedented distinction and load you with honours." My answer was so positive against having recourse to this talisman that the poor Marquis, losing every hope, relapsed into gloomy reverie and left me with a heart full of heaviness.

Tuesday 2 October

Instead of sitting down to write, I mounted my horse, and picking up Bezerra by the way, galloped to Colares. As we passed Sintra on our return, the Abbade joined us, and I acquainted him with my hopes of walking in the cloisters of the Escorial before many weeks were elapsed. The poor old man, who had only heard a faint whisper of my intentions at Horne's, bowed low to the neck of his horse upon receiving the full confirmation of these evil tidings, and could hardly summon up spirits to say three words during the remainder of our ride. "Now," said he, "I comprehend too plainly the cause of the Marquis' dejection last night, and the reason why he went supperless to bed without speaking a word to any one of his family." Bezerra fidgeted away soon after dinner. Towards night, the wind blew chill and rainy, whirling ugly crumpled leaves about the verandas, and kept hammering against the windows. I cushioned myself up in a corner of the sofa, whilst Franchi played an adagio of Haydn, and the Abbade took snuff with sorrow and despondency.

* Wednesday 3 October [242]

I took a wild ride over the desert mountains which surround the eyrie-like Convent of Nossa Senhora da Pena. The toll of its bells was borne by my ear as I rode musing along. I returned by the neat paved route of Colares, and called at Horne's in my way, whom I found in a strong fit of elevation and pomposity. He had penetrated into the great hall of the Palace, called the Casa dos Cignos,[243] and had kissed the Princess of Brazil's hand, and had spoken to the Marquis this and Count t'other. Much and loudly did he talk of the grand appearance of the hall, its august portal and superb view discovered from its lofty windows. The turkey poult[244] sat by, stretching out its silly neck and gobbling up the narration with avidity. I was called home to dinner in a violent hurry, the Marquis, attended by the Prior of S. Julião, being in waiting for me, with his watch on the table counting the minutes. The Marquis returned in the evening and stayed till near ten. I avoided talking with him about my journey. Our conversation turned upon indifferent matters. He told me many strange improbable stories about Pekin and the Emperor of China, which had been palmed upon him by one Pacheco, a fellow who had resided at Pekin eight years as a sort of ambassador.[245]

* Thursday 4 October [246]

The mildness of the morning tempted me early on horseback. I took the road of the ancient Convent of Hieronymites near the Penedo dos Ovos. The larks were singing and a vast profusion of wild flowers opening into bloom. The pleasantness of the weather detained me later than usual. Upon my return home I found the Marquis, Horne, the Miss Sills, Street and Bezerra all in a violent uproar for dinner, which was hardly despatched before Mme Arriaga, the two Lacerdas, D. Ana Brigida and D. Emilia O'Dempsy arrived.[247] This last mentioned Irish dame is in high favour with the Spanish Infanta[248] whom she followed from Madrid. She has a sly smooth specious manner, well calculated to make its way in Courts. Her utmost art was exerted to discover whether I had any thoughts of establishing myself in Portugal by an alliance with the Marialvas. Instead of adding to her stock in the gossiping branch of business, the chief trade of all Courts without any exception, I flew to the harpsicord and sung *Pietoso Enea* and two or three more arias of Lima and João de Sousa with so much effect that Franchi for the first time in his life attended.

Friday 5 October

Languid and unwell. I sat down to write but could make nothing of it. We rode
out and crossed the dismal stony plain towards Cascais. Some miserable peasants
were grubbing up the stunted ilex for fuel. Sea glittering at a distance and many
ships sailing in; happy those that sail out, say I. The evening cold, the sky had a red
frosty look, and the windows clattered. I kept walking to and fro in the saloon with
Verdeil to keep myself warm. Seeing the train of torchlight pass by after the Queen,
I sallied forth according to appointment and met the Marquis at Rocha's. Rocha
bewailed pathetically the timidity of the Court, and the irresolute weakness of the
Queen. <The> Marquis returned with me. I hope to get such letters for Spain as
will prevent my baggage from being ransacked by Custom House officers.

Saturday 6 October

I have not seen so delightful a morning this many a day. The clear beams of the
sun, the prospect of the blue glittering sea, have given a flow to my spirits. I am
all eagerness and curiosity this morning to traverse Spain, and view my journey in
a flattering light. Verdeil and I rode to Colares. Azure bloom of the hills, round
heads of the orange trees, clustered with fruit. After dinner the Abbade came in
with a blue mantle; he <looked> like a New Zealand chief. Verdeil romped with
Franchi. The Marquis came in unexpectedly and sat fixed on the sofa four long
hours sinking from thought to thought a vast profound.[249]

Sunday 7 October

Franchi left me; I gave him the best advice in my power. Rode out after Mass.
Bezerra and Abbade at dinner, full of the news of war.[250] My nose burns after dinner;
I shall end with a flaming red nose. Chill evening; I long for <a> fire.

Monday 8 October

I went to the Archbishop's and found him in all his native frowziness wrapped
up in an old snuff-coloured greatcoat sadly patched and tattered, his paunch
left at full liberty to hang as low as it pleased, no breeches to keep it up. He was
very hugging[251] and kind, but I believe is heartily glad to get rid of me. The story
of Walpole's having protested in the name of his Court against my presentation

is, I believe, a plump lie. Forbes was in the right; the poor Marquis is the dupe. The Archbishop and his Royal mistress are persuaded that I am <a> very formidable personage and that my stay in their domain might occasion them more trouble than profit. My old bird, conscious of having fibbed, seemed upon thorns. "So," says he, "my Beckford, you are going to leave us. Pray get that rascal Walpole a good trimming and make haste back again." "That is more than I will promise," answered I. The Archbishop went to feed,[252] and I drove back, and mounting my horse, rode towards Penha Longa. The birds singing, and a soft air blowing over the turf. We had the Abbade at dinner. I am perplexed how to contrive my journey with tolerable convenience. <In the> evening entered the Penalvas, father and son. At seven the Marquis and D. Thomaz de Noronha. The Marquis still brim-full of projects. He wrote himself to Bandeira for mules.

Tuesday 9 October

My excursion on horseback was short this morning, we only went half way to Colares. I stopped at the Marquis', who was in a dreadful hurry as usual. As I was standing on the veranda towards sunset, an old Irish woman who lives with the Marchioness of Marialva and carries on a little smuggling business under her auspices crept up to me. She came to offer me a parcel of Irish linen very cheap, etc. I learnt from her the desolation and the disappointment of the whole family at my sudden departure, and particularly that D. Pedro had taken my going away so much to heart that he said he could no longer bear the sight of my habitation since I was so soon to abandon it. We drove out. The musicians are gone. Lima played and I sung the whole evening. Abbé at dinner. I dread my journey through Spain. Talk of war.

Wednesday 10 October

Rare weather for my ride to Lisbon. We were two hours and a quarter, the atmosphere pearly, the sun bright. I found the house in confusion, Berti dawdling. We did not sit down to table till half past four. I have brought Lima with me. The views of the river bar, capes etc. from the leagues beyond Queluz are striking enough. Forbes hurried to see me and the Grand Prior soon followed him. The Grand Prior looks rueful, all the agreeable castles he had built in concert with me are dissolved into air. I am grieved at the thoughts of leaving him. Mme Franchi has not yet sent her son to the Seminary, and he too came posting to kiss my hand.

There are stories innumerable of the cause of my quitting Portugal flying about, but none of them true. Many believe that the Queen has ordered me to quit her dominions in four and twenty hours; others pretend that I am summoned home by order of Parliament;[253] other fools say I have quarrelled with Assumar, and that we are to cut each other's throats the first opportunity. The difference of climate between Sintra and Lisbon is still greater than I imagined. The evening was so mild and warm that I walked with Franchi in the square before the Palace of the Necessidades.

Thursday 11 October

Melancholy and dejected. A lowering day. Franchi sneaked in as if ashamed of himself for not having yet surrendered up to the Seminary. I soon dismissed him. My time drags heavily. I am in a sad desultory mood and can settle to nothing. My voice however was in tolerable tune, and I was singing with Lima when Polycarpo came in, reeking and stinking. The news of my approaching departure had brought him trotting all the way from the Ajuda through pools and puddles; he has spoiled my mat. I am taking leave of my books and packing them in their case. Forbes found me so employed.

M. Verdeil, who likes gadding better than I do, persuaded me to go to the play at the Salitri Theatre.[254] We took Lima and Polycarpo with us. I was better amused than I expected, though the performance lasted above four hours and a half, from seven till near twelve. It consisted of a ranting prose tragedy in three acts called *Sesostris,*[255] two ballets, a pastoral, and a farce. The decorations were not amiss and the dresses showy. A shambling blear-eyed boy dressed in the sable garb of woe squeaked and bellowed alternately the part of a widowed princess. Another hobbledehoy tottering on high-heeled shoes represented Her Egyptian Majesty, and warbled two airs with all the nauseous sweetness of a fluted falsetto. I could have boxed his ears for surfeiting mine so filthily. The audience was numerous and warm in their applause. In the stage-box sat the mincing Countess of Pombeiro, whose light hair and waxed complexion was finely contrasted by the sable hue of two little negro attendants perched on each side of her.[256] It is the high *ton* at present in this Court to be surrounded by African implings, the more hideous the better, and to dress them out as fine as you are able. The Queen has set the example: the Royal family vie with each other in spoiling and caressing D. Rosa, Her Majesty's dark-skinned, blubber-lipped, flat-nosed favourite. One of the dances pleased me exceedingly. Upon the rise of the curtain, an astrologer's apartments, tables, spheres, astrolabes and cabalistic images is discovered. The astrologer appears very busy arranging certain cabalistic images and pinking their eyes with a gigantic pair of black compasses. A sort of pierrot enters and announces some inquisitive travellers who enter with many bows and scrapings. One of them, an old dapper beau in pink and silver, reminded me very much of the Duke de Lafões, and sidled along, and tossed his cane about, and asked questions and never waited for answers, with as good a grace as that jaunty General. The Astrologer, after explaining the wonders of his apartment with many pantomimical contortions, makes signs for his company <to follow him>, and the scene changes to a long gallery illuminated with a profusion of lights in gilt branches. The perspective terminates in a flight of steps upon each of which stands a row of figures, pantaloons, harlequins, sultans, sultanas, Indian chiefs, devils and savages, to all appearance motionless. Pierrot brings in a machine like a hand-organ and his master begins to grind, the music accompanying. At the first chord, down drop the arms of all the figures; at the second, each rank descends a step, and so on till gaining the level of the stage; and the astrologer grinding faster and faster, the supposed clockwork assembly begin a general dance. Their ballet ended, the same accords are repeated and all hop up in the same stiff manner as they hopped down. The travellers, highly pleased with the show, pouring their purses into the astrologer's sleeves with the usual stage liberality, depart.

Pierrot, who longs to be grinding, persuades his master to take a walk and leave him in possession of the gallery. He consents, but leaves a strict charge with the gaping oaf upon no account to meddle with the machine or set the figures in motion. But vain are his direction<s>! No sooner has he turned his back, than to work Pierrot goes with all his strength. The figures fall a-shaking as if on the point of disjointing themselves; creak-crack grinds the machine with horrid harshness; legs, arms, and noddles are thrown into convulsions; three steps are jumped at once. Pierrot, frightened out of his senses at the goggle-eyed crowd advancing upon him, clings close to the machine and gives the handle no respite. The music too degenerates into the most jarring shrieking sounds, and the figures, knocking against each other, and whirling round and round in utter confusion, fall flat on the stage. Pierrot runs from group to group in rueful despair, tries in vain to re-animate them, and at length losing all patience, throws one over the other, and heaps sultanas upon savages and shepherds upon devilkins. Most of these personages, being represented by boys of twelve or thirteen, were easily wielded. After Pierrot has finished tossing and tumbling, he drops down exhausted, and lays as dead as his neighbours, hoping to escape unnoticed amongst them; but this subterfuge saves not his bacon. In comes the astrologer, armed with his compasses. Back he starts at sight of the confounded jumble. Pierrot pays for it all, is soon drawn forth from his lurking place, soundly thrashed, and the astrologer, grinding in a moderate and scientific manner, the figures lift themselves up, and returning all in statu quo, the ballet finishes.

I am not ashamed to say how lively a pleasure this nonsense afforded me, having still the happiness of feeling myself a child in many moments. Of all the favours gracious Heaven has bestowed on me, the one I esteem the most is the still retaining the appearance, the agility and the fancy of a stripling. I——— [257]

Sunday 14 October

As it was in the beginning so shall it be in the end. I will make a good finish at Lisbon and part friends with St. Anthony. I despatched Berti this morning to the Antonine Convent with ten moidores and a message to the monks that I intended hearing Mass in their church. Accordingly I went, and was received by a universal grin of the whole fraternity, conducted in processions along the cloister, and placed on a bright new carpet just before the image of my protector. There was a prodigious crowd, all the blackguards in Lisbon with their wrinkled aunts and toothless grandmothers. The crowd pressed hard upon me and would have scared a less devout mortal out of countenance. High Mass was just ending when I came in, and the low roar of the monks shaking the vaulted ceiling. I kept my eyes lifted up inflexibly to the image of the saint, whose silver crown and glory shone bright with the reflection of flaming tapers. Mass began and the kneeling crowd waddled forwards in waves. Two or three scabby boys scratching their lousy pates encroached upon my carpet, but I was too deeply employed in my orisons to have them got rid of. The whole congregation seemed animated with the same fervour that lengthened my chin and rolled my eyeballs. A deep silence prevailed, interrupted alone by a few puffs of wind and snuffling aspirations, for of snuff takers there were many dozens. Berti distinguished himself by frequent thumps and crossings. I thump pretty well, but have not yet learnt to keep perfect time. For flippery in crossing myself and goosishness in poking out my head I will turn my back to no one.

The service ended, I walk forth followed by a train of reverend fathers, and having recommended myself to their especial prayers for the success of my voyage, I drove home, and mounted my horse, for the day is bright, clear and enlivening. We rode along the shore of Belem. The hills in the opposite shore are clothed in the liveliest verdure, the sunbeams played on the surface of the river, and the streamers of innumerable vessels floated in the soft breezes. I enjoyed this luxury of sunshine, and sighed at the thoughts of journeying to the North and abandoning this serene sky. The Grand Prior and Rumi dined with me. Forbes came to take leave: he sets off tomorrow to join his regiment; happiness and prosperity go with him—he is the honestest man I have known in Portugal. The Grand Prior and I had another tête-à-tête in the coach this evening, Verdeil having again sallied forth to see sights, and satisfy his craving curiosity.

I went to the Monastery of Belem, ascended the grand staircase constructed at the expense of Queen Catherine, Charles the Second's dowager, and after walking in the cloister of Manoel, visited the library. The cloisters are spacious, lofty, and present a fine spread of Gothic arches; red-coloured stone. The corridor which leads to the cells <is> above five hundred feet long. In the windows are commodious resting places where the monks loll at their ease and enjoy the view of the river. We saw <the> treasure by candlelight; a custodium of the pure gold of Quiloa, made <in> 1506, the shape light, pyramids enamelled, twelve apostles, their hair beautiful.[258]

Afterwards to the old Marquis <of Marialva>, all the rooms lighted, fifty servants in waiting. I came home from the Marquis at seven. Verdeil was not returned. I drank tea alone and turned over the *Voyage pittoresque d'Italie*,[259] then took up *Julia Mandeville*[260] and read till I was frozen with horror. I looked around. The candles were burning dim with long dismal snuffs. A superstitious eye would have seen in them shrouds and ghastly images. There was a time when even the most ridiculous childish superstitions swayed my mind, when I dreaded night solitude and darkness. At present my imagination is wonderfully calmed. The sudden transition from the gayest happiness to the most mournful sorrow described in *Julia Mandeville* <re>called all my sufferings in a similar situation. I leaned upon the table, bending over the last pages of this admirable novel, till the recollection of my agonies last year, when I lost the very Being I ever truly loved, poured in so thick upon me that the tears started in my eyes, and the swelling of my heart almost deprived me of respiration. I still kept reading in spite of myself till I seemed to behold Julia's and her lover's corpses lying extended in the once festive saloon. My imagination soon ceasing to prey on these imaginary horrors, took its flight to Fonthill, and pictured to itself the pale image of my Margaret. This vision often recurs to me, and fills my soul with terror and bitterness. I think of the peaceful hours we passed together at Vevey. I know they are gone without return, and that no power can recover them.

Monday 15 October

I had a scorching ride this morning through the heart of the city and along the quays near Marvila. The sun in meridian splendour darted his fiercest rays upon my head and half blinded me. I was in no very pleasant temper and found in my heart to have rated Verdeil for having so vigorously forwarded every disposition I happened to have shewn towards leaving Portugal. My Spanish journey appears in a formidable light now the term approaches for putting it into execution. I have not spirits to encounter it, and had much rather bask the winter away in some snug palace at Lisbon with a view of the Tagus and a garden well filled with early flowers and orange trees, than traverse the windy plains of Castille, exposed to the inconvenience of hoggish inns and the wearisome paces of mule drivers. I by no means like the thoughts of bidding Marialva and D. Pedro an eternal adieu, and if I once leave Portugal what chance have I of ever returning to it. I am tired to death of travelling, and my curiosity burns dim like a lamp on the point of extinguishing. Lisbon, now I am going to leave it, appears not half so dull, so noisy or so disagreeable. I could hardly take my eyes off the gay glittering expanse of the river, and began forming a thousand projects of sailing on its surface and enjoying music and collations under the vine arbours on its banks. Such is the perversity of human nature that the moments in which objects appear the most estimable are those when we have lost or are going to lose them.

At three, M. Verdeil and I sat down to one of the worst dinners that ever was served up to me—a dish-clout soup, wizzled chicken and flabby turbot. If M. du Noyer treats me so a second time it shall be the last. Whilst we were nibbling at a dessert right worthy of the repast which had preceded it, the Grand Prior lifted up amongst us the light of his good-natured countenance, and stayed chatting till it was time for him to go to a christening where he was to stand proxy for the Patriarch. After tea we went, that is to say Verdeil and I, to the theatre in the Rua dos Condes, a more tolerable edifice than that of the Salitri, but sorry enough on conscience. I was surprised at finding the scenery very good and the dresses splendid and well fancied. The actors, too, were not half so abominable as those at the other house. Our play was a translation of Voltaire's *Mérope*, with ballets and a farce. The actor who represented Mérope had bundled himself out with great adroitness, managed his hoop with ease, and sailed about the stage with as good a grace as many an old drawing-room dowager. Several scenes in the farce made me laugh heartily as I begin to enter into the force and idiom of the language. A few months more would perfectly initiate me.

Two young fellows, one dressed as a girl and very becomingly, sung an enchanting *modinha*. Those who have never heard *modinhas* must and will remain ignorant of the most voluptuous and bewitching music that ever existed since the days of the Sybarites. They consist of languid interrupted measures, as if the breath was gone with excess of rapture, and the soul panting to fly out of you and incorporate itself with the beloved object. With a childish carelessness they steal into the heart before it has time to arm itself against their enervating influence. You fancy you are swallowing milk and you are swallowing poison. As to myself, I must confess I am a slave to *modinhas,* and when I think of them cannot endure the idea of quitting Portugal. Could I indulge the least hopes of surviving a two months' voyage, nothing should prevent my setting off for Brazil, the native land of *modinhas*, and living in tents, decorated like those the Chevalier de Parny describes in his agreeable little *Voyage*,[261] and swinging in hammocks and gliding over smooth mats with youths crowned with jasmine and girls diffusing at every motion the perfumes of roses.

Tuesday 16 October

Berti, alias Twiddleman, is a severe clog upon active proceedings. He never gets up till half-past eight and diffuses his sluggishness and stupor over my whole family. Owing to this double-distilled spirit of slothfulness, the cook, instead of setting out at six, was only getting in order to depart at ten, so I am obliged to dine here instead of going to Sintra as I proposed (?), or stand a chance of faring worse than I did yesterday. The flies will not let me write in peace, and tickle the tip of my nose and insult me continually. There has been that turkey poult Sill and two or three other fowls of the same feather looking over my furniture; I hear they pecked hard at the dearness of several articles.

By twelve the Grand Prior was with us. We dined at three and set off all together for Ramalhão. The valley of Alcantara, so parched and blasted a month ago, partially discovered between the arches of the colossal aqueduct now presents a delightful scene of verdure. The orange and citron trees, washed by frequent showers, are once more clothed with the brightest green. Even the olives have lost their rustiness. We met numbers of *saloias*[262] singing and giggling as they drove their *burras* along; our heavy coach, which justly deserves to be called, as well as a galleon, the *Nostra Señora de Carvadonza*,[263] afforded them great amusement. However, notwithstanding its heaviness and the books, plate, and bodies with which it was loaded, my mules drew it without even stopping to breathe, in two hours and <a> half to Ramalhão. The sun set in troubled clouds just as we reached Rio de Mouro, and the plains of flowering heath at the base of the Sintra mountains, tinged by his last beams, exhibited rich shades of purple, which as night came on sunk into total blackness. The Grand Prior suffered all the miseries of low spirits, to which he is more subject than any man; however, thanks be to Heaven, they fled before a dish of tea with a spoonful of rum in it, prescribed by M. Verdeil the moment of our arrival. The mildness of the evening tempted me to remain till about supper time on the verandas, breathing the woody fragrance of the thickets below. At intervals I entered the saloon and sung *seguidillas* with Lima. 'Tis lucky the weather is so warm and genial. Did the north wind bluster, I should feel shivery and very uncomfortable, the saloon being stripped of all its drapery and the glasses and tables removed.

Wednesday 17 October

Rode to Horne's. A long conversation with him; convinced of his shabby interested views. Then to the Marquis; miserable we are both at parting. D. Pedro clinging round me as if unwilling to let me go. How grieved I am to quit this family. Not a blot in their conduct to me, affectionate, open, and disinterested. Abbé at dinner.[264]

The month wears apace, and owing to Berti's sluggishness the preparations for my journey are but little advanced. It will be rare pleasant travelling from one crazy *venta*[265] to another in the heart of the winter. I rode to Horne's, whom I found in a strong fit of gout and selfishness. He hinted and hinted again and again that it might be as well if I made a few presents before my departure to the veterans who had fought and suffered in my cause, meaning himself I suppose and the Marquis of Marialva. Two pieces of worked muslin, the most dingy coloured I ever beheld, were at the same time produced, and recommended at the *low* price of thirty guineas apiece, as pretty offerings for the Marchioness and D. Henriqueta. I begged leave to assure this worthy mentor of mine that the friendship between the Marquis and myself was founded upon a very different basis than that of giving or receiving presents, and that I would not for all the palimpores[266] or muslins of the Indies shock his sincere and genuine delicacy. These sentiments were received with a wink of the eye and a shrug of the shoulders, and other means of squeezing something out of me were essayed. I was told by the virtuous Horne, in a tone at once solemn and menacing, that Her Majesty, irritated by the constant insinuations of my enemies, would in all probability prevent the sale of my furniture, and that of course I had better not wait for this moment of royal anger, but give some articles away with a noble spirit and send the rest to England. This idea I treated with the contempt it merited, and making my bow with more than a smile on my countenance, mounted my horse and galloped to the Marquis.

There was I received with open arms by the whole family, and obliquely reproached for staying away so long. I told Marialva everything that had passed between me and Horne, and he coloured up to his eyes with anger. I had some difficulty in prevailing on him not to show the mean trader public marks of his indignation. "Are such shameful lies as that of the Queen's intentions to[267] impede the sale of your furniture, the return this fellow makes you for your solicitations in his behalf with the Archbishop?" said my friend with unusual vehemence. "He a sufferer in your cause! Does he pretend to be ignorant that for your sake alone the Archbishop has shewn him those very civilities which seem to have overturned his understanding? Give him not a farthing, and banish him eternally from your esteem and your recollection." So saying the Marquis embraced me and hurried off to the Palace. I returned soberly to dinner with the Abbade and Lima.

In the dusk Verdeil and I walked back to the Marquis', where the Queen and all the Royal Family were assembled to partake of a splendid *merenda* and see fireworks. D. Pedro and the Grand Prior conducted us into a snug boudoir that looks into the great pavilion, whose gay and fantastic scenery appeared to infinite advantage by the light of innumerable tapers reflected on all sides from lustres of glittering crystal. The little Infanta D. Carlota was perched on a sofa in conversation with the Marchioness and D. Henriqueta, who in the true Oriental fashion had placed themselves cross-legged on the floor. A troop of Maids-of-Honour commanded by the Countess of Lumiares[268] sat in the same posture at a little distance. D. Rosa, though not so frolicsome as the last time I had the pleasure of seeing her in this fairy bower, was more sentimental, leaned against the door ogling and flirting with a handsome Moor belonging to the Marquis.

Presently the Queen and Princess of Brazil came forth from their *merenda* and seated themselves directly under the window behind which I had placed myself. A mournful silence prevailed. The Count de Sampaio[269] and the Viscount Ponte de Lima knelt by the Royal personages with as much abject devotion as Mussulmans before the tomb of their prophet or Tartars in the presence of the Dalai Lama. My friend alone, who stood right opposite Her Majesty, seemed to preserve his ease and cheerfulness. The Prince of Brazil and D. João[270] stalked about with their hands in their pockets, their mouths in a perpetual yawn, and their eyes wandering from object to object with a stare of royal vacancy. Few princes are more to be pitied than these. Condemned by a ridiculous etiquette to strict confinement within the walls of their palaces, and never allowed even to mix incognito with the crowd, they experience all the *gêne* of sultans, without their power or their luxuries. The Count de Sampaio, who happened to be the Lord-in-Waiting, handed the tea to the Queen and Princess and fell down on both knees to present it.

This ceremony over, for everything is a ceremony at this servile Court, the fireworks were announced and the royal sufferers, followed by their sufferees, adjourned to a neighbouring apartment. The Marchioness, her daughter, the Countess of Lumiares, D. Emilia[271] and another *açafata* mounted up to the boudoir where I was sitting and took possession of its windows. Seven or eight wheels and as many tourbillions began whirling and whizzing. A succession of line-rockets darted backwards and forwards with sputtering velocity, and to the infinite delight of the little Countess of Lumiares,[272] who, though hardly sixteen, has been married four years. Her youthful cheerfulness, light hair and fair complexion put me so much in mind of my Margaret that I could not help looking at her with a melancholy tenderness that filled my eyes with tears. Her being with child too increased the resemblance, and as she sat in a corner of the window, discovered at intervals by the blue light of rockets bursting high in the air, I felt my blood thrill as if I beheld a phantom. The last firework being played off, the Queen and the Infantas departed, and the Marchioness and the other ladies descended into the pavilion, where we drank tea, whilst the Grand Prior and D. Pedro attacked the remains of the royal collation, consisting of ham pies, quivering jellies and larded turkeys. D. Maria[273] and her little sister, animated by the bright illuminations, tripped about in their light muslin dresses with all the sportiveness of fairy beings, such as might be supposed to have dropped down from the floating clouds Pillement has so well represented on the ceiling.

The Marquis, who had been obliged to accompany Her Majesty to the Palace, returned at ten; we supped immediately. He sighed bitterly at the thought of my approaching departure, and assured me it was also much regretted by the Prince and Princess of Brazil, who openly taxed the Queen and her Minister with the meanest cowardice for suffering me to leave Portugal so gravely dissatisfied. God knows, though I feel more compassion for the Queen than anger, I cannot but reserve a larger portion of pity for the miseries of two millions of human beings who in affairs of the most serious moment are equally the victims of her timidity and irresolution.

Thursday 18 October

There is a sympathy I am convinced between toads and witch-like old women. Mother Morgan[274] descended this morning, not into the infernal regions, but into the cellar, and immediately five or six spanking toads hopped around her. She treated the poor things rather scurvily and laid three of the fattest sprawling. I saw them lying breathless in the court as I got on horseback. The largest measured half a foot in diameter. Your Portuguese toads may be of a finer size, but are not half so amiably speckled as ours in England. Miss Sill and Bezerra were seated on the veranda as I passed by Horne's, enjoying their daily chat. We proceeded only half way to Colares, though the weather was truly vernal, and the prospect of the wild rocks beyond Penha Verde diversified by plats of springing herbage.

The Marquis was at table when I called in upon him on my return. He told me D. Pedro and his uncle were gone to dine with me, so I hurried home and found the Grand Prior expanded on his beloved sofa. Bezerra was also there. After dinner I lighted up his imagination into a fervent blaze by reading him part of this scrawl of a journal. I thought he would have bounced into the air, especially at hearing certain passages in which Daddy Horne is celebrated, with whose virtues he is fully acquainted. I defy the wildest Brazilian to possess a larger portion of that ethereal fire which warms the heart into ecstasy, but misleads the understanding. The Grand Prior presented J. Antonio Castro[275] to me. It was this ingenious mechanician who invented the present method of lighting Lisbon.

He appeared to have taste as well as science, and his observations on the Abbé <de> St. Non's *Voyage pittoresque de Naples*, which happened to lay open on the table, were those of a man highly sensible of the beauties of art and nature. Lima often contrives to be out of the way when I most want him. I was seized with a vehement desire to sing and had no one to accompany me. During an hour my voice seemed to stick in my throat and I suffered a severe indigestion of sharps and quavers. The softness of the evening invited D. Pedro and myself to take a run in our favourite alleys, which being strewed with fallen leaves, red, black and yellow, appeared in the dusk to be paved with mosaic. I believe D. Pedro and I are never happy asunder. To leave him will cost me many a pang. He has become so lively and so engaging, so different from what I found him six months ago, that I cannot help thinking some friendly magician by a whisk of his wand has lent me his power to produce this metamorphosis for my pleasure and entertainment.[276]

Friday 19 October

The day clear and exhilarating. Rode towards Colares. Met Horne, his nieces and Bezerra. Horne quite dulcified. I told him I had the best authority from disavowing any objection from the Queen on the score of my furniture. He told me that he had offered a bribe <of> 250 <moidores> to the *leigo*[277] and the Abbade, and was refused by both. < > I am, and more and more averse to quitting this country. I cling to every rock, to every tree, <and> look at Mafra with eager eyes. D. Pedro and the Grand Prior came in at the dark and stayed the whole evening; the Marquis also.[278]

My health improves every day. The clear exhilarating weather we now enjoy infuses new life into my veins. I ride and walk and climb as long as I please without fatiguing myself. The valley of Colares affords me a source of perpetual amusement, and I have discovered a variety of shady paths which lead through copses and orchards to the greenest spots imaginable, where self-sown bays and orange bushes hang wild over gushing rivulets, and drop their fruit and blossoms into the streams. You may ride for miles on the bank of this delightful water, catching endless perspectives of flowery thickets between the stems of poplar and walnut. This scenery is truly Elysian, and worthy to be the lounge of happy souls. The mossy fragments, grotesque pollards <and> rustic bridges which occur at every step remind me of Savoy and Switzerland. But the vivid green of the citron, the golden fruitage of the orange, the blossoming myrtle, and the rich fragrance of a turf embroidered with aromatic flowers allow me without a violent stretch of fancy to believe myself in the Gardens of the Hesperides and to expect the Dragon under every tree. Oh how I wished for a *quinta* at Colares. It cuts through my heart to abandon these smiling regions, whose charms I have now health and spirits to enjoy. Twenty times I have been on the point this very day of revoking the orders I have given for my journey and determining to remain here in spite of every objection.

I met a caravan composed of Horne, his nieces and Bezerra, on my return from my excursion. Horne, quite altered and dulcified, favoured me with many confidential stories, as how he had offered 250 moidores to the lay brother to prevail with the Archbishop to——[279]

* *Saturday 20 October* [280]

The myrtles which cover a wild slope in my garden, are covered with the most beautiful luxuriant blossoms. I was enjoying their fragrance and reading Theocritus when Bezerra arrived and persuaded me to accompany him on horseback to Colares. 'Twas a charming serene day and the distant hills invested with a pearly bloom. Notwithstanding the softness of the weather I was in a turbulent mood, and had much strange conversation with Bezerra, one moment exalting D. Pedro to the skies and the next levelling all his merit with the ground. I could not help saying a thousand things which ought never to have been uttered. *Faire sans dire* is an excellent maxim, and it would have been better for me had I paid it a stricter attention. I have more profligacy of tongue than of character and often do my utmost to make myself appear worse than I am in reality. We penetrated almost to the extremity of the valley of Colares, whose thickets of orange and wild pomegranate I had not yet explored. Bezerra wished me to have traced the course of a rivulet which < > these wild shrubberies quite to the sea, and to have visited the caverns and grottos near the Pedra de Alvidrar, but I recollected Marialva was to dine with me, and rode back as fast as I was able that I might not make him wait.

We will visit these grottos tomorrow—I long to see them. I fancy it was beneath their craggy arches that the ancients imagined the tritons used to sleep and revel. There is a strange story of the Lusitanians having sent a message or embassy to Tiberius, informing him in the most solemn manner that they had seen the marine divinities sporting in these grottos and playing upon their twisted conchs. Marialva stared when I quoted this odd piece of erudition,—nay, more, shewed it him in print in Colmenar and Udal ap Rhys.[281] It seemed to arouse D. Pedro's fancy mightily, for he begged his father to allow him to ride with me to the Pedra de Alvidrar tomorrow and go a-triton hunting. The weather promises to be so warm and fine that the Grand Prior intends to be of the party. The Abbade will certainly not be left behind, and three or four of the Marquis' equerries are ordered to attend, to take care I suppose that no triton or dolphin swims away with the Heir of the

Marialvas. We shall compose a formidable caravan, to the great joy of the poor fishermen in the neighbourhood of the Pedra de Alvidrar, who gain their livelihood from the liberality of strangers who pay them for ascending and descending the almost perpendicular rocks with the same ease as the angels are represented on Jacob's Ladder. I hate precipices myself and shudder when others are climbing them, so I shall not enjoy this part of the exhibition.

Sunday 21 October

Never did I behold so divine a day or a sky of such lovely azure. The Grand Prior and D. Pedro were with me by half past eight, and after hearing Mass most devoutly we breakfasted and sallied out, all in high spirits. The Abbade and Bezerra joined us as we passed Horne<'s>. We followed the road to Colares, and then leaving those woody regions, traversed wild barren eminences towards the sea-shore and the famous rock Pedra de Alvidrar, which composes one of the most striking features of that famous promontory called the Rock of Lisbon. I advanced to the margin of the cliff which is nearly perpendicular. A rabble of boys followed at the heels of our horses and five young fellows descended with the most perfect unconcern the dreadful precipice. One in particular walked down with his arms expanded majestically like a being of a superior order. The sea roars horribly below and covers the shelving rocks with sparkling foam. The coast is truly picturesque and consists of bold projections intermixed with pyramidical rocks succeeding each other in a theatrical perspective, the most distant crowned by a lofty tower which serves as a lighthouse. No words can convey an adequate idea of the bloom of the atmosphere and the silvery light of the sea. I stood in raptures gazing on the cerulean prospect. My nerves are strengthened. I could bear advancing to the very edge of the abyss and see the men go down.

From the summit we descended a winding road about half a mile to the smooth beach. Such coves, such caverns, such a noise of rushing waters, such a flow of waves I never beheld. We were shut in on every side by cliffs and grottos, a fantastic amphitheatre, the true abode of marine divinities. No wonder the ancients, inflamed by the scenery of the place, imagined they heard the conchs of triton sounding in these secret caves. Verdeil, D. Pedro, Bezerra, the Grand Prior all left me musing, lulled by the murmuring waves, surrounded by the men who had so boldly set their face against the terror of precipices. I thought there was a wan and fatal paleness in some of their countenances, a look as if their fate awaited them in these cliffs and that they were destined on some future day to be dashed in pieces. The sides of the rocks are encrusted with beautiful limpets and a variety of small shells grouped together. The waves swell against some rocks with violence, rush into the air, form instantaneous canopies of foam, then fall down in a thousand trickling rills of silver. Of such cascades no monarch can boast. The whole time I remained—and I stayed a full hour—one solitary *corvo marino*[282] sat perched on an insulated rock about 100 paces from the shore. Like myself, he moped alone.[283]

I suppose it was too cold for tritons to leave their elements. We had not the pleasure of seeing any. In the days of Tiberius, certain < > Lusitanians sent a special messenger to Rome to acquaint the Emperor with their having seen a group of these marine deities playing on their twisted shells in this very cavern. We dined at five and drank champagne and burgundy till Bezerra, after spinning round the room like a moth on the point of singeing itself, fell down dead drunk and was carried off to bed. D. Pedro and I were wild with spirits. I could have sat up all night.

Monday 22 October

I was in too good spirits to sleep well; my slumbers were broken and agitated. My happiness yesterday was too excessive to be of long duration. I fear a change. I passed the Marquis' villa in my usual ride with a beating heart. I fear D. Pedro fatigued himself too much yesterday. I tremble, and when I foresee events to interrupt our intercourse I feel cold at heart. 'Tis certain I dote on him with too much fondness, that I am growing blind to his imperfections and can hardly exist without him. Talking with Verdeil today, I tried my utmost to extort from him some approbation of my stay in Portugal, but to no purpose; he remained inflexibly bent on my departure. As I walked from my room through the long suite of apartments I saw the Grand Prior's capote lying on a chair which terminated the perspective. My heart leapt; I thought D. Pedro might be at the other end of the saloon looking over my prints. I entered, but no D. Pedro was there. I felt the chill of disappointment, <and was> deprived of the power of embracing the Grand Prior with that heartiness his affection for me deserved. At table the Abbade told me D. Pedro had been obliged to accompany his mother and the *Camareira-mor* to the Pena, but that he lamented sorely not coming to me, and had told everybody at home that yesterday was the happiest day of his life, that the whole day had passed agreeably, but that the hour in it he chiefly liked was that when he was walking to and fro with his dearest friend. I must confess this intelligence filled me with joy and <I was> triumphant. The idea that my affection is so tenderly returned gave me such transports that I could not eat. Verdeil had the kindness to contrive a party for tomorrow so that D. Pedro <and I> will pass the whole day together. Tomorrow! Tomorrow! He loves me. I have tasted the sweetness of his lips; his dear eyes have confessed the secret of his bosom. I felt after dinner in so lively and restless a mood that I could not sit still, but flew from one extremity of the house to the other.

It was a clear evening and the Grand Prior expressing a desire of taking the air, we got into my light carriage with four mules, and I bid them drive full speed to their destination. We passed that village and, turning round, beheld the mountains of Sintra obscured by clouds of the saddest purple. The lights in the windows of Ramalhão twinkled in the gloom. We had not been long returned when the Marquis appeared. We took our usual walk and had much conversation. He told me in the strictest confidence that the Queen had thoughts of retiring from government, that she was worn out with the intrigues of the Court and sick of her existence. The Marquis long persuaded (?) me to talk with Melo and prevail with him to settle matters in such a manner as will permit my stay here with honour and triumph.

Tuesday 23 October

My blood flows so briskly that I could hardly sleep. The beams of the sun woke me early. I lay an hour tossing and tumbling. As soon as I was up, in came the Grand Prior—without D. Pedro. He talked a deal of stuff about headaches and lassitudes, and told me D. Pedro, having climbed the Pena on foot yesterday, could not stir this morning, and was under coddle-ation with < > and < > at home; perhaps that he might come to dinner. The day is changing: watery clouds have eclipsed the sun. I care not what becomes of me. I shall shut myself up in the carriage with the Grand Prior and have at least the satisfaction of talking of dear Pedrinho.[284] At Penha Longa we left the carriage and mounted our horses. The softest breezes played over the flowery moors, and the sunbeams twinkled on the distant sea, but I was languid and melancholy, shifting uneasily from side to side of my saddle. We reached Cascais and were shewn the citadel by the Lieutenant-Colonel. There are noble batteries towards the sea. I suppose the fort mounts not less than 170 bronze cannon. The town has an air of cleanliness very unusual in Portugal. The environs are barren and naked; a flourishing palm was the only tree I saw tossing itself above the walls of the gardens.

We found Martinho Antonio Castro in the saloon expecting our return. The Abbade came in at dinner time and told me the Marchioness had taken D. Pedro with her an airing towards Colares. This intelligence contributed to sink my spirits to the lowest abyss, and what did not restore <them> was a long conversation I had at sunset with Verdeil as we walked in the alleys of the *quinta*. More bent than ever upon unrooting me from < >, he exerted his whole eloquence to display the folly and ignominy of my stay, and the danger which might arise from D. Pedro conceiving for me too fond and unlimited an attachment. He has staggered me. I am lost in an ocean of perplexities. The dew falling heavy, we hastened home. I threw myself disconsolately on the sofa alongside of the Grand Prior. The Abbade taking a chair, perched himself opposite to me and talked me deaf. The saloon, being stripped of its curtains, is relapsed into its primitive state of naked lanthornism, and as I had forgot calling for lights the moon cast a ghastly gleam through the window and threw the shadows of waving branches on the mat. We drank tea late. I sung over six or seven times that passionate aria of Sacchini, *Poveri affetti miei* with such energy that drew tears from the eyes of the Grand Prior. Lima has been soliciting me to obtain an addition to his salary by once more speaking to the Marquis in his behalf. I hate asking favours. The petition he has presented me lies like a dead weight in my pocket.

Wednesday 24 October

I slept ill and woke in a feverish tremor. Read Theocritus. Verdeil sticks close to his point and will not allow me to think of a conversation with Melo or any measure to facilitate my stay here. After passing two hours in discourse upon this subject and exhausting every argument for and against it, we rode out but went no further than Horne's. There was Bezerra, looking half dead. At the Marquis', where I stopped in my way home, I found all at table. D. Pedro guards every look in his favourite's presence. He coloured several times, and there was a misty softness in his eyes, inexpressibly tender. I plucked up courage to ask the Marquis to let him accompany his uncle and me to Peninha tomorrow if the day should be bright and cloudless. After staying with my friend till he was obliged to drive off to the Palace, I returned home to dinner. The Grand Prior soon followed me and sat by us at table. I expected D. Pedro, and when the door opened and his uncle alone appeared, I <was> struck with a sudden coldness at my heart and could not eat. I passed an agitated melancholy evening. The Grand Prior went with me to Horne's where we drank some vile slop. As soon as the Queen had passed by, we hastened home and drank tea in reality with the Marquis, who, whilst I was singing, closeted Verdeil and tried without effect to gain him over to his own way of thinking. I learnt from Verdeil after my friend left me that he had not even yet abandon<ed> his project of marrying <me> in Portugal, and that he still blindly entertained hopes of turning the tide Melo has poured against me once more in my favour.

Thursday 25 October

My agitations are somewhat diminished and I enjoyed last night a more sound and uninterrupted repose than for these last three days I have experienced. The day was glorious but a gloom I could hardly account for hung on my spirits. After breakfast

I set out in the chaise to take up the Grand Prior and D. Pedro according to our yesterday's appointment. I found them halfway on the road on foot. I thought D. Pedro looked dejected but perhaps I am mistaken. However, be that as it will, our schemes of passing the day together are destroyed. The Queen is to take her *merenda* this evening in the Marquis' pavilion and my poor little friend is obliged to wait her arrival at three o'clock and cannot dine with me, nor shall we have time to go to the Peninha. The Grand Prior and his nephew getting into the chaise to me, we drove to Colares. There we stopped before the door of a chapel. The Grand Prior went to his devotions. D. Pedro and I mounted our horses and descending into the valley rode amongst the orchards to the Quinta do Vinagre.[290] This shady garden extends along the banks of a rivulet under a craggy hill overgrown with Italian pines, arbutus, and a variety of fragrant shrubs, many of which, however, in spite of their lovely blossoms, the tasteless proprietor has destroyed to make room for a vile range of terraces in the Portuguese style, with reservoirs and glassy parapets neatly plastered and striped with crimson. D. Pedro and I scrambled up amongst the shrubberies <and> gathered the arbutus berries, which in this happy climate are nearly as large as plums and glow with the brightest vermilion.

There was a calm in the air today and a genial mildness in the sunbeams that I think would have infused peace and contentment into any breast but mine; but alas, a dark cloud of thought had rolled over me. To my shame, however, be it written that I was insensible to the charms of the prospect before me, disgusted with myself, with my companion, and with every object on the earth or in the heavens. It may be supposed, then, that I was in no mood to loiter amongst the pine trees or relish the flavour of the arbutus D. Pedro was swallowing with avidity. I passed hastily through the garden, vaulted on my horse and galloped off, leaving D. Pedro to make the best speed he was able. It was the resigned indifference of D. Pedro that filled me with indignation—instead of straggling against the silly obligation of putting himself in the Queen's way this evening, or shewing a lively sense of disappointment, he took a very slight hint of his presence being necessary, and submitted with all the stupid tameness of a sheep that cares not to what pasture it is driven. I abhor from my soul such passive character, and will attempt at least tearing out by the roots my affection for D. Pedro.

Before I went home I passed an hour with the Marquis, whose cordial, affectionate behaviour afforded me some consolation. Upon my return I found D. Luis de Miranda and an attendant captain walking to and fro in my lantern apartment, waiting for dinner. I wished them heartily in their citadel and had some difficulty in masking the uneasiness of my heart. Bezerra came in and I felt a strong impulse after dinner to have had some conversation with him, but he vanished before I had time to call him back. At sunset D. Luis and his captain made their bows and departed. The remainder of the evening I passed in solitary dullness.

Friday 26 October

The tumult of my blood, which has not even yet entirely subsided, prevented my sleeping well and gave birth to frightful dreams. I fancied my dear mother was no more, and that a phantom, seizing me by the hair, was transporting me through the clouds to Fonthill, where I beheld her breathless body extended in a gloomy vault. I thought also that my eldest infant lay strangled on the steps which lead down to its dark abode. My heart seemed to die within me and I awoke with a start that threw me from my bed three or four paces. I had not spirits sufficient to undertake a long ride across the mountains, but tamely contented myself with ambling to Penha Longa. The Marquis made his escape from the Palace rather earlier than usual and stayed with me the whole evening. With all possible respect for Her Majesty I thought him highly incensed by her timid irresolute proceeding.

Saturday 27 October

I went directly to the Marquis, who was in consultation with Martinho Antonio Castro about some additions to his villa. Then we went into dinner and D. Pedro advanced to embrace me, but the disgust I have conceived to his coldness is so strong that I shrank and hardly looked at him. The Abbade, I suspect, perceived the cause of my aversion. He dined with us; I sat sullen and sad. The Grand Prior is gone to Lisbon and I feel deserted. Verdeil and I drove to Horne's who introduced to me Captain Macdonald. He came in the evening with the Marquis, and we had much <conversation> about London, our families, etc. etc., to the great delight of my friend who loves genealogical prattle as dearly as <an> old Dowager.

Sunday 28 October

I can boast no longer of my health! My digestion is sadly deranged; I sleep indifferently. This morning I felt unable to run or disport (?) myself. I crawled to Mass and then rode to Penha Longa full in the face of the sun which almost burnt my eyes out. I could not support a long ride, but returned back in a feverish feeble state. At dinner, besides Lima and the Abbade who never fail, we had Horne and the Miss Sills. I sat by Miss Sill at least two hours tracing back the series of my adventures in Portugal till she left me with her sister and uncle to go to a ball at the Count de S. Vicente, who attempts at least escaping the horrors of a disturbed conscience in the tumult of company. His palace is perhaps the only one in Portugal where the lowest ranks of people have an opportunity of dancing, feasting and flirting with the highest.

Monday 29 October

Unless I remain in torpid quietness, read stupid books, and frequent dull harmless animals, I shall fall seriously ill. My bile is in a ferment, I squitter and feel the giddiness and nausea of sea-sickness. I rode to Horne's and heard from Miss Sill how gay they had all been last night at the Count de S. Vicente<'s>. The Count had waddled out after supper by moonlight on the terrace where they played at Blind Man's Buff and were as lively as children. The veranda is arched over with lofty trees. It must have been a fairy scene from Horne's. My course as usual was directed to the Marquis, whose countenance brightens up the moment he beholds me. D. Pedro appeared somewhat ashamed of his coldness and stood by—like a slave—the sofa where his father and I were sitting. I treated him with some little kindness and I thought he revived. When I went away he held my stirrup. We had more company at table than I wished for in my present state of debility and dejection. There was D. Luis de Miranda, Martinho Antonio Castro, and Caldas[286] the poet, who, as soon as the dessert was brought in, poured forth a torrent of extempore verses and continued above half an hour lamenting my departure in very harmonious numbers. I could not help being warmed by the strain into a glow of enthusiasm which hurried me to the harpsichord and obliged me to sing in defiance of my indisposition. The consequence was a violent palpitation and a considerable degree of fever. I painted the imbecility of the Portuguese Court to Caldas in such colours, and I daresay <they> will long dance before the eye of his vivid imagination. Verdeil, perceiving <to> what lengths this false flow of spirits was hurrying <me>, persuaded the Abbade to put me in mind of moving off to the Marquis. He succeeded. I left the poet, and walked soberly in the twilight to my friend's. Mounting into the closet which looks into the pavilion, I saw the Queen and the Infantas sitting like a row of waxwork images in the midst of a dazzling illumination, whilst an ill-looking dirty fellow was soothing their royal dullness with a sonata on the dulcimer. What instrument is so detestable as a dulcimer? I know none. A spinet, such as Misses at a boarding school thump upon with whimpering perseverance could not have affected my ears more disagreeably. As soon as this pert tinkling ceased, a buffoon began roaring a Portuguese opera song and straining hard to be comical. Notwithstanding the wretchedness of the performance, Her Majesty and the whole audience appeared amused, except the dwarf negress D. Rosa who shrugged up her shoulder and lolled her tongue at the virtuoso. D. Pedro, I believe, was extremely delighted with him, having a true Portuguese relish for coarse buffoonery. He danced a minuet with D. Henriqueta before the Queen with the most freezing composure. Nothing discourages this hopeful youth. His sister, though visibly abashed by the Royal presence, danced with infinite grace and gave her hand with that modest dignity no dancing-master can teach, and which springs from a consciousness of high blood, candour and innocence. As soon as the Queen and her suite were departed, I joined the Marchioness and D. Henriqueta in the pavilion, but remained with them only a few minutes. I drank tea at home and walked on the veranda till supper was ready, enjoying the serene rays of the full moon and fanned by mild and fragrant breezes.

Tuesday 30 October

I was dosed at daybreak with a vile beverage of salts and rhubarb. Lima came early and I was fool enough to sing nine or ten arias. The Queen passed by Ramalhão at eleven o'clock, followed by a hundred and fifty shabby two-wheeled chaises drawn by some of the most wretched mules and escorted by the lousiest grooms and footmen I ever set eyes upon. We had the Abbade at dinner and he stunned us with the praises of a certain Cabinet courier he wishes much I would take with me into Spain. The Queen having dispensed with the Marquis' attendance for a few days in order that he might settle his affairs at Sintra, he returned full speed from Queluz[287] and was with me before sunset. We sat the whole evening with the folding doors which lead out upon the veranda wide open, blessing the climate of Portugal. My friend described to me the lovely nights he had often experienced in the neighbourhood of Porto on the Tagus sailing down to Salvaterra, and on the shrubby hills of Trasos-Montes, in such terms as make me more loath than ever to go away. I am not even yet reconciled to the idea of my departure and shall for ever regret leaving the province of Minho unvisited.

Wednesday 31 October

A rawness in the air like England, mists on the mountains, and the plains tinted by the grey clouds, which hung over them, with dingy hues. D. Pedro overtook me as I was riding through Sintra. I felt melancholy and oppressed. There was more frankness than I could have expected in his manner.[288]

The sun found great difficulty in bursting through the clouds and I in persuading myself to ride out. The vast plains in which Mafra is situated were tinted by the clouds, which hung over them, with dingy hues. Sintra appeared quite forlorn. Baggage waggons standing before every door, and hectic mules looking doleful and famished. As we were passing under the elms by the Count de S. Vicente<'s>, somebody hailed. I looked round and saw D. Pedro galloping along and waving his hand. He soon came up with us and we proceeded together towards Colares. There is a small chapel built by João de Castro near the Duchess of Cadaval's villa[289] on the border of a grove of pine and cork trees, into which I entered, and began praying with great fervour, whilst D. Pedro went to his aunt the Duchess.

* Several circumstances united to inspire me with devout enthusiastic feelings; the dark awful colour of the sky, the solemn wave of the pines, whose branches seemed agitated without any apparent cause, and the thoughts of my approaching separation from the most affectionate friend Heaven ever bestowed upon me. All his expressions of regard and attachment, all his zealous exertions in my favour, crowded into my mind as I knelt in this solitary chapel. During my ride home, I was haunted by the most gloomy ideas and a presentiment that if I quitted the Marialvas it would be for ever. Verdeil, perceiving the turn of my reverie, attempted to rouse me from it by reading some letters he had just received from Paris, which painted in the brightest colour the flourishing state of the arts and the varied amusements of that gay capital. His manoeuvres succeeded, and my spirits revived.

Thursday 1 November

Bells jingling. Mass. I stayed at home sorting my papers, and heaving many a sigh at reading over some letters of my dear Margaret's. D. Pedro and the Marquis, Abbade, Bezerra and Martinho Antonio Castro at dinner. Bezerra returned from Lisbon with an ample collection of gossiping tales. The evening neither dull nor pleasant. We drove out in the *carrinho* to a *quinta* of the Marquis about a quarter of a mile from this villa, and sprang D. Henriqueta and a flock of *criadas*, who had been taking a *merenda* in a snug sheltered spot closely wrapped up in bays and citrons. D. Henriqueta was perfectly at her ease and in high spirits. D. Pedro ran about and brought me branches of arbutus. I cannot help being attached to him in spite of his tameness. His father treats him too roughly and subdues what little spirit there is in him by harsh words and severe looks. The poor boy I do believe feels more kindness for me than for any other human being except D. Henriqueta. He has no friend, no companion, no opportunities of relaxation except at my house. If he dared, could he but conquer the timidity which scares him, I fancy he would throw himself into my arms.

Friday 2 November

Three Mass<es> running did I hear without rising from my knees. The chapel was full. I have a new coat that stinks of the tailor enough to poison one. As soon as I had arranged my papers I hurried to the Marquis, and found the family on their knees before an altar praying for the souls of their ancestors. Verdeil stayed at home to the great joy of the Marquis, who abhors heretics. We were all at our ease, cheerful and comfortable, D. Henriqueta more gay and lively than I ever beheld her. After dinner the whole family moved forth bag and baggage. D. Pedro and I clung fondly round each other. I accompanied my friend in his chaise and we set off at a quarter past four and reached Bemfica just as five was striking.

The Marquis having a mind to show me the interior of a pompous glaring villa[290] belonging to Quintela,[291] a rich merchant, we drove up to it. The whole front is painted yellow and red in compartments, and the garden a dead sandy flat as full of huge urns and squat obelisks as a churchyard of tombstones. What pleased me most in the apartments were the floors, neatly laid and formed of the first Brazil woods, smoothly polished. 'Twas a pleasure to glide along them. Vast sums have been expended on this mansion. The verandas are paved with marble, the courts guarded (?) with iron gates of the most complicated workmanship, and the walls hung with silvered India taffeties and crowded with the most delicate Chinese paintings on glass. The chairs, beds, and sofas are more elegantly designed than any I have yet seen in Portugal, but the shape of the rooms is unpleasing, and the doors wretchedly proportioned. We returned to my house, which being stripped of its furniture, makes a comfortless appearance. My friends' spirits sunk upon hearing some dismal bells tolling in commemoration of the deceased. The news too which Berti brought of my mules being arrived at Aldea Gallega did not contribute to render him more cheerful. Amply did I partake of his dejection. The thoughts of my departure sink heavy on my mind.

Saturday 3 November

Verdeil wonders I have not sent for Franchi. What care I for Franchi? Is he not under the thumb of João Antonio and should I not set the whole Patriarchal in an uproar if I was to send for him? The view from the square before the Necessidades has gained considerably by the mild weather with which it has pleased Heaven of late to favour us. I walked to and fro by the obelisk[292] this morning till my feet were galled by the craggy pavement, and I was forced to hobble home. The Marquis and Grand Prior came late to dinner; the latter looked piteous and rueful. I have every reason to flatter myself his countenance would clear up were I to alter my resolution of leaving Portugal. As we dined uncommonly late, it fell dark when coffee was brought in. Having no long suite of apartments to range in like those at Ramalhão, and wanting exercise, I persuaded my friend, who always drives at a furious rate, to jumble me half over Lisbon in his two-wheeled carriage. 'Twas a mercy we crippled no one: the people had enough to do to get out of our mules' way, who advanced foaming and prancing like the coursers in the Apocalypse. Hard by the church of the Santos[293] we met the *Bon Dieu* attended as usual by Vila Nova and his brothers, two chubby lads of fifteen or sixteen. Out we jumped, <you> may be sure, and saw the *Bon Dieu* home and safely deposited in the Tabernacle. Passing through the Terreiro do Paço, we took a circumbendibus, and mounting a sharp ascent[294] between heaps of stones and shattered arches, thrown down by the earthquake, gained the Barro Alto. The Marquis pointed to the remains of his once magnificent palace in which many capital pictures by Rubens and the first Masters, gold and silver, tapestry and Persian carpets sixty or seventy feet in length were destroyed. The Barros Altos is an irregular opening on the summit of a lofty hill, surrounded by churches and palaces and adorned by a pompous fountain.[295] Seeing lights in one of the churches we entered and did homage before the High Altar. The priest<s> were extinguishing the tapers, and the curling smoke which rose from them produced a mysterious effect. I believe the church is dedicated to Our Lady of Loreto.[296] It has not been long built, and there is a grandeur in the dimensions and spread of the vaulted roof that strikes with awe before one has time to be put out of humour by the bad taste and frivolity of the ornaments. On each side are rows of altars. In front an arch sixty or seventy feet high and a flight of marble steps divides the sanctuary from the rest of the edifice.

Our devotions finished we rambled on foot through several streets and alleys and went to see an enormous house which Quintela the merchant is building.[297] An old snuffling servant lighted us up a staircase large enough for a town hall or a theatre, <and> taking us both for strangers, favoured the Marquis with a description of the Court in general, Her Majesty and the Prince of Brazil. It was almost too dark to distinguish the doors from the windows. Most of the apartments are of an extraordinary height. I should imagine one of the halls, an awkward shaped narrow octagon, cannot have less than forty feet <of height>. The Marquis enjoyed his incognito prodigiously, and laughed heartily at the information given him by our guide and the nasal twang with which it was accompanied. We returned home and drank tea precisely at the hour fashionable fools in England are sitting down to dinner, that is to say a little before seven. The whole evening passed in earnest conversation, the Marquis contriving ways and means to put off at least for a short space of time the evil day of my departure.

Sunday 4 November

Precisely at ten my friend was at my door waiting to take me with him to Mass in the Convent of Boa Morte. This is a true Golgotha, a place of many skulls, for its inhabitants, though they live and move and have a sort of being, are little better than skeletons. The priest who said Mass appeared so pale, weak, so dismally emaciated, that I hardly imagined he would have had strength to elevate the chalice. It did not, however, fall from his hands, and having ended one Mass, God gave him strength to begin another for our especial benefit and consolation. From the ghastly pictures which cover the walls of this mansion of penitence and mortification, and from the deep contrition apparent in the tears, gestures and ejaculations of the faithful who resort to them, I fancy no convent in Lisbon can be compared with this for austerity and devotion. I shook all over with piety and so did the Marquis, and my knees are become horny with frequent kneelings. Verdeil thinks I shall end in a hermitage or go mad—perhaps both; he says, too, I have rendered the Marquis ten times more fervent than before and that by mutually encouraging each other we shall soon produce fruits worthy of Bedlam. To be sure I have a devout turn and a pretty manner of thumping myself, but there are twenty or thirty thousand good souls who thump better than me. This morning at Boa Morte one shrivelled sinner remained, the whole time our Masses lasted, with outstretched arms in the attitude and with the inflexible stiffness of an old-fashioned branch<ed> candlestick. Another contrite personage was so affected at the moment of consecration that he flattened his nose on the ground and licked the pavement. When shall I have sufficient grace to be so beastly![298]

I must confess that, notwithstanding all my sanctity, I was not sorry to escape from the dingy cloisters of the convent and breathe the pure air, and look up at the blue exhilarating sky. The weather being so delightful, we drove to several parts of the town to which I was yet a stranger. Returning back by the Barros Alto, we looked into a new house just finished building at an enormous expense by João Ferreira,[299] who from an humble retailer of leather has risen by the Archbishop's favour to the possession of the most lucrative contracts in Portugal. Uglier shaped apartments than those the poor shoe-man has contrived for himself I never beheld. The hangings are of satins, of the deepest blue and the fiercest and most sulphurous yellow. The whole ceiling is daubed with allegorical paintings most indifferently executed, and loaded with gilt ornaments in the style of those splendid signposts which some years past were the boast of High Holborn and St. Giles'. The Marquis and I were soon tired of this glaring display of false taste and ill-judged magnificence, and as it was growing late made the best of our way to Belem. Whilst he was writing letters, I walked out with D. Pedro on the verandas of the palace,[300] which are washed by the Tagus and flanked by turrets, in one of which roosts the good old Abbade. The views are enchanting, and the day being warm and serene I enjoyed them in all their beauty. Several large vessels passed by as we were leaning over the balustrades and almost touched us with their streamers. Even frigates and ships of the first rate approached within twenty feet of the palace.

* There was a greater crowd than usual of attendants round our table at dinner today. Seven or eight of the old Marquis' confidants and buffoons crept forth to have a peep at me and hear me descant upon the glorious deeds and miracles of St. Anthony. The scenery of Boa Morte was still fresh in my thoughts, and my descriptions were gloomy and appalling. D. Pedro, his sisters and his cousin Duarte[301] gathered round me with all the trembling eagerness of children who hunger and thirst after hobgoblin stories. You may be sure I sent them not empty away. A blacker dose of legendary superstition was never administered. The Marchioness seemed to swallow my narration with nearly as much avidity as her children, and the old Abbade, dropping his chin in a woeful manner, produced an enormous rosary and accompanied my pious discourse by thumbing his beads and mumbling orisons. The Marquis luckily had been summoned to the palace by a special mandate from his royal mistress. Had he been at the party, I fear Verdeil's prophecy would have been accomplished, for never in my life did I hold forth with so much scaring energy. The most horrible denunciations of divine wrath which ever were sounded forth by ancient or modern writers of sermons and homilies, recurred to my memory, and I dealt them about me with a vengeance. The last half hour of my discourse we were all in total darkness—nobody had thought of calling for candles; the children were huddled together, scarce venturing to move or breathe. It was a most singular scene. Full of the ghastly images which I had conjured up in my imagination, I returned home alone in my carriage, shivering and shuddering. Verdeil was out, and half the servants, and nothing could be more dreary than the appearance of my fireless apartments.

* *Monday 5 November*[302]

The Marquis had a long conversation with Melo, but I could make little of the result of it: my poor friend's mind seems in woeful confusion. The Grand Prior and D. Pedro came with him to dinner. As soon as it was despatched we all set off together on the wings of holiness to pay our devoirs to the Holy Crows. A certain sum has been allotted these many centuries for the maintenance of two birds of this species. They are kept in a dark recess of a venerable cloister adjoining the Cathedral,[303] most plentifully fed and most devoutly venerated.

The origin of this singular custom dates as high as the days of St. Vincent, who was martyrised at the Cape which bears his name,[304] and whose body was miraculously conveyed to Lisbon in a boat attended by crows, which after seeing it decently interred, pursued his murderers with dreadful screams and tore their eyes out. The boat and the crows appear painted or sculptured in every corner of the cathedral.

It was late when we entered this gloomy edifice, and the crows, I believe, were gone quietly to roost, but a sacristan, seeing us approach, officiously roused them. Oh, how sleek and plump and glossy they are. My admiration of their size, their plumage and their deep-toned croakings carried me, I fear, beyond the bounds of saintly decorum. I was just stretching forth my hand to stroke their feather<s> when the Marquis checked me with a solemn forbidding look. D. Pedro and the Grand Prior, aware of the proper ceremonial, kept a respectful distance, whilst the sacristan and an old toothless priest, almost bent double, communicated a long string of anecdotes concerning these present Holy Crows, their immediate predecessors, and other crows in the old time before them. The Marquis listened with implicit faith and attention, never opened his lips during the half hour we remained, except to enforce our veneration and to exclaim with the most pious composure *Honrado Corvo*.

I believe we should have stayed till midnight had not a page arrived from Her Majesty to summon the Marquis away. Leaving the Grand Prior and D. Pedro to their meditations, I returned home and refreshed myself with tea and profane music. Lima and Polycarpo were in waiting. They persuaded me to go to the theatre in the Rua dos Condes, to hear my favourite *modinha* in the intermezzo, but it was not so well sung as before. Polycarpo entertained me at supper with many curious anecdotes of the Portuguese nobility, not greatly to their honour. I longed in return to have treated him with the adventures of the Holy Crows, but prudently repressed my inclination. It would ill become St. Anthony's especial favourite to treat such subjects with any degree of levity.

Tuesday 6 November

The Marquis abhors not the tolling of bells more than I do. My ears have been regaled with their sounds the whole morning, and they have lowered my spirits. The morning began with fogs but cleared up. I rode out on the shore of Belem: the sea sparkling, ships with crowded sails. It was so hot that I could hardly bear my heavy coat of Saragossa cloth. Polycarpo and Bezerra at dinner. The Grand Prior came in and I set him down at the Marialva Palace. The door was beset with buffoons, of which the old Marquis harbours a tribe. D. Pedro ran down and talked with me a moment. I was as spiteful as an aspic, and returned home in a venomous mood. Verdeil laughing heartily at hearing my declamations in pure Italian—fine, flourishing phrases and sounding words. Notwithstanding my evil temper, I never sung so well in my life—three octaves clear, falling as plump on the note as a hawk on its prey. Polycarpo howls and hoots with infinite execution; he is a perfect master of his art, and composes with science and judgment.

Wednesday 7 November

The Hornes have been arrived here from Sintra four days, and I have seen nothing of them. At eleven I went to Melo who was over head and ears in business with the Spanish and Sardinian Ministers. The Marquis was there waiting for me, and we walked about the garden, which is pleasantly situated on the slope of the Ajuda Hill, commanding a vast prospect of the Tagus. The jasmine arbours are still covered with blossoms. Melo was in a most gracious mood, and paid me the highest compliments in the name of the Court and nation. Though upon no bad footing with Walpole, he could not help for my sake mentioning his name with some epithet of talk not the most flattering.

From Melo I went in the Marquis' chaise to the Ajuda Palace, and he shewed me all the apartments. Nothing can be well shabbier. The audience chamber is a vile low barn, not above fourteen feet high, spread with greasy Persian carpets and hung with the coarsest hobgoblin tapestry. The throne is a pretty mass of gilding <and> cut velvet. The Queen's bedroom is strewed over with books of devotion and saintly dolls of all sorts and sizes. In the Princess' room are many daubs. All doors open upon the Marquis' approach, and notwithstanding the etiquette which forbids the entrance of the Palace to males whilst the Ladies of the Bedchamber are lodged in it, we penetrated into every apartment.

At dinner we had the Marquis, D. Diogo de Noronha, the Grand Prior and the Abbade. The evening turning out bright and vernal, we went to Quintela's villa at Bemfica. The sun set in a fiery glow, the air was perfumed like spring. The Marquis wishes to make a last effort to detain me by attacking Walpole through the channel[305] of Macdonald. He read to me some of the pious dismal tales of Arnauld.[306]

* Thursday 8 November

I went to Horne's, whom the turkey poult[307] contrives to render very disagreeable and suspicious. Were it not for the narrow, interested schemes of this odious animal we should agree perfectly. A bright gleam of sunshine invited me about one o'clock to the shore of Belem, and there I rode to and fro refreshing and calming myself with the view of the azure Tagus and the hills on its opposite shore, now clothed with a lively verdure. The Grand Prior and the Abbade dined with us. D. Bernardo de Lorena came in whilst we were still at table. As soon as it fell dark, the Grand Prior persuaded me to drive through the principal streets to see the illuminations in honour of the Infanta, wife to D. Gabriel of Spain, who had produced a Prince.[308] A great many idlers being abroad upon the same errand, we proceeded with difficulty, and were very near having the wheels of our carriage forced off in attempting to pass an old-fashioned preposterous coach belonging to one of the dignitaries of the Patriarchal cathedral. I cannot boast much of the splendour and beauty of the illuminations, but some rockets which were let off in the Terreiro do Paço surprised me by the vast height to which they rose and the innumerable clear blue stars into which they burst. I should think the Portuguese tolerably ingenious in making fireworks. The late poor drivelling, saintly king, D. Pedro,[309] expended vast sums in bringing this art to perfection.

From the Terreiro do Paço, we directed our course to the great square in which the Palace of the Inquisition is situated.[310] Here a vast mob was assembled, and two or three Capuchin preachers holding forth upon the illuminations and glories of the world to come. I should have listened with pleasure to their harangues, which appeared from the short specimen I caught of them to be full of diabolical fire and frenzy; but the Grand Prior, who lives in perpetual awe of the rheumatism, complained of the night air, so we drove home. Every apartment of my house was filled with the thick vapour of wax torches which Berti had set most loyally a-blazing. I fumed and fretted and threw open the windows. Away went the Grand Prior and in came Polycarpo, who supped with us and brought me a cargo of new Brazilian music, very quaint and original, which kept me employed till one in the morning.

Friday 9 November

I communicated the Marquis' project of gaining Walpole through Macdonald, and he[311] approves it. I walked towards the powder mills at Alcantara through a compost of dust and rotten shoes. After dinner the Marquis entered in a violent hurry. As he had not a moment to spare, I accompanied him as far as the Palace, and he told me that he had been at Boa Morte yesterday to make his vow for the success of our scheme upon Walpole. The evening was so mild that Verdeil and I rode after tea all over Lisbon. I passed under the dark walls of the Patriarchal and could not help wishing to have entered and consoled Franchi. I gaped and yawned and passed the rest of the evening dismally.

Saturday 10 November

Letters to England. It rains. The Marquis has found means to come to me; he was fresh from Court. Walpole presented Mr. North, a jaundiced, shambling figure. The Queen treated Walpole coolly. We were a trio at dinner —the Marquis, Verdeil and I; D. Bernardo came in at dusk. Lima and a brother of his, a gawky, pedantic owl.[312] The Marquis wrote again to Pinto[313] whatever I chose to dictate. He did not leave till after eleven. As soon as Lima was gone, Polycarpo arrived, and I sung a cantata of Bertoni's, *Va ma conserva i ridei* (?) in a style which almost transported Verdeil, who has warm musical feelings, beside himself.

Sunday 11 November

I waded through mire to the church of St. Francis de Paul,[314] where I heard High Mass and had my ears put to severe torture by a harsh swelling organ completely out of tune. At my return I found the Grand Prior, who takes my departure to heart sincerely and has tears in his eye whenever he thinks of it. Bezerra whisked in and out in a twinkling, after having laid a few gossiping stories begotten at Horne's about my having run away with some mattresses belonging to Ramalhão and having sold a pennyworth of bottles to the Countess of S. Vicente. He drops these silly tales as fast as a hen lays eggs and with the same cackling. What a misfortune it is to have no employment! The Marquis, Captain Macdonald and Verdeil had a consultation together upon the means of producing a total change in Walpole's behaviour. Could this be compassed, I shall remain at Lisbon. Macdonald has an opportunity of making his fortune, for if he succeeds in dulcifying the brutal Envoy, my friend will use every effort to procure his advancement. The council, which was supposed to be held without my knowledge, having broken up, we all sat down to dinner. The Abbade and Lima were of the party. I went no further in the evening than to the Palace with the Marquis, and he drove back again. The days are shortening dismally, and winter coming on. Polycarpo came, and I sung not absolutely ill.

Monday 12 November

Finding myself in a shivering sickly mood like a bird that is moulting, I took advantage of an interval of fair weather and rode along the shore of Belem. As I passed the Marquis of Angeja's[315] I espied his grandson, D. Pedro de Noronha,[316] sitting at his harpsichord. I am extremely partial to youths who play on the harpsichord. 'Tis a sweet, soothing, effeminate employment. To avoid a soaking

with which we were menaced by angry-looking clouds, we rode home full speed
at the risk of our necks, and were received by Bezerra, who, thank God, happened
to have no tittle-tattle ready cut and dried to serve up to us. We dined therefore in
peace. Early in the evening he whisked away, leaving me in. Verdeil oppressed with
a violent fit of ennui. Our solitude was interrupted by the Marquis' arrival, who put
my patience to the severest trial by humming a sort of second to every air I sung
with Polycarpo. Horne called at the door, but finding the Marquis with me, seized
that pretext for driving away.

Undated entry [317]

... I could make nothing of my voice, and was reduced to playing *capriccio,* in
which there was less melody than modulation.

Sunday 18 November

Every day I remain at Lisbon costs me at least four guineas in mule money. Did
ever mortal pay so dear for dawdling? It is certainly no difficult matter to lose one's
time at a cheaper rate. The weather is clearing. Seven or eight vessels are entering
the port, and the sun beamed cheerfully in the blue sky when the Grand Prior came
to take me with him to Mass in the Church of St. Isabel. Our devotions performed,
we went to the Theatine Convent[318] and looked in to the library, which seemed to
lie in the same confusion in which it was left by the earthquake—half the books out
of their shelves, tumbled one over the other in dusty heaps without any distinction
of size or subject. I spied out a few curious Voyages, a tolerable set of de Bry,[319] and
some account of Japan with which I am totally unacquainted. A shrewd-looking
monk,[320] who I am told has written a voluminous *History of the House of Braganza*
not yet printed,[321] guided our steps through this chaos of literature, and after
searching in vain for some first edition of the classics he wished to display to us, led
us into his cell and pressed my attention to a sorry cabinet of medals he pretended
to have been at much pains and expense in collecting. I have seldom seen coins
which give finer scope to the imagination, as scarce one in fifty can boast above a
letter and a half of inscription, and the greatest number none at all.[322]

We had not been returned above a few minutes, when the Marquis came in
with D. Pedro and the Abbade. I plainly perceived my friend was much incensed
and agitated. He soon burst forth into a torrent of abuse against Walpole, who
had carried so far his audacity as to write a furious letter to the Secretary of State
complaining of the Marquis' menaces, and claiming the Queen's support and

protection. This epistle having thrown Melo into great confusion, he had sent for the Marquis and lain it before him. I find the Envoy is ready to sacrifice truth, prudence and propriety, everything in short, to the indulgence of his resentment. We all went to dine at Horne's, who had invited D. Federico de Sousa Calhariz,[323] the Governor of Goa, and his constant attendant Count Lucatelli, to meet us. D. Federico's manners are the most graceful and conciliating imaginable; those of his friend, the rashest and most bullying I have ever observed. They form a perfect contrast and mutually set off each other's merits and deficiencies. D. Pedro had not a word to say for himself, but sat in a corner abandoned to silence and melancholy. The Abbade too, for a wonder, scarce opened his mouth during the whole repast. Count Lucatelli alone engrossed the conversation, and bounced and rattled away without mercy or moderation. After the Marquis' departure, which took place very early on account of the Queen's party. Horne and I began a conversation which lasted us three hours. Captain Babel is arrived, and I hope to get my travelling bed unshipped the day after tomorrow.

Monday 19 November

If the least prating or snoring goes forward in my neighbourhood of a night I cannot sleep. My servants lie higgledy-piggledy on the floor, next room to me, in our present most uncomfortable state of confusion. I heard them puff and toss and tumble, and for a long while I could not shut my eyes, so it may be imagined I arose but little refreshed in the morning. Two Packets sailed in yesterday and have brought me a great many letters, which I opened and read as I followed my usual track on horseback along the shore of the Tagus. I see by an epistle of Mrs. Hervey's, that Walpole has been inventing a thousand lies to my prejudice and dispersing them amongst all his acquaintance in England. My poor sister, who notwithstanding her geographical acquisitions, knows little of the customs and manners of Portugal, imagines that assassinations and poisonings are common at Lisbon; that I have offended this revengeful nation by mimicking and insulting some of its principal characters, and shall probably fall a prey to the bowl or the dagger. With what empty phantoms do my worthy relations scare themselves. Instead of applying to Pinto as the fountainhead of information, they lap up every petty stream of calumny that crosses their footsteps, taking whatever fall<s> in their way for granted, like dumb creatures unblessed with the powers of enquiry or disquisition.

Just as I was committing to the winds the cover of one of Mr. Collett's circumstantial epistles, I caught sight of the *Bon Dieu* moving in pomp towards the monastery of Belem, and immediately dismounting, joined myself to the faithful who were following in crowds. The tide carried me into the great church, vast, solemn and fantastic, like the prints of the Temple of Jerusalem in old German bibles. The awful sound of the organ and choir proceeded from a dark recess at the farthest extremity of the edifice, one of the largest in Portugal. A procession of priests, with censers smoking and tapers lighted, deposited the Host in the tabernacle under a stately canopy, after reciting the usual prayers and pronouncing the Benediction, which I received on my knees with profound humility. M. Verdeil, who has not sufficient warmth of fancy to enjoy these pompous rites in their full perfection, remained at the entrance of the church, scraping the dirt of his boots against the angular bend of a Gothic column. I continued all the way home reading my letters, at the risk of being thrown off my horse, who by no means relished the abrupt and absent twitches I gave my bridle.

Horne favoured us with his company at dinner and brought me news of another Captain's arrival with some cases of books and clothes I have been long expecting. This intelligence putting me into good humour, I was peculiarly gracious and communicative to D. Bernardo de Lorena, who came in at coffee. 'Tis true I owe him great attention, and have reason to believe his attachment to me warm and sincere. Polycarpo and Lima took their posts at the pianoforte when candles were lighted, but I was too much engaged in talking with D. Bernardo to sing myself, or lend an ear to their warblings. Macdonald and the Marquis spent part of the evening with me, both foaming and fretting at Walpole's obstinacy. How tired I am of this cursed subject!

Tuesday 20 November

I passed the whole morning jammed up in a two-wheeled chaise with Horne, jumbling through the most crooked and hideous streets of Lisbon to pay Manique a visit, whom we found at home,[324] surrounded as usual by a crowd of lousy supplicants. I asked him for an order to have my cases released from the Custom House, which was immediately granted with many smiles and expressions of regard. This business despatched, we drove to the great Dominican Convent,[325] and I took leave of Rocha and Frei José do Rosario. Horne could not stay to dinner, but his place was supplied by D. Bernardo, who has of late been extremely assiduous in shewing me attentions. For a wonder, neither the Marquis nor the Grand Prior have made their appearance today. The Abbade, who dined with us, could give no account of them. Lima and the never-failing Polycarpo arrived at their usual hour. I could have dispensed with the company of Lima's brother Signor Biaggio, an odd mysterious character, no indifferent composer as I am told, but who for what reason I have not discovered, thought proper to be introduced to me as a merchant totally ignorant of music.[326]

Wednesday 21 November

The Marquis cannot bear to hear of my passport, and has not yet, I suppose, taken any steps to procure it, for I expected it this morning to no purpose. He called in his way to the Duke de Lafões', where he was obliged to dine, and could not help still persuading me to remain here in spite of reason and comfort. Just as he left me and I was going to get on horseback, Berti, lifting up his eyes and his shoulders, announced Lima, who, with a most submissive simper, presented on the knee a trifling bill of £200 sterling and upwards for his attendance at Ramalhão. Had not this worthy artist always declaimed against extortion, fleecing of strangers etc., I should have been more astonished. I kept my temper admirably well and ordered a receipt to be taken for the money, and did not kick *il Signor Maestro* out of doors as he merited, but gave him a gentle hint that his visits in future would be dispensed with. Signor Lima with many modest shrugs retreated downstairs, assuring me that it was no <more> than barely his due, and that he had too much veneration for my exalted character to suppose that I would wish a poor artist to have thrown away his precious time upon me.

I took a longer ride than usual along the shore of Belem, and when I returned found the Grand Prior, the Abbade and D. José de Menezes. We sat down to table immediately and were very cheerful. The Abbade'<s> tongue, moistened by repeated draughts of rose-coloured champagne, never lay quiet an instant. D. José laughed heartily at Signor Lima's confounded (?) scoundrelism, and though it must be allowed I have paid for the jest, I could not help enjoying it. The Abbade's<s> pockets <were filled> with dried raisins and pears his friend D. Federico[327] brought him from the Cape of Good Hope. These good things he crammed down our throat with as much energy as <if> we had been turkeys and he a poulterer whose future depended on our fattening. For patriotic flourishes and rodomontades no nation excels the Portuguese and no Portuguese the Abbade. I thought he would have stunned me today with a panegyric of D. Vicente de Sousa, the Ambassador at Paris, and J. Antonio, the Cabinet courier who goes with me. He likewise passed off as a prodigy a young nephew of the Marquis of Marialva, now at Paris pursuing his studies, I know not as yet in what College; however I am to see him and send an exact account of his proceedings. "Oh! he is a sweet youth," said the Abbade, "and you will delight in him, for he is the image of the Marialvas and will recall them to your remembrance. The Marchioness has his picture; if you have a mind I will show it to you. He is her darling favourite and she has taken upon herself the expense of his education. Perhaps at this very moment she is writing to him how much the family are attached to you, and the attention she wishes him to pay your advice and instructions." [Rare sport, thought I.]

In this strain did the Abbade continue chanting, till G. Luis Texeira and Father Mota,[328] a Dominican, entered the room. G. Luis is one of the best hearted and humoured men, perhaps the very best, I have known in Lisbon, but he has always some friar or other in his sleeve, whose keen looks and sharp visage form a striking contrast to his good-natured open countenance. I had not much time to improve my acquaintance with Father Mota, being engaged to accompany the Grand Prior to Vespers in the Church of the Martires[329] at the Barro Alto. It was dark when we arrived. Having driven at a rapid rate, we seemed suddenly transported not to a church, but to a splendid theatre, glittering with lights and spangled friezes. Every altar on a blaze with tapers, every tribune festooned with curtains of the gaudiest Indian damask. A hundred singers and musicians executing the liveliest and most brilliant symphonies. Much fanning, giggling, and flirting going on in the spacious nave, which was comfortably carpeted for the accommodation of a numerous group of ladies. A recess in front of the great entrance, in which the high altar is placed, looked so like a stage and was decorated in so very operatical a manner that I expected every moment the triumphant entrance of a hero or the descent of some pagan divinity, surrounded by cupids and turtle doves. All this display was in honour of St. Cecilia and at the expense of the brotherhood of musicians.[330] I must confess it exhilarated my spirits and filled me with pagan ideas. We returned to tea. The Marquis passed the evening with me. He is sadly disconsolate and loath to forward the expedition of my passport.

Thursday 22 November

I breakfasted early with the Grand Prior, who accompanied me afterwards to High Mass in the Church of the Martires. We were placed in a tribune immediately over the altar, so far removed from the orchestra that we could hardly distinguish one singer from another. I was but little pleased with the music, it had nothing solemn or pathetic, but was made up of odds and ends of overtures and the beginnings and cadences of opera arias; in short, I was much jaded with the performance, yawned piteously, and rejoiced when it was ended. As I went out I spied Franchi amongst the crowd, who immediately making up to me, entreated with tears in his eyes that I would obtain João Antonio'<s> permission for him to pass still another evening with me. I know not whom to send to this cursed J. Antonio, and have still less inclination to write to him upon this subject, and yet I would give a good deal to cheer up the poor boy's spirits by granting him this small consolation.

* *Friday 23 November*

I would give a great deal to send my muleteers away, and remain here in defiance of every inconvenience. Marialva's spirits are sunk still lower than mine. He tossed my passport upon a chair and cursed Walpole by all his saints. After dinner we went to his Palace. The Marchioness was seated in the midst of a circle of *criadas* and attendants, who, like the chorus in a Greek tragedy, seemed to share the sensations of their superiors and lament my departure. D. Pedro came forth from his sister's apartment and embraced me with tears in his eyes. I was moved, and could hardly refrain from bursting into tears. The Marquis had retired to talk with the Abbade, observing how greatly I was moved, lest his own sorrow should add to mine. We have few if any examples of such warm friendship in our phlegmatic England.

* *Saturday 24 November*

A bleak cold day, dark and gloomy. There was an alarm of fire at the Ajuda Palace, and a violent stir in the streets occasioned by the passing and re-passing of troops and rabble. Both the Duke de Lafões and the Marquis were obliged to attend, which prevented the latter from dining with me. The Grand Prior took his place. About five he came in, the fire being extinguished. I was seized with feverish shiverings. The Marquis cursed Walpole by all his saints, and went to the Queen with a firm resolution of speaking his mind; but I know these resolutions will dissolve in the Royal presence. After my friend was gone, I went to Horne's and sat by his fire till I grew drowsy.

Sunday 25 November

I had strange dreams last night. I was riding with Lady Loughborough on hills which overlooked my plantations at Fonthill, and then was transported to a house of old Lady Ilchester,[331] who shewed me herself the apartments. I cannot imagine what put this old Dowager into my head. I awoke full of the recollections of the days I passed at Redlynch seventeen or eighteen years ago—the broad gravel walk leading up to the house, the picture of Queen Elizabeth walking in procession to Lord Hunsdon's surrounded by her pompous Court,[332] and the figure of Charles Strangways,[333] then a child of five or six year<s> old, hiding himself in the red curtains of an old fashioned State bedchamber.[334]

[Since this period, how many events have befallen me! Could my dear Mother then have imagined the perverse fate which was waiting her darling child? An oracle might have said with truth: He will be rich and wealthy (?), the affectionate husband of the best of wives, the father of two lovely infants, and yet an exile from his country, shunned by his countrymen.]

*335 As soon as my eyes were open, I ran to the window to bask in the rays of the sun which was shining most brilliantly. I breakfasted alone, Verdeil being gone to S. Roque to see the ceremony of publishing the Crusade Bull which allows good Christians to eat eggs and butter and other good things during Lent, upon paying His Holiness a few shillings.[336] I stayed at home composing *seguidillas* till the hour of Mass was over, then getting into the Portuguese chaise drove headlong to the Palace in the Praça do Comerçio, and hastened to the Marquis' apartments. All his family were assembled to dine with him. Had it not been for the thoughts of my approaching departure, I should have felt more comfort and happiness than has fallen to my lot this many a day. Marialva, whose attendance upon the Queen may be too justly termed a state of downright slavery, had hardly sat down to table before he was called away. The Marchioness, D. Henriqueta and her little sisters soon retreated to the old Marchioness of Tancos <in> the *Camareira-mor's* apartments, and I was left alone with Pedro and Duarte.

They seized fast hold each of a hand, and running like greyhounds along the vast corridors of the Palace, took me to a balcony which overlooks one of the greatest thoroughfares in Lisbon. The evening was delightful and vast crowds of people moving about, of all degrees, colours and nations, old and young, active and crippled, monks and officers. Shoals of beggars kept pouring in from all quarters to take their stands at the gates of the Palace and watch the Queen's going out; for Her Majesty is a most indulgent mother to these sturdy sons of idleness, and hardly ever steps into her carriage without distributing considerable alms amongst them. By this misplaced charity, hundreds of stout fellows are taught the management of a crutch instead of a musket, and the art of manufacturing sores, ulcers and scabby pates in most loathsome perfection. Duarte, who is all life and gaiety, vaulted upon the railing of the balcony, and hung for a moment or two suspended in a manner that would have frightened mothers and nurses into convulsions. The beggars, having nothing to do till Her Majesty should be forthcoming, seemed to be vastly entertained with these feats of activity.

They soon spied me out, and two brawny lubbers, whom a happy mixture of smallpox and King's Evil had deprived of eyesight, informed no doubt by their comrades of what was going forwards, began a curious dialogue with voices still deeper and harsher than those of the Holy Crows. "Heaven prosper his noble Excellency D. Duarte Manoel, and D. Pedro and all the Marialvas, sweet dear youths; long may they enjoy the use of their limbs. Is that the blessed Englishman in their sweet company?" "Yes my comrade," answered the second blind. "What!", said the first, "that generous favourite of the most glorious Lord St. Anthony"—

o gloriosissimo Senhor Sant Antonio? "Yes my comrade." "Oh that I had but my precious eyes that I might see his heavenly countenance," exclaimed both together. By the time the duet was thus far advanced, the halt, the maimed and the scabby, having tied some greasy night caps to the end of long poles, pushed them up through the very railing of the balcony, roaring and bawling out "Charity, charity, for the sake of the Holy One of Lisbon." Never was I looked up to by a more distorted or hideous collection of countenances. I made haste to throw down a plentiful shower of small copper money, or else Duarte would have twitched away both poles and nightcaps, a frolic I was anxious to prevent as it would have marred my reputation for sanctity. Just as the orators were receiving their portion of pence and farthings, a cry of "There's the Queen, there's the Princess" carried the whole hideous crowd away to another scene of action, and left me at full liberty to be amused in my turn with the squirrel-like feats of my lively companion. He is really a charming boy, bold, alert and sprightly, quite different from the rest of the young Portuguese nobility, an effeminate, degenerate race.

D. Pedro perhaps thought me too partial to his cousin, and after scolding him for skipping about so hazardously, begged and entreated me to take him to the Salitri Theatre, where a box had been prepared for us by the Marquis' orders. This box happened to be exactly opposite to one in which Walpole and his relations had taken places. The Theatre was uncommonly crowded, Her Majesty being there in state with the little Infanta D. Carlota, as mischievous and as full of frolic as Duarte. The Prince of Brazil and his brother D. João never opened their mouth during the whole performance but to gape. The Queen talked a great deal to Marialva. Her manner is uncommonly graceful and dignified. The play ended, D. Pedro and I returned to the Palace to supper, which was almost over before the Marquis could escape from the Royal apartments.

Monday 26 November

I went to the Martires to hear the Matins of Perez. The music august and affecting beyond the power of description. The splendid decoration of the Church was changed into mourning, the orchestra hung with black, the altars veiled, a solemn flow of purple and gold drapery on the High Altar, and in the middle of the choir a catafalque, surrounded by candelabrums and tall tapers, priests in black and gold standing around. An awful silence and then the solemn service of the Dead. The singers pale as they sung *Timor mortis* etc. All exerted themselves. After the Requiem, the High Mass of Jommelli in commemoration of the deceased. It closed with the *Libera me, Domine*. I was thrilled and on the point of bursting into the tears. I went to the Palace, being sent for by the poor Marquis, who seizes every interval of peace the Queen allows him to talk with me. How loath he is to see me depart. Poor Franchi is ill; his uncle brought me a message from him. I dined at home with the Grand Prior and Abbade; at tea Franchi. Went to Horne's and then to the Palace. The Marquis stupefied with grief. Returned to supper: Polycarpo; Franchi—caresses (?) < > fondness.

*[337] I went to the Martires to hear the famous Matins of Perez and the Dead Mass of Jommelli performed by all the principal musicians of the Royal Chapel, for the repose of the souls of their predecessors. Such august, such affecting music I never heard and perhaps may never hear again, for the flame of devout enthusiasm burns dim in almost every part of Europe and threatens total extinction in a very few years. As yet it glows at Lisbon and produced this day the most striking musical expression. Every individual of the band seemed penetrated with the spirit of those awful words which Perez and Jommelli have set with tremendous sublimity. Not only the music, but the serious demeanour of the performers, of the officiating priest, and indeed of the whole congregation was calculated to impress a solemn pious terror of the world beyond the grave. The splendid decoration of the church was changed into mourning, the tribunes hung with black, and a veil of gold and purple cast over the High Altar. In the midst of the choir a catafalque surrounded with tapers in lofty candelabrums, a row of priests standing on each side. There was an awful silence for several minutes and then the solemn service of the Dead. The singers turned pale as they sung *Timor mortis me conturbat*. [Ferracuti and Totti exerted themselves in a wonderful manner, particularly in some of those pathetic deprecations of the divine wrath.]

After the Requiem, the High Mass of Jommelli in commemoration of the deceased, which begins with a movement imitative of the tolling of bells,

Swinging slow with solemn roar.[338]

It closed with the *Libera me, Domine, de morte aeternai* which thrilled every nerve in my frame and affected me so deeply that I burst into tears. My knees knocked against each other, a cold sweat moistened my forehead. I scarcely know how I was conveyed to the Palace, where the Marquis expected my coming with the utmost impatience, [and had sent for, several times, one of his pages to call me away, but he had not been able, or willing perhaps, to traverse the crowd and disturb their devotions. When I entered Marialva's apartment I found him leaning upon a table.] Our conversation took a most serious turn. He entreated me not to forget Portugal, to meditate upon the awful service I had been hearing, and to remember he should not die in peace unless I was present to close his eyes. In the actual tone of my mind, I was doubly touched by this melancholy affectionate address. It seemed to cut through my soul, and I execrated Verdeil and all those who had been instrumental in persuading me to abandon such a friend. The Grand Prior wept bitterly at seeing my agitation. Marialva went to the Queen, and the Grand Prior home with me. We dined alone, my heart was full of heaviness and I could not eat. At night we returned to the Palace, and there all my sorrow and anxiety was renewed.

Tuesday 27 November

The wind prevented my setting off as I intended. It blew so fresh in our teeth that no bark would venture over to Aldea Gallega. I might have crossed in the old Marquis' *scalera* with thirty oars in defiance of the wind and waves which, by the bye, raged furiously; but for the sake of the Grand Prior, I consented to put off my departure till tomorrow. Franchi was with me soon after I got up, looking [so deeply dejected (?) and so sorrowful that I could hardly refrain from kissing (?) < >]. My time at present is almost entirely engrossed with the melancholy occupation of taking leave. Upon this errand I went to the Marialva Palace and bid the old Marquis, the Marchioness, D. Pedro and the little girls an eternal adieu. The Abbade made a piteous moaning. I fear I have seen him for the last time and that his days will not be long in the land. Everything being in confusion at home, I dined with Horne. The Grand Prior never left me a moment. In the dusk I went to Francisco José's, who has done his utmost to oblige me, and having embraced him, drove to the Palace with the Grand Prior. My friend and I passed two hours in earnest conversation, and to revive his drooping spirits I gave him some hope of my returning in a year or two. On his part he promised never to lose sight an instant of Melo's ruin and that of the English interest at Lisbon.

SPANISH JOURNAL 1787–1788

Monday 10 December

[339] <Not far from Nuestra Señora del Prayo we crossed the Tagus and continued dragging through> heavy sands for five tedious hours without perceiving a habitation or meeting any animals, biped or quadrupeds, except herds of swine in which I believe consist the principal riches of this part of the Spanish dominions. I doubt whether the Royal stye of Ithaca were half so well garnished as many private ones in New Castile and Estremadura. Having nothing to look at except a dreary plain bounded by barren, uninteresting mountains, I was reduced to tumbling over the trashy collection of books with which I happen in this journey to be provided:[340] poor fiddle-faddle Derrick's *Letters from Cork, Chester and Tunbridge; John Buncle, Esquire's, Life,* holy rhapsodies and peregrinations; Shenstone's, Mr. Whistler's, and the good Duchess of Somerset's *Correspondence;* Bray's *Tour,* right worthy of an ass; Heely's fulsome description of the Leasowes and Hagley; Clarke's ponderous account of Spain, and Major Dalrymple's dry, tiresome and splenetic excursion. There's a set, equal it if you can! I hope to get a better at Madrid and throw my old stock into the Manzanares.[341]

We dined at a village called Brabo not in the least worth mentioning, and arrived in due, tiresome course about six in the evening at Santa Olalla, where my courier had procured us an admirable lodging in the house of a veteran Colonel. The principal apartment, in which I pitched my bed, was a sort of gallery with large folding glazed doors gilt and varnished, had its white walls almost covered with saintly pictures and small mirrors stuck near the ceiling out of the reach of mortal sight, as if their proprietor was afraid they would wear out by being looked into. On low tables to the right and left of the door stood glass cases filled with relics and artificial flowers. Stools covered with velvet and raised not above a foot from the floor were stationed all round the room. On one of these I squatted like an Oriental, warming my hands over a brazier of coals.

The old lady of the house, followed by a train of curtseying handmaids and sniffling lapdogs favoured me with her company the best part of the evening. Her spouse the Colonel, being indisposed, did not make his appearance. Whilst we were talking of the excellent qualities and wonderful acquisitions of the Infant D. Luis,[342] who died about two years ago at his villa in this neighbourhood, some very grotesque figures entered the ante-chamber, and tinkling their guitars struck up a *seguidilla* that in a minute or two set all the feet in the house in motion. Amongst the dancers two young girls, whose jetty locks were braided with some degree of elegance, shone forth in a fandango, beating the ground and snapping their fingers with amazing agility. This sport lasted a full hour before they discovered the least sign of being tired. Then succeeded some drawling *tiranas,* by no means so delightful as I expected. I was not sorry when the ball ceased and my kind hostess, moving off with all her dogs and dancers, left me to sup and sleep in tranquillity.

Tuesday 11–Wednesday 12 December

In the Book.[343]

Thursday 13 December

It was a heavy damp morning, and I could hardly prevail upon myself to quit my fire-side[344] and deliver a letter I have brought from Marialva to the Portuguese Ambassador, D. Diogo de Noronha. The Ambassador being gone to the palace, I drove to the Duchess of Berwick,[345] my old acquaintance with whom I passed the chief part of my time at Paris eight years ago. Her dear spouse, so well known at Spa, Brussels, Aix-la-Chapelle and all the gaming places in Europe by the name, style and title of Marquis of Jamaica, has been departed these five or six months, and she is now mistress of the most splendid palace in Madrid,[346] one of the first fortunes, and the affairs of her only son, the present Duke of Berwick,[347] to whom she is guardian. The façade of the Palace and the spacious court before it please me extremely. It is in the best style of modern Parisian architecture—simple and graceful, no elaborate sculptures, cracked pediments and projecting cornices. I was shewn up a majestic staircase adorned with Corinthian columns, and through a long suite of apartments, lofty and well-proportioned, at the end of which, in a saloon hung with embroidered India satin, sat reclined Mme la Duchesse in all her accustomed listlessness. She seemed never to have moved from her chair since I last had the pleasure of seeing her. She is a good-natured, indolent soul, free from malice or uncharitableness. I wish the world was fuller of this harmless, dozing species.

The morning passed swiftly away in talking over old times. I returned home to dine with Verdeil, and as soon as it was dark went back again to Mme de Berwick's, who was waiting tea for me. I like her apartments very much; the angles are taken off by low semi-circular sofas, and the space between them and the wall filled up by slabs <of Granadian marble>,[348] on which are placed large vases of mignonette and rose-trees in full bloom. The fire burned cheerfully, the table was drawn close to it; the Duchess' little girl, D. Fernanda,[349] sat playing and smiling upon a dog, whom she had in her lap and had swaddled up like an infant. Soon after tea the young Duke of Berwick and a French Abbé his preceptor came in, and stayed with us the remainder of the evening. The Duke is only fourteen and some months, but he is taller and sleeker than I am, though I have increased in size during my absence in Portugal. His manners are French, and his address as prematurely formed as his figure. Few if any fortunes in Europe equal that of which he has expectations, being heir to the <House of> Alba, seventy thousand a year at least, and in possession of the Veragua and Liria estates. These immense properties are underlet and wretchedly cultivated. If proper exertions were made in their management, his income might be doubled.

Mme de Berwick has not lost her passion for music. Operas, arias, and sonatas lie scattered all over her apartment. She soon sat me down to the pianoforte, and as I happened to be in voice, I sung an air which Burton composed for me upon my return from Venice in 1780, when Miss Seymour[350] was my confidante-in-chief and had the patience to listen hour after hour to my romantic effusions. What a strange exotic animal I was in those days, abandoned to all the wildness of my imagination, and setting no bounds to my caprices. Never was I quiet a single instant. I seemed like the antique Mercury perpetually on tip-toe on the point of darting through the air. The Duchess says I am wonderfully sobered and that there is now some chance of my going through the world without losing my senses by the way.

Friday 14 December

A little lively Spaniard called the Chevalier de Rojas,[351] who had been very intimate with Verdeil at Lausanne, came in a violent hurry here this morning to pay us a visit. He seems to have set his heart upon shewing us about Madrid and rendering our stay here agreeable. Fifty schemes did he propose in half a minute of visiting museums, churches and public buildings, of going to balls, theatres, assemblies and tertulias, and of posting immediately to a Mr. Listen's,[352] the English Chargé d'affaires, in order to be introduced to His Majesty. I took alarm at this bustling prospect, drew back into my shell and began wishing myself in the most perfect incognito, but alas, it will be no easy matter to keep myself to myself in this capital. I am sorry to find that my arrival is already notified to half the idlers within its precincts, and ten to one but I must enter the lists with M. le Chargé d'affaires and be plunged into another Walpolian contest. I expect D. Diogo de Noronha every minute. After sounding him I shall be able to fix upon some plan for my proceedings.

M. de Rojas, all eagerness to enter upon his office of cicerone, fidgetted backwards to the window, observed the day was clearing, and proposed an excursion to the Palace and gardens of Buen Retiro.[353] They are just by, so we were not above a quarter of an hour in driving to them, for the *remise*[354] I am blessed with is rather deliberate in its motions. Upon entering the large court of the Palace, which is surrounded by low buildings with plastered fronts, sadly battered by wind and weather, I spied some venerable figures in caftans and turbans leaning against a doorway. I have still sufficient sparks of Orientalism about me to catch fire at such a sight. "Who are those picturesque animals?" said I to our conductor. "Is it lawful to approach them?" "As often as you please to," answered Rojas. "They belong to the Turkish Ambassador,[355] who is lodged with all his train at the Buen Retire. If you have a mind we will go upstairs and examine the whole menagerie."

No sooner said, no sooner done. I cleared four steps at a leap, to the great delight of his whiskered Excellency<'s> pages and attendants. Never was I more delighted than upon entering a stately saloon,[356] spread with the richest carpets and perfumed with the fragrance of wood of aloes. In a corner of the apartment sat the Ambassador, wrapped up in a pelisse <of the most precious sables>,[357] playing with a light cane he held in his hand, and every now and then passing it under the noses of some tall slaves who were standing in a row before him. These figures were motionless as statues and neither moved hand nor eye as I passed them to make my salaam to the Ambassador, who received me with a most gracious nod of the head. His interpreter explained my nation and the respect which I had always conceived for the Sublime Porte. As soon as I had taken my seat in a ponderous fauteuil of figured velvet, coffee was brought in cups of most beautiful china with gold enamelled saucers. Notwithstanding my predilection for the East and its customs, I could hardly get down this beverage, it was so thick and bitter. Whilst I was sipping it and making, I fear, wry faces, a low sound of music like flutes and dulcimers, accompanied by a sort of tabor, issued from behind a curtain which separated us from another apartment. There was a melancholy softness in the air and a continual repetition of the same plaintive cadences, that soothed and affected me. The Ambassador kept poring upon my countenance and appeared much delighted with the effect his music seemed to have upon it. I began asking many questions concerning Constantinople and the state of modern Turkish literature and received the most satisfactory answers indeed. I could not have addressed myself to a person better calculated to give me information, the Ambassador being one of the first scholars in the Empire and commissioned by the Sultan to write the history of his ancestors.

Monday 17 December

I am determined to come to an explanation with Mr. Listen, and wrote him a note to desire he would name an hour for me to wait upon him. He returned for answer that at half past one he would be happy to receive me at his own house or come to mine. So this point is settled and I shall soon know to what a degree of Latitude Walpole has been able to spread his malign influence. Though the streets were half-a-foot thick in mud, I waded out to rummage the booksellers' shops in search of ancient Spanish travellers, but my pains were lost. I have met with nothing curious. At Ibarra's,[358] who is printer to the Academy, I was shewn into a shop not much larger and full as dirty as a cobbler's stall. There I found the third edition of Ponz' *Travels through Spain*, the plates of which are worn to the stumps and so coarsely retouched as to be no longer intelligible. I took up Senor Ponz' last performances, two volumes of travels in France and England,[359] full of mistakes and absurdities.[360]

At Mr. L<iston's>. Dined at home. Verdeil went to the Cabinet <of Natural History>[361] and I to D. Diogo's.[362] Pisani[363] talked over the Cornari, etc. Whilst I was there, the packet of letters arrived; two for me from Marialva and one <from> the Abbade. Answered my letters.

Tuesday 18 December

Walked in the Pardo;[364] went to Carmona's;[365] found <a> curious book. Rojas at dinner. Went to the Turk's at supper, and then to the Opera with him and Masserano (?): Masserano,[366] humpy, < > at his button-hole, staring and drumming out of time.

Wednesday 19 December

Morning: pictures at the Carmelites.[367] They are perishing in a damp sacristy. On the staircase which leads up to a range of apartments, a Rosa da Tivoli,[368] eight to ten feet in length, one of the first pictures of the master I ever beheld: goats, turkeys, geese huddled together on the brow of a hill under a troubled sky that throws over the whole group the strangest effect of light and shade.

Rojas went with us to the bookseller Sanchez.[369] I enquired after Spanish travellers; none to be met with. The most curious M.S. relations imaginable of Mexican, Californian and American travels, lies buried by order of the King at the ———.[370] Sanchez has them often in his hands to bind; amongst others, a voyage to Tahiti <and> Raiatea in the same year <as that> under Cook, for whilst Cook landed at one end of the Island, the Spaniards were employed in burying their Commander at the other.[371] There is at present in Madrid a sea officer just returned from an expedition to Kamchatka, during which he made the most accurate charts of the shores and penetrated to the 80th degree of Northern Latitude.[372] His maps <and> journals are all entombed in the same sepulchre which has swallowed up so many interesting performances. Let us pray for the day of their blessed resurrection when the discoveries of so many voyages will come to light. The Spanish Ministry affects even in affairs of the smallest moment a most mysterious secrecy. Their ships steal privately out of their harbours and the Commanders are not allowed to open their instructions. Dined at D. Diogo's with the Sardinian Ambassadress and her cuckoldy spouse.[373] Drank tea with Mme de Berwick.

Thursday 19 December.[374] Escorial

Broad, noble road; desert ploign[375] between the rocks. As you approach the Escorial, level parks, deer; mountains picturesque. Church heavy as if hewn out of rock. In the Sacristy, the Peria[376] in a sad condition. The altar-piece superb, <of> the grandest nature. In the Sala de Capitulo, Baroccio d'Urbin<o>:[377] an Annunciation < > in the corner; its companion. A Vandyck. The ceilings grotesque; colours lively as new.

I hate being roused out of bed by candlelight of a sharp, wintry morning, but as I had fixed to-day for visiting the Escorial and had stationed three relays on the road in order to perform the journey expeditiously, I was obliged to carry my plans into execution. The weather was cold and threatening, the sky red and deeply coloured. Rojas was to be of our party, so we drove to his brother the Marquis of Villanueva's[378] to take him up. He is one of the best-natured and most friendly of human beings, and I would not have gone without him upon any account, though in general I abhor turning and twisting about a town in search of anybody, let their merit be ever so transcendent. It was after eight before we issued out of the gates of Madrid and rattled along full gallop an avenue on the banks of the Manzanares, which brought us to the Casa del Campo, one of the King's palaces, wrapped up in groves and thickets. We continued a mile or two by the wall of this enclosure, and leaving La Sarsuela, another royal villa surrounded by shrubby hillocks, on the right, traversed three or four leagues of wild naked country, and after ascending several considerable eminences, the sun broke out, the clouds rolled away, and we discovered the white buildings of the Escorial with its dome and towers detaching themselves from the bold background of a lofty, irregular mountain. We were now about a league off, the country wore a better aspect than round Madrid. To the right and left of the road, which is of a noble width and perfectly well made, lie extensive parks of greensward scattered over with fragments of rock and stumps of oak and ash trees. Numerous herds of deer were ranging about and staring us full in the face, secure of remaining unmolested, for the King never permits a gun to be discharged in these enclosures. The Escorial, though overhung by melancholy mountains, is placed itself on a very considerable eminence up which we were full half an hour toiling, the late rains having washed this part of the road into utter confusion.

Friday 21 December

The cursed water of the Escorial has given me a pain in the guts. Walked in the Prado. The Director[379] of the Cabinet of Natural History came up to me and shewed me the new Museum etc. which joins the Prado. It will be magnificent—an obelisk, fountains etc. As we were walking along the great alley we met the French Ambassadress, Mme de la Vauguyon,[380] and her daughter[381] in Spanish mantillas. The Director presented me to them. Dined at home with Verdeil. At three, Rojas accompanied me to the Palace.[382] <The> staircase the most majestic imaginable: broad steps, figures in marbles reclined on them; a stately descent. Grand confusion of arcades in the Palace. Could not see the apartments without an order from the Captain of the Guard—humpy Masserano. Heard a *Salve Regina* in the chapel ill-executed. King's tribune like a coffee room with sconces. The gilt ceiling and polished marble pillars give the chapel an air of regal magnificence, but the altar is poorly adorned and without effect. Went from the Palace to Mme de Santa Cruz',[383] whom we found sitting by her fire-side with Mme de Berwick; a lovely woman. Drank tea, played on a cracked pianoforte. Then to the Marquis of Villanueva's, Roja's brother. A suite of galleries, splendid, furnished in the Spanish taste, glass doors, silver braziers, japan panels etc., and Persian carpets. Then to D. Diogo's who took me to de Aranda's.[384] His house half-Spanish, half-French, small glasses in heavy frames, fuming braziers that made my head swim. I was plagued too with gripes in the gizzard. There were eleven or twelve rooms open, a lotto table with twenty fools gaping round it. I was presented to the Duchess of Alba[385] and God knows who beside. Old de Aranda's wife is an elegant childish-looking girl full of grace and sweetness.[386] Mr. Liston presented the American Resident, Mr. Carmichael,[387] to me, whom I believe a man of sense and abilities, but whose appearance is stark and manner embarrassed. I was horribly out of sorts with the pain in my gizzard and very dull. The Countess of Benavente,[388] a mischievous old hag in the style of Lady Harrowby, was beating about for recruits to her faro bank, and Pisani was to have presented me to her, but I got out of the way, returned home at tea, and supped voraciously.

Saturday 22 December

The weather has rained itself fair. Do you understand me? In plain terms it poured hard all night, but is now blue and sunshiny. I have the devil of an appetite and queer feverish tremors. I breakfasted twice: first at home, and then with Rojas, who gave me some marvellous coffee, not Mocha but Udeim[389] he had from <the> Abbé (?) Raynal,[390] and the best chocolate I have tasted in Spain. We went to the

King's Library and then to Selma[391] the engraver's where I saw several drawings after the *Madonna del Pesce*,[392] the *Perla* and other pictures in the Escorial executed with the most scrupulous exactness. Selma is an honest plain-dealing man. I could not prevail on him to take the money for a beautiful proof of the *Madonna del Pesce*. Dinner at home. At four went to the Sardinian Ambassador's and was let in. The Ambassadress shewed me about her home, which is large and dull. I called a moment upon D. Diogo, who scolded me for not coming oftener to dine with him. <He> offered the key of his box at the Opera and was all graciousness and cordiality. I believe he likes me for my own sake as well as for Marialva's. There was nobody with him but a Saxon Count called Buest or Beist.[393]

I could not stay above half an hour, having promised to go to my dearly beloved Mahomet<an>, Ahmed Vassif. I found him in his interior apartment, seated in pomp under the canopy of a huge embroidered State bed that looked like the pavilion of Darius in an opera dance. His attendants were standing silently around. Mr. Timon his interpreter has a pert, squirrelish countenance and has certain spiteful nibbling ways that I don't relish. The Ambassador and I are great friends and all his whiskered suite are enchanted whenever I make my appearance. For my amusement they performed a sort of pantomimical dance with the strangest leapings, wrigglings, and scrambling I ever beheld. The music played doleful piteous strains that grated my ears most cruelly, and two old fellows with black rusty beards sung. My dear Ambassador takes no exercise and is for ever lolling in his sofa, fumigating himself with the vapour of wood of aloes. No wonder that he complains of the headache and lassitude. I cannot help thinking how perfectly he and the Grand Prior would agree in supineness and indolence. Paid a visit to Pisani; called at Mme de Berwick's, who was out, and came home early.

Sunday 23 December

Every morning I have the pleasure of supplying the Grand Signior's representative with rolls and *brioches* baked at home for my breakfast. I have quite won his heart by these attentions and he will miss me < > when I depart. After Mass, which I heard devoutly in the Carmelite Church just opposite my windows, Verdeil and I took a walk in the Buen Retiro gardens.[394] The gardens of Buen Retire contain neither statues or fountains worth describing. They cover a vast extent of sandy ground in which there is no prevailing upon trees to flourish.

Rojas dined with us and presented me in the early part of the evening at the French Ambassador's, the Duc de la Vauguyon,[395] whose daughter, a fine young woman of eighteen or nineteen, is married to the Prince de Listenais,[396] a smart stripling with wild hair and a low grecian forehead, who has not yet entered his fifteenth year. The Ambassador is not without knowledge of books as well as men. His manners are easy and polished without affectation. Mme la Duchesse talks more elaborately and uses fine phrases. Their son M. de Carency[397] and another young man, perhaps his brother,[398] are perfectly well-bred and amused me by the justness of their remarks on Madrid and its society. Upon the whole I like this family extremely and should be happy if they would like me.

I could not stay with them so long as I wished, Rojas having promised to take me to Mme de Aranda's, whose obedient humble servant and *cortejo* he has the honour and pleasure to be. I should not dislike being *cortejo* to such a charming little creature as Mme de Aranda, so full of candour and innocence, but in general the state of cortejoism is not very enviable. You are the sworn victim, as it were, of all the lady's caprices, must be always ready to attend her to whatever society, however stupid, to which she chooses to go, and can never move from her apron-string without her express permission. I imagine she has very good-naturedly given him leave of absence to shew me about this royal village, or else I should think he would be hardly able to spare me so much of his company.

We found her sitting *en famille* with her sister and two young boys her brothers over a silver brazier in a snug interior apartment hung with a beautiful Valencia satin. She shewed me every mark of attention and civility, <and> ordered her own apartment to be lighted up in order that I might see its magnificent furniture to advantage. The bed is beautifully shaped and placed in a recess formed by ample curtains which are festooned with infinite elegance and produce a striking theatrical effect. I have often wondered architects and fitters-up of apartments have not more availed themselves of the powers of drapery. There is no ornament I like so well or that admits of more variety. The moment I have an opportunity I will set about making to myself a tabernacle and indulge myself in all the plaits and frills that can be thought of. Mme de Aranda's toilet is a chef d'oeuvre of chased work, as well designed as executed. Poor thing! She has every exterior delight the pomp and vanity of this world can give, but she is married to a man old enough to be her grandfather, and looks as sickly and drooping as a narcissus or lily of the valley would appear if stuck in Abraham's bosom and continually breathed upon by that venerable patriarch.

After passing an hour very agreeably in her company, we went to a Mme Badaan's, who is so obliging as to give assemblies once or twice a week in no very large apartment, where people have the comfort of being jammed close together this cold weather. I repented having clothed myself in ermine and was sadly sweltered. There were forty or fifty females at least, all dressed in a fantastic blowsy style. My friend Ahmed Vassif stalked in with his Turkish interpreter, who is much more to my liking than Mr. Timon, and taking me by the hand made me sit down

by him in a corner of the room. We were just settled, when two or three young tits
with sparkling eyes and streaming ribbons drew their chairs round us and began
talking a strange lively gibberish neither French, Spanish nor Italian. I think we
must have formed a curious group: I was declaiming and gesticulating with all
my might, quoting Hafiz and Mesihi;[399] the ladies, who were rather short and
seated on very low chairs, were perking up their faces in the beard of the venerable
Mussulman, whose solemn grave demeanour formed a striking contrast with their
thoughtless vivacity. Mme Badaan and her spouse, the best sort of people in the
world and the most ready to oblige and amuse their company, sent for music and
proposed a dance for the entertainment of the Ambassador. Accordingly thirteen
or fourteen couples started, and footed away an hour or two without intermission
upon a thick carpet. Much good may it do them, thought I; the Devil wrap me
up in a blanket warmed at his own fire if I follow your example. There are scarcely
any floors boarded in Madrid, so the custom of dancing upon rugs is universally
established.

Monday 24 December

I shall have the megrims for want of exercise, like my friend Ahmed Vassif, if
I don't alter my way of life. This morning I only took a few turns in the Prado
and returned home early to dinner with a very slight provision of fresh air in
my lungs. Rojas was with me, hurrying us out of our appetite that we might
see the Palace[400] by daylight, and so to the Palace we went, and it was luckily
a bright ruddy evening, the sun gilding a grand confusion of mountainous
clouds and chequering the wild extent of country between Madrid and the
Escorial with glorious effects of light and shade. I say nothing of the front
of the Palace. It has neither elegance nor majesty, and in the centre of the
edifice starts up a gimcrack sort of belfry with chimes and bells, gilt, and the
vilest ornament that could possibly have been imagined. The interior court is
handsome and the great staircase so spacious, easy and well contrived that you
arrive almost imperceptibly at the great portal of the guard-chamber. Door-cases
and window recesses all gleam with the richest polished marbles. The immense
and fortress-like thickness of the walls and double panes of superb plate glass
exclude the keen blasts which range almost uninterrupted over the wide plains
of Castile, and preserve an admirable temperature throughout the whole suite of
apartments. The grandeur and at the same time comfort of this truly royal range
of rooms cannot be exceeded.[401]

Tuesday 25 December

I got up late and stayed at home like a simpleton playing forsooth on the p<iano> and forte (?). The Comte de Beust called on me. I felt unwell—an eager craving appetite. Dined at D. Diogo's. He is < > and always the same; he has a noble spirit and deserves five times the sum of forty-six thousand cruzados which the Queen pays him. The Opera: sat the first act in M.[402] Bendice'<s> box; M. de Aranda and French Ambassador.

Wednesday 26 December

The Prince de Carency with me, candid and ingenuous, desperately fond of the Englishman. In the evening at the Turk's then Mme de Aranda's—a brilliant assembly. M. de Rangeneck (?)[403] an impertinent puppy.

Thursday 27 December

Kauffman[404] brings (?) me a miniature copy of Paul Veronese. Received a letter from Marialva reproaching me for not having written to him; I have written eleven or twelve times: what are become of my letters? I had a < > levee: Kauffman, M. d' < >, Silva,[405] etc. Dined at Pisani's; sat between Vialli and the American Resident. Faro, lost ten *doblons*.[406] Sat with M. de la Vauguyon, then M. de Aranda's. Mme Badaan's; danced. Closed the evening at old Benavente's, and wore out my purse and my patience like a simpleton.

Friday 28 December

Rojas with me at breakfast. I made him go to Mass with me at the Church of the Carmelites. Then rode out along a vile sloppy (?) road leading to the Convent of Nuestra Señora de Atocha. Then paid visits. Evening, sat with Mme de Santa Cruz, and then to M. de Aranda's. Danced solemn minuets. Mme O'Reilly opened the ball and I with her. Danced with the Princesse de Listenais; we like each other. Went to Benavente and won what I lost last night.

Saturday 29 December

Sitting up late and consuming an hour or two after midnight at a faro table, inhaling the noxious breath of such hags as the Benavente and the Sardinian Ambassadress will not agree with me. I rose today quite disordered and feverish. Ahmed Vassif and his train arrived in one of the King's lumbering state coaches to pay me a visit. They only stayed a few minutes. I then went to see a Colonel Eustace[407] who has made some noise in the American world. He lodges in the same hotel with myself, so I had not far to go. I found him in a dark dismal room in a piteous condition, p——d over head and ears and covered with ulcers. His finances, are, I fear, in no flourishing condition and I am apt to suspect, from the very respectful message and compliments I received from him yesterday, that he has some design of being obliged to me for the loan of a few *medals* as they call their £3 12s. in this country. However he did not open his business and we talked upon indifferent matters.

I rode to and fro the avenues of the Prado with Verdeil; met Mme de la Vauguyon <and> the Princesse de Listenais walking in spite of the dirt. I am in raptures with the youthful lively manner of the Princess. She has made more impression upon me than any woman I have seen this long while and I cannot help flattering myself that she thinks me an original open-hearted being, not absolutely disagreeable. Kauffman dined with us, and just as day closed we went to the French Ambassador's. There was Mme O'Reilly and her daughter, laughing and giggling with all their soul and all their strength. Young Listenais began singing *tiranas*, with one of the best-tuned and sweetest voices I ever heard.

I too fell a-warbling and could have sung on till midnight had I not been engaged to go to Pacheco's,[408] Mme Arriaga's uncle, where there was a solemn concert and gathering together of diplomatic and Ministerial personages in honour of the Sublime Ahmed Vassif, whose musicians were seated like dogs on a carpet, piping, drumming, and howling a doleful ditty composed at Baghdad by one of the first dilettantes of the East, as an Armenian interpreter assured me. The Archbishop of Toledo[409] and the Grand Inquisitor[410] sat listening to these grating sounds with evangelical patience and resignation. Both these prelates have an air of frankness and beneficence that promises a truce to autos-da-fé and persecutions. The Archbishop came up to me the moment I entered, and without waiting for any ceremonious introduction, began addressing me in French with most good-humoured civility. Pacheco's apartments are like an auction room, small, low and lined with pictures not very skilfully selected. The *rinfresco*[411] was magnificent, the instrumental concert <executed> with taste and spirit, but if there are no better singers than those I was condemned to hear, sad is the condition of vocal music in His Catholic Majesty's dominions. A Jewish-looking Portuguese, who I am told is a mighty favourite with Pacheco, sweated up to A in alt in a nauseous falsetto, and having saddled his nose with an enormous pair of spectacles, favoured us with the old hackneyed song of *La pauvre bourbonnaise*,[412] which greatly delighted his Turkish Excellency. Ahmed Vassif made me sit by him the whole night in state and form. I could not get away till twelve. Old Benavente invited me cordially to faro, but happily for the repose of my purse and my body I went to bed.

Sunday 30 December

I dined at M. de la Vauguyon's, and am more enchanted than ever with Mme de Listenais. She is sensible, I believe, of the pleasure I take in conversing with her, but Papa and Mamma have opened the eyes of suspicion. The little Prince and his governor accompanied me to the Prado. We were all together at the Opera in the Ambassador's box, and adjourned from thence to Mme Badaan's.

Monday 31 December

Mme de Listenais runs in my head, I insensibly bend my course to the Prado in hopes of meeting her. There she was, true enough, and stopped the moment she saw me, and admired my horses and seemed to wish I would dismount and walk with her. But I dared not follow the impulse of my heart. The severe eye of her father, hitherto at least, keeps me within bounds. Were I to seize every opportunity that presents itself and wear it out, there would soon be an end of opportunities. It is a heavenly day, the air has all the mildness of spring, and the sky the glow of summer. Verdeil and I rode up and down the wild sandy hillocks which skirt the town and command a vast prospect of sterility and desolation. But its ugliness was lost upon me, so constantly did I keep my eyes fixed on the soft blue ether and the beautifully tinted clouds that were continuously shifting their forms and colours. My mind was absorbed in a reverie, and I hardly knew where my horse was carrying me. At two I perceived we were entering the street of Alcala, and at sight of M. de la Vauguyon's hotel my heart gave a leap that restored me to my senses.

Just as dinner was bringing in—for which, by the bye, I had no appetite—the Prince de Listenais and his governor M. d'Elmas entered. The governor has conceived a strong prepossession in my favour, which the young one, if I read him right, will take care to augment rather than diminish. They only stayed a few minutes, seeing me on the point of sitting down to table. Rojas came to us early, and we went together, first to D. Diogo's and then to Mme de Berwick's, then to the Opera, and then to old Benavente's, where I lost my money, twenty guineas at least.

Tuesday 1 January 1788

I never passed in all my life a day more agreeably. In the morning Carency, Listenais and the young Infantado[413] came in and breakfasted, and we all mounted our horses and scampered along a broad level road in high glee and spirits. Verdeil and the governor, who has such an excellent opinion of my head and heart, followed at a distance. The governor let fall in confidence that the young Princess was rather too fond of talking about me. I must take care, or I shall kindle a flame not easily extinguished. I am surrounded with fires; it is delightful to be warmed, but unless I summon up every atom of prudence in my composition I shall be reduced to ashes.

Rojas and Kauffman dined with us. The latter accompanied me to the Prado and from thence to Ahmed Vassif's, whom we found in all his glory surrounded by twenty or thirty of his attendants in their most splendid dress, giving audience to the Tripolitan Ambassador,[414] whom he had invited to supper. He is a young man of two-and-twenty, son of the *Chaid* or First Minister of Tripoli. His brother, a boy of twelve, was seated next to him, and behind the sofa stood a rank of venerable grey-bearded Africans, the most picturesque figures I ever beheld. The little boy's name is Mohammed. There is a languid tenderness in his eyes, a softness in the contour of his face, and a bewitching < > in his smile that enchanted me. We conserved[415] in lingua franca. I was seated on the carpet like an Oriental, to the great delight of Ahmed Vassif, who has hopes of alluring me to Constantinople; but still more to that of little Mohammed, who kept whispering to me with a tone of voice that went to my soul, and pressing my hands with inconceivable tenderness. I thought myself in a dream—nay, I still think myself so, and expect to wake. What is there in me to attract the affections of these infidels at first sight, I cannot imagine. Mohammed and I continued drinking each other's looks, to use the phraseology of Hafiz, with such avidity that we forgot how the time passed, and were startled upon quitting one instant the contemplation of each other to find the saloon illuminated with three vast lustres, the musicians placed in due order, the pages standing in solemn rows, and Mme de Santa Cruz, the little Villamayors and Sabatinis[416] with high plumed heads and streaming ribbons, taking their places to the right and left of Ahmed Vassif. Presently in came the Prince Masserano, who followed my example, and throwing himself cross-legged on the carpet at the feet of his divinity Mme Villamayor, where he looked like a crump-backed tailor stitching the hem of her garment. Mme de Santa Cruz looked in high beauty, her hair fell wildly over her ivory forehead, and——.[417]

Wednesday 2 January

Feverish. Rode out with Verdeil. After dinner presented him to the French Ambassadress. Returned home. To tea with Listenais, his governor and Gaudin.[418] Carency sat with me all the evening; I love his candour and sincerity.

Thursday 3 January

Laid up with a sore leg; I got it sprawling at the Turk's. Verdeil cooked me, and the inflammation subsiding, I went to Ahmed Vassif in search of Kauffman, that I might go to my dear Mohammed; but instead of meeting him, the old Effendi laid hold of me and dragged me in his coach to Mme Badaan's. I only stayed half an hour, then to the Opera; chatted with Mme Santa Cruz, Imperiali[419] etc., and got home early. Wrote to Marialva.

Friday 4 January

Carency, Infantado and the little Prince at breakfast, and then a scampering ride; we rode into Mme de Berwick's court; weather pleasant. After dinner, M. de Aranda's, where I met Mme Santa Cruz, who took me and Infantado to a play at the College of the Nobles acted by boys. Then back again to M. de Aranda's. Princesse de Listenais far gone, I believe. To M. Bendicho's; I went at twelve.

Saturday 5 January

Visit D. Diogo. Rojas and Kauffman at dinner, M. Gaudin at tea. Went to Ahmed's, who took me to the Opera, there I flirted with Mme Villamayor and Mme de Santa Cruz. Carency and Listenais very fond and loving. We returned home a coachful.

Sunday 6 January

At Mass at the Carmelites, then to Mme Villamayor's with Minutoto.[420] Dined at home. Again to Mme Villamayor's, then to the French Ambassador's ball, where I danced till three in the morning.

Monday 7 January

Rose late; hardly out of bed when Carency, Listenais, Infantado etc. came to breakfast. It was bright sunshine, we rode all together to see the troops drawn out and the King pass, who set off for the Pardo. Mme de Berwick gave us a collation and we rewarded her by making a choice racket. The young Duke very pawing and lecherous. At five, we dined with Masserano and thirty officers. Carency went home, and Listenais to bed. I had better have followed his example, but was fool enough to be led gadding about to puppet shows and whores' party by M. Gaudin.

Tuesday 8 January

I rode to the Prado. Walked in the Retire with Ahmed Vassif, whose slaves were romping. Tired and yawning. Dined at the French Ambassador's and felt profoundly stupid. Mme de Listenais frets to death upon my account, I fear. At tea, Listenais, his governor, Gaudin, Kauffman and a M. de la Chaise. Kauffman went with me to < > Zamora the Tripolitan Ambassador, where I sat an hour with Mohammed. Then to the Opera; sat with M. Bendicho and Mme Santa Cruz. Received a letter today from Marialva announcing his daughter's marriage with the Duke de Lafões.

Wednesday 9 January

Bright and cold. Pisani, Infantado and M. d'Elmas rode out with me. Dined at the Portuguese Ambassador's, then to Ahmed Vassif, where there was romping and dancing. I felt tired and returned home with the Comte de Beust. Kauffman supped with me. The Comte de Beust has a taste for hobgoblin stories and has assisted at magical operations.

Thursday 10 January

I rode out as usual. Evening, went to the French Ambassador's, then to Badaan's: a ball, hot and stewing, but well illuminated.

Friday 11 January

In the morning went to Infantado's Palace with Listenais and his governor. The pictures by Rubens and Velasquez are glorious. Then to the tennis court; I sat with Listenais whilst his governor and Infantado played. Infantado dined with me; he is a good-natured ignorant animal. Beust at tea and the whole troop of young Frenchmen. Beust went with me to Villamayor's then to de Aranda's, dull and solemn. Then with Infantado to the Marquis of Villanueva's, where I flirted with Mme Villamayor. The apartments were dark and favourable for flirtations. The glowing embers in the braziers taught light to counterfeit a gloom. Low murmurs and whispering. Ahmed Vassif in the midst with his chicks all round him. I led Mme Villamayor to her carriage, and was swayed and pressed significantly.

Saturday 12 January

Beust and Carency at breakfast. Ahmed Vassif sent me his favourite slave Taker with a magnificent present of wood of aloes, amber and odour of roses; by this token of regard I conclude that I am in high favour. Carency and I went together to Mme de Berwick's to comfort the young Duke, who has bruised himself by a fall down stairs; a giddy pate. We found him snug in his bed, full of wantonness. After trifling away an hour with the Duchess we returned home, dressed and hurried to Pisani's where we were engaged to dinner. We were all very gay and I was in such spirits that I began imitating Pacchierotti,[421] the Grand Opera, and my friend Ahmed Vassif's Turkish howlings. There was at dinner the Swedish sleek, smirking Minister,[422] a lusty young man with a broad countenance shining with the oil of gladness, old Silesian Beust, Rojas etc. We all went in a body to Mme de Berwick's, and I sat down to the pianoforte and ranted and roared till my throat was parched up. Liston heard me and was convulsed into laughter. From Mme de Berwick's we went to the Opera and from thence to the Marquis of Cogolludo's[423] ball. A long gallery hung with yellow damask, richly carpeted. Mme de Listenais soon came in and scolded me for having flirted at the Opera with the Villamayors a little too conspicuously. We mutually promised to meet at Paris and gave way to the enchanting delirium of a rising passion. The ball was splendid, the orchestra full and spirited. I danced with the Imperiali, Mme de Listenais not daring on account of her father to give me her hand. Cogolludo is a mean little figure unworthy of the race of heroes from which we are to believe he is sprung, but he was civil and attentive and I have no reason to complain of him.

Sunday 13 January

Kauffman sallied out with me to the Prado after breakfast. It was excellent basking in the sunshine. We met Mme Bendicho and her faithful Expilly, who told me Mme de Listenais was not far off. This intelligence made me double my speed; Kauffman was obliged to take long strides to keep pace with me. I traversed all the Prado without meeting the object of my pursuit, and found myself in the court before the hideous front of the Church of Atocha. A tide of devotees carried me into the chapel of the Virgin which is hung round with trophies and ex-votos—legs, arms, and fingers in wax and plaster. Kauffman is a sturdy infidel, but I made him kneel by me and hear out a Mass which was none of the shortest, the priest being old and sadly addicted to the wiping and adjusting of spectacle<s>; I thought he would never have succeeded in fitting them to his nose. I knelt under the shade of some banners which the British Lion was simple enough to let slip out of his paws during the last war: the colours of Fort St. Philip[424] dangled immediately above my head. Amongst the crowd of worshippers I espied the young Duke of Arion,[425] one of the hopeful heirs of the Medinaceli, looking like a strayed sheep and smiting his breast with exemplary energy. I measured back my steps to the Prado and at length discovered Mme de Listenais strictly guarded by Mamma. I accompanied them to their door and returned sheepishly home. Infantado was waiting for me. I rode out with him. Dined alone. [Then to the French Ambassador's ball, dancing till three in the morning, where I saw the semi-royal race][426] of the Medinaceli glittering with jewels and dancing abominably.

Monday 14 January

Infantado and I went a-cavalcading with Ahmed Vassif, whose principal favourites were mounted on Spanish prancers almost hid by enormous Turkish trappings, glittering and clattering with thin plates of gold. Masserano on his beautiful parade horse curvetted on the left of the Ambassador and looked more like an unlucky crook-backed groom than the Captain of His Catholic Majesty's Guards. Timoni the interpreter was likewise of the party, which was twenty-five or thirty strong. We sallied out from the Buen Retiro and passing through the gate of Atocha met Mme Santa Cruz and Imperiali, who followed us in their carriage. Soon after the Venetian Ambassador joined our cavalcade, which was accompanied also by a numerous rabble. The mildness of the day invited us to dismount and walk along the bank of a canal still clad with fresh herbage. Ahmed Vassif ordered his pages to spread out carpets, fringed with gold, on a pleasant level spot, so down we all squatted, and after reposing ourselves half an hour and basking delightfully in the sunbeams,

Infantado and I run races with the Turks. This frolic ended, we all repaired, except Masserano, to dinner at Mme Imperiali's. Ahmed's messes were cooked by his own slaves; a wild gaiety prevailed that completely intoxicated my imagination and set me a-talking nonsense to Mme de Santa Cruz without intermission. In the evening the flow of our spirits carried Infantado and me on foot through thick and thin to Mme de Berwick's where we rattled away to the infinite delight of the young Duke and his little blowsy sister. At length, fatigued and burnt out, I retired home to supper calmly with Infantado, whom I sent off sooner than he wished.

Tuesday 15 January

My eyes were not open till eleven and then it was the tumultuous entry of the French band that dispelled my slumbers. After swallowing my breakfast in uncomfortable haste, they persuaded me to go with them to the tennis court, where I *ennuied* myself not a little. Carency returned home with me in the carriage. He is still limping lame and seizes every opportunity of leaping and hopping that a mortal desirous of crippling himself would desire. In the evening I went to the Opera and sat by Mme de Santa Cruz with dog-like (?) fidelity.

Wednesday 16 January

I rode out with Listenais to the pleasant lawn where Ahmed's attendants performed their evolutions last Monday, and dined at the French Ambassador's, papa being absent, and Mme de Listenais and I felt a little more at our ease. In the evening <at> M. de Aranda's; my poor friend the Venetian Ambassador upon thorns, wishing and yet not daring to ask me to a solemn diplomatic dinner he gives tomorrow. As I have not been presented he knows not how to act; at length, however, he pressed me to come in spite of all the rules of the Diplomatic body.

Thursday 17 January

The dinner was pompous and formal. All the ambassadors and the first grandees of the Court were assembled. Carency, Listenais, Infantado and I surrounded Mme de Santa Cruz, and laughed and sported and snorted our fill. The apartment is spacious and magnificent, but had a bewildering enchanted air, one of the long galleries being panelled with japan, flamingly < > and bedraggled, and the lustres crowded with tapers three or four feet high. Infantado consorts with me as much as he is able, and we drove home together to tea. These youths have caught such a trick of drinking tea that they will miss me sadly when I leave Madrid. After swilling four or five dishes, we went to the Opera and then to Badaan's ball, which was as crowded as usual. The Duchess of la Vauguyon and Mme de Listenais were there for a wonder. Mme de Listenais wastes away visibly and looks completely wretched. She would fain have danced with me, but trembled and coloured and looked at her mother, and with a faltering voice told me she was engaged.

Friday 18 January

Though I am sadly jaded with late hours, balls, operas and *tertulias,* I suffered myself to be roused out early by Carency and galloped with him a full league on the road to Toledo. We met again at M. de Aranda's in the evening, where there was a ball in the great saloon which looks like a tabernacle or sanctuary set apart for the rites of some austere religion. The Count de Aranda officiates as high priest with much severity. The Count de St. Simon,[427] a French Colonel just imported, returned with me and Infantado to supper, and made me sit up later than I wished.

Saturday 19 January

I am so worn down with late hours that I can hardly keep my eyes open. However I made an effort to dine with the Venetian Ambassador who had collected a singing party, which I deserted as soon as was decent and drove to Ahmed Vassif, where I reposed on sofas in perfect idleness. At nine I got home intending to dress for Cogolludo's, but had not the power, and after swallowing some rice broth, hurried to bed and sunk into profound sleep before eleven.

Sunday 20 January

A whirlwind seemed to have carried off the inhabitants of Madrid to the Pardo. It is the King's birthday. Not a coach was visible in the avenues of the Prado. I walked out with d'Elmas and the Comte de Beust at the risk of being blinded by dust, and heard Mass at the Puerto del Sol.[428] Beust dined with me. All the infidels were assembled at the Duc de la Vauguyon's ball; Ahmed and Zamora, the Tripolitan Ambassador, both sweltering in ermine and sables, wedged close by Mme Torre de Manzanares, Mme O'Reilly and other potent females. I sat by Mohammed the best part of the evening, and took vehement delight in his African remarks and original ideas.

Monday 21 January

To comply with a whim of Beust's I dined at Noronha's [429] and eat myself hoggish dull. Our party consisted solely of Silva the Secretary and two sorrowful beings, the Duke of Sangro[430] and the Russian Minister,[431] one of the quaintest of God's creatures. I got away as soon as I could and accompanied Beust to the French Ambassador's. My Journal is in sad confusion. I have no time to write. From the moment my eyes open to that in which they close, I think confusedly of Mme de Santa Cruz, the Turks, Mohammed, Listenais etc.

Wednesday 23 January

At Mme de Aranda's. I was surrounded by a rabble of young officers who talk me crazy; my head swims round. I never was in such confusion in all my days, or occasioned more to others. Papa Vauguyon wishes me at Hell for having engrossed all the thoughts of his young ones, male and female. He has learnt certain anecdotes of me that are far from calming his inquietudes.

Saturday 26 January

At Cogulludo's. Mme de Listenais talked to me without reserve and gave me clearly to understand that her affections were mine beyond the power of control.

Sunday 27 January

I have acquired a confirmed habit of going to Mass.

APPENDIX I

MARIALVA'S VILLA AND SETEAIS

It has long been thought that Marialva's new villa in the Sintra area, with its "gay pavilion designed by Pillement and elegantly decorated" (p. 128, and Letter 18 of *Portugal*), was the well-known Palace of Seteais.[432] Seteais is on the Sintra-Colares road, about three miles from Ramalhão, on the further side of S. Pedro and Sintra. The *Journal* shows that Marialva could not have been as far away from Beckford as that. For example, on October 17 and 29 Beckford "walked soberly in the twilight" after dinner from Ramalhão to his friend's villa, where the Queen was being entertained. In such circumstances a gentleman would not have dreamed of walking such a long distance: he would have gone by carriage. On September 25 after seeing Rocha at the Royal Palace at Sintra, Beckford returned to Ramalhão, and on the way back there "stopped to take up Verdeil, whom I had left by the way at the Marquis'." On October 24, Beckford rode to Horne's (Q. do Relogio), which was on the Sintra side of Seteais, and on his way home stopped at Marialva's. These and other similar examples show that Marialva could not have been at Seteais, and was, as we would expect, much nearer Beckford.

The approximate whereabouts of the villa is given in Marialva's letter in Portuguese to Beckford, in the Hamilton Papers, dated 31 January 1788; Marialva wishes himself sitting "quietly on a sofa with you by my side at Sintra in the Quinta do Ramalhão or in the house built by Pillement at S. Pedro."[433] This fits in with the topography of the Journal. But which villa was it? The *quinta* at S. Pedro inherited by the Lafões family through the 2nd Duke's marriage in 1788 with

Marialva's daughter Henriqueta was that now known as the *Quinta do Marquez de Valada*, a half-mile walk from Ramalhão. That the Lafões got it through their Marialva marriage is proved by a document in the present Duke's possession, a *livro de apontamentos* written by the last *administrador* of the last Marquis of Marialva (d. 1823) about the family's property, to aid the formalities of inheritance; it describes the *quinta*. The villa itself was rebuilt in the last century, and there are now no signs of Pillement's work. But the spacious grounds correspond to Beckford's description, are laid out in the style of Queluz and bear traces of the 18th century; they used to contain false ruins, probably of 18th century work, and statues. Moreover, it is the only *quinta* in S. Pedro which crowns a hill (the hill of S. Pedro itself), and Beckford spoke of it as "perched on the summit of a bleak hill", and mentions that the hillside below was planted up by Marialva and enclosed for his garden. The cliff below Seteais is so steep that it could not have been similarly planted up and enclosed; nor, just before it was built on, could the site of Seteais ever have been described as "a wild hill bestrewn with flints and rocky fragments" (Letter 18), for it had from time immemorial been laid out as a flat space upon which cavalry exercised.

The history of Seteais will help to show how the legend arose that Beckford was entertained here by Marialva in 1787. It has always been known that it was built at this period by Daniel Gildemeester *pere,* Dutch Consul in Lisbon. Cunha[434] gives 1778 as the date, but this may be a misprint for 1787. The Deed[435] leasing the common space in front of Seteais to Marialva on 19 May 1801 mentions some old walls there being demolished in 1788 when Gildemeester was building the houses and stables of his *quinta*. In passing, we may note that since Gildemeester had only just built Seteais, it was unlikely that he would at once have sold it to Marialva or that Beckford would have failed to mention this in his description of Marialva's villa, which reads as if Marialva had just built it for himself. It must be the opening of Seteais which Beckford describes on 25 July 1787, when the building, decoration and surroundings were still unfinished; he mentions the *space* (July 25) and *flat space* (August 31) in front of the Dutch Consul's new building.

Gildemeester's *quinta* was still owned by his family when J.B.F. Carrère wrote his anonymous *Tableau de Lisbonne en 1796*, in which at p. 90 (Paris, 1797 edn.) he says "the largest <quinta at Sintra>, the most beautiful, the worthiest of being seen is that of Gildemeester, the wealthy Dutchman, whose astonishing fortune was found to be almost dissipated at his death; it is now in the possession of his widow, who with difficulty permits entry to the curious." It was then sold by Daniel Gildemeester *fils,* also Dutch Consul at Lisbon, to Marialva.[436] This accounts for the fact that Portuguese articles and books on Sintra constantly state that Gildemeester, tired of business in Portugal, sold Seteais to Marialva and retired to England. Gildemeester *père* was buried in the English Cemetery at Lisbon in 1793, but his son did retire to England (it has not hitherto been appreciated that two Daniel Gildemeesters succeeded each other as Dutch Consul).

Unfortunately we do not know what date it was sold. The flat space in front of it was rented, as we have seen, to Marialva in May 1801. The undated request[437] to the Prince Regent for this lease mentions that Marialva had already started to plant the space with woodland trees which were being gnawed by other people's cattle; it was partly for this reason that he wanted to rent the ground—to be able to keep out the cattle. This suggests that the trees had not been planted long and that Marialva had not long had the property. The 1798 *Almanac* gives Gildemeester *fils* as Dutch Consul; he is still listed in 1800 (there is no copy of the 1799 *Almanac* in British libraries), but the man who later succeeded him as Consul is listed with him *serve*, i.e. as deputising for him in his absence; it looks as if young Gildemeester had left before 1800.

It is understandable that tradition became confused and that Marialva was thought to have entertained Beckford at Seteais in 1787: Marialva bought it so soon afterwards, added to it, and improved it; he entertained Royalty there, as well as at S. Pedro in Beckford's time; there was confusion over the two Gildemeesters; Seteais has frescoes which are guessed to be by Pillement, although M.N. Benisovich[438] questions this attribution; and finally, Beckford was last in Portugal from October 1798 to about July 1799, during which period he would have been entertained at Seteais if by that time Marialva was (as seems likely) its owner.

APPENDIX II

GENEALOGICAL TABLES OF THE CONNECTIONS
OF THE MARIALVAS

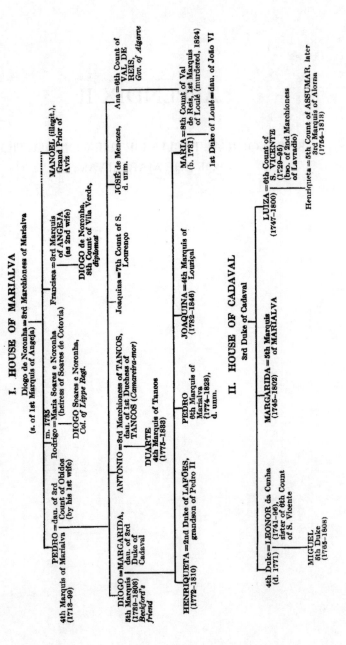

Genealogy and Connections of the Marialvas

I. HOUSE OF MARIALVA

II. HOUSE OF CADAVAL

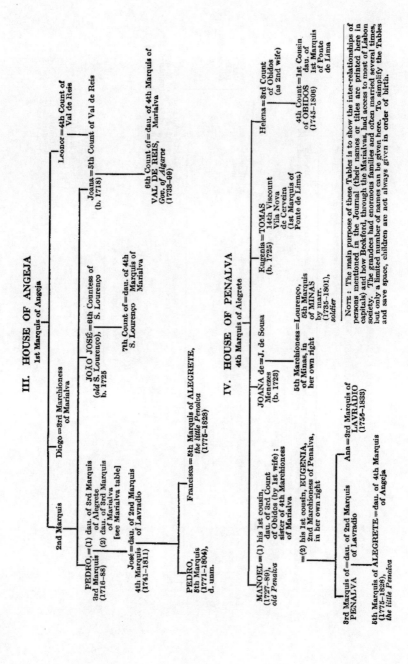

III. HOUSE OF ANGEJA
1st Marquis of Angeja

- **2nd Marquis**

    - **PEDRO,** =(1) dau. of 3rd Marquis
      3rd Marquis   of Alegrete
      (1716–88)   =(2) dau. of 3rd Marquis
                        of Marialva
                        [see Marialva table]

        - **José** = dau. of 2nd Marquis
          4th Marquis   of Lavradio
          (1741–1811)

- **Diogo** = 3rd Marchioness
            of Marialva

    - **JOÃO JOSÉ** = 6th Countess of
      (old S. Lourenço),   S. Lourenço
      b. 1725

        - **7th Count** = of dau. of 4th
          of   Marquis of
          S. Lourenço   Marialva

    - **Francisca** = 5th Marquis of ALEGRETE,
                      the little Penalva
                      (1775–1828)

        - **PEDRO,**
          5th Marquis
          (1771–1804),
          d. unm.

- **Leonor** = 4th Count of
             Val de Reis

    - **Joana** = 5th Count of Val de Reis
      (b. 1718)

        - **6th Count** = of dau. of 4th Marquis of
          VAL DE REIS,   Marialva
          Gov. of Algarve
          (1738–99)

IV. HOUSE OF PENALVA
4th Marquis of Alegrete

- **MANOEL** =(1) his 1st cousin,
  (1727–89),   dau. of 3rd Count
  old Penalva   of Obidos (by 1st wife);
                    sister of 4th Marchioness
                    of Marialva
  =(2) his 1st cousin, EUGENIA,
       2nd Marchioness of Penalva,
       in her own right

    - **Ana** = 3rd Marquis of
              LAVRADIO
              (1756–1833)

        - **3rd Marquis** = of dau. of 2nd Marquis
          of   of Lavradio
          PENALVA

            - **5th Marquis of ALEGRETE** = dau. of 4th Marquis
              (1775–1828),   of Angeja
              the little Penalva

- **JOANA** de = J. de Sousa
  Menezes   Menezes
  (b. 1728)

    - **5th Marchioness** = Lourenço,
      of Minas, in   5th Marquis of
      her own right   MINAS
                          by marr.
                          (1735–1801),
                          soldier

- **Eugenia** = TOMAS
  (b. 1725)   14th Viscount
                de Cerveira
                Vila Nova
                (1st Marquis of
                Ponte de Lima)

- **Helena** = 3rd Count
             of Obidos
             (as 2nd wife)

    - **4th Count** = 1st Cousin
      of **OBIDOS**   dau. of
      (1745–1806)   1st Marquis of
                      Ponte
                      de Lima

NOTE : The main purpose of these Tables is to show the inter-relationships of persons mentioned in the Journal (their names or titles are printed here in capitals) and how Beckford, through the Marialvas, had access to most of Lisbon society. The grandees had enormous families and often married several times, but only a limited number of names can be given here. To simplify the Tables and save space, children are not always given in order of birth.

NOTES

1   In accordance with Portuguese usage, Beckford calls monasteries "convents." They were secularised in 1834 and their buildings, when not demolished, used for other purposes, although some of their churches have been retained for worship. Belem (Bethlehem) Monastery, in a W. suburb of Lisbon, now houses Casa Pia and the Ethnological Museum. Beckford was driving W. from his house in the Necessidades Palace area, along the great coast road.

2   Usually called "the Abbade" (Abbé) by Beckford. Aged 92, he had been in the Marialvas' service most of his life, starting as their foster-father, and was on intimate footing with the family. He was an uncle of Pina Manique, the great administrator.

3   Quinta da Praia in Praga do Imperio, just beyond Belem Monastery. José I gave it to his friend "old" Marialva when he lost his Loreto Palace in the 1755 earthquake.

4   The "old" 4th Marquis of Marialva (his son, Beckford's friend, is nearly always called "the Marquis" in the Journal). Pedro José de Menezes Coutinho (1718–99), 4th Marquis, was Grand Master of the Horse, General of Cavalry and Councillor of War, and was reputed to be one of the finest riders in Europe, founding the system of equitation still called after him. See also Genealogical Table in Appendix II.

5   Pedro José Joaquim Vito de Menezes (1774–1828), 6th and last Marquis of Marialva, Grand Master of the Horse and Gentleman of the Bedchamber. In 1807 he was sent as Ambassador to Napoleon, but on his way in 1808 joined the Bayonne delegation, which treacherously asked Napoleon for a King in place of the Braganças; with the other Delegates, he retired under duress with the retreating French armies and remained in France in honourable confinement until 1814, when he became Ambassador in Paris.

6   Diogo José Vito de Menezes Coutinho (1739–1808), 5th Marquis, Grand Master
     of the Horse and Gentleman of the Bedchamber, General and Councillor of War.
     Adjutant-General to the Forces in 1797, and in 1801 during Spanish invasion.

7   Polycarpo José Antonio da Suva.

8   Henriqueta Maria Julia de Lorena e Menezes (1772–1810). Married 68-year-old 2nd
     Duke of Lafões, 29 January 1788. She and her two younger sisters were called "The
     Three Graces" because of their beauty and charm.

9   The death in childbed of his wife.

10   His half-sister, Mrs. Hervey.

11   The Church occupied by the Patriarch of Lisbon, which in 1787 was the Church of
     S. Vicente da Fora in E. Lisbon.

12   Dr. Francois Verdeil (1747–1832) of Lausanne, where he held administrative posts
     connected with local education and health; married in 1786 Sophie Dufey, natural
     daughter of Benjamin Constant's uncle, the Seigneur of Hermenches. Verdeil
     temporarily left his wife to follow Beckford as his physician.

13   João Paulo Bezerra de Seixas (1756–1817). Later, Ambassador to several countries and
     Secretary of State for War and Foreign Affairs.

14   Joseph Sill (1743–1824). Admitted to Lisbon Factory, 1769; in partnership with
     Thomas Horne, his cousin.

15   Gregorio Fellipe Franchi (1770–1828), b. Lisbon, buried in Marylebone. Son of
     Loreto Franchi, Italian singer at the Portuguese Court, and his Tuscan wife. Entered
     Patriarchal Seminary, 1788. See Introduction, p. 16.

16   Niccolo Jommelli (1714–74), Neapolitan composer. His setting of the Mass for the
     Dead (1755), which Beckford admired, was long famous.

17   Thomas Horne (1722–92), b. Wakefleld, buried in English Cemetery, Lisbon, owner
     of a business. Horne & Sill had part of the State contract in whale oil. He was
     Beckford's agent and banker.

18   Beckford spells him variously, usually Mateos, but I have standardised it to Mateus.
     He is most often simply called D. José, Bezerra's friend. The entries for September 2,
     3 and 4 make it clear that he is the same as José de Sousa, a landowner with an estate
     in Tras-os-Montes. Mme Bezerra's letters to Beckford in H.P. show that this is José
     Maria do Carmo de Sousa Botelho (1758–1825), the well-known Ambassador who
     sumptuously edited Os Lusiadas in Paris, 1817. From the family estate of Mateus he
     had the official title of Morgado de Mateus—hence Beckford first knew him as D.
     José de Mateus.

19   The elder sister was Betty Sill (1758–1885), who married Bezerra c. 1788. For his
     services to the State she was made Viscondessa de Tagoahi, 1819. Died in London.
     Her sister Sophia died unmarried, 1827.

20   One of the names of the Royal Palace at Belem, now the Presidential Palace, which
     has always been reserved for the use of the Head of the State or his official guests

of royal or princely rank. Horne's unpublished letter to Beckford in *H.P.* from the Royal Court at Caldas, 28 June 1787, shows that the plan to lease the Palace to Beckford was a serious one. Such a possibility illustrates Beckford's remarkable position, due to Marialva's friendship. The Palace was called Q. dos Bichos (Wild Beasts) because at one time Moroccan lions were kept in cages in one of its courtyards.

21 Maria I (1734–1816), succeeded her father José I (Pombal's friend), 1777. Married her uncle, 1760, who became her consort Pedro III (*d.* 1786). A prey to religious melancholia, incurably insane from 1792, when her surviving son João (later Regent and King) governed.

22 Beckford's aunt Elizabeth (1725–91), widow of 2nd Earl of Effingham, and wife of Field-Marshal Sir George Howard. She had been a Lady of the Bedchamber to Queen Charlotte, and one of her sons had an important Court post.

23 Hon. Robert Walpole (1736–1810), youngest son of 1st Baron Walpole of Wolterton; nephew of the Prime Minister, and cousin of Horace Walpole. Envoy at Lisbon, 1772–1800; twice married, to daughters of Lisbon Factory merchants.

24 The Patriarch of Lisbon, elected 1786 and inducted 1788: José F.M.A. de Mendoça (1725–1803).

25 José de Seabra da Silva (1733–1818) was in 1771 appointed Secretary of State assisting Pombal. It is thought that he was banished in 1774 for disclosing to Princess Maria Pombal's plan to replace her as Heir Apparent by her son José, later Prince of Brazil. The interest that he, Angeja and Lavradio took in Beckford's case is a measure of the importance it had begun to assume in Portuguese politics.

26 Pedro José de Noronha (1716–88), 3rd Marquis, acknowledged leader of the nobility. Maria's first Prime Minister and Chancellor of the Exchequer until 1783.

27 Luis de Almeida Soares e Portugal (1727–90), 2nd Marquis. Viceroy of Brazil, 1769–79. At this time he was the President of the Supreme Royal Court (Mesa do Desembargo do Paço), Comptroller of the Queen's Household, and Councillor for War.

28 João Carlos de Bragança (1719–1806), 2nd Duke, "Uncle of the Queen" and grandson of Pedro II. Married Henriqueta (Marialva's daughter), 1788. He was later Prime Minister and C.-in-C. of the Portuguese army. His Palace was at Grilo, E. of Lisbon.

29 Frederick North (1766–1827), bachelor, later 5th Earl of Guilford, and son of the Prime Minister. In his own copy of Fanny Burney's *Memoirs of Dr. Burney*, 1832, which eulogised North, Beckford sarcastically jotted:

> But who can escape calumny? Even the maimed, distorted, puny
> but truly amiable and witty Frederick North was accused by some
> of the vigorous young ladies of the British Factory at Lisbon …

of a mighty cool indifference to their charms. I once heard 3 or 4
of these commercial Amazons declare in chorus that they always
understood he was reckoned a nasty man. What they could possibly
mean by the application of such an epithet to so spotless a character,
I am at a total loss to conjecture.

30   Manoel de Noronha e Menezes, Grand Prior of Military Order of S. Bento of
Aviz, to which he was appointed at some date after Maria's accession (1777);
died in office, 1794, after accompanying Beckford to Alcobaça and Batalha.
Beckford sometimes calls him "Prior-mor," and usually speaks of him as D.
Pedro's uncle, whereas he was his great-uncle, being the natural brother of "old"
Marialva (*b.* 1713). By "the young Marialva," Beckford here means the "young"
Marquis, Diogo.

31   Baby's napkins.

32   This monastery has disappeared. Its site is now apparently occupied by the Casino
at Alges, a suburb beyond Belem. Founded in 1559 for barefoot Franciscans of
the Order of Arrabida. During his second stay in Portugal, Beckford rented the
adjoining *quinta* of the same name, 1794.

33   Gerard Devisme (*c.* 1725–98), millionaire Lisbon merchant. His *quinta* is now a
reformatory, near the Church of S. Domingos. Bagnigge Wells and White Conduit
House were fashionable pleasure resorts in Finsbury.

34   A poem in Dryden's *Fables ... from Homer, Ovid, Boccace and Chaucer*, 1700.

35   William Courtenay (1768–1835), instrument of Beckford's ruin, was later 3rd
Viscount Courtenay and 9th Earl of Devon. He led a scandalous life, fled the
country in 1811 to escape arrest, and died unmarried in Paris in obscurity.

36   Palace of Palhava, now the Spanish Embassy, is on Bemfica road. Its owner, 3rd
Marquis of Louriçal, became father-in-law of Marialva's youngest daughter Joaquina.
The bastards, uncles of Maria I, were Antonio; Gaspar, Archbishop of Braga; and
José, Inquisitor-General.

37   Elizabeth (1750–1828), 6th Baroness Craven by marriage. She was separated from her
husband and living on an easy footing with the Margrave of Anspach, whom she
later married; this was the last of her several liaisons.

38   A royal Palace near Lisbon.

39   From Dryden's *Absalom and Achitophel*, i, 8–9.

40   The Rock of Lisbon.

41   These were Custom House guards, Health Officers, minions of the Inquisition,
and a consular official. No wonder that Beckford laughed, for the Captain of his
ship had to sign on behalf of himself and his crew a curious set of Articles, some of
which, in translation, would have run as follows: "that they will take off their hats
to the clergy ... that they will kneel at the elevation of the Host; that they will in no

way insult the Cross, wherever set up, by making [water], but however urgent their Necessities may be, will retain the same till a proper and lawful distance."

(Miss J. Schaw's *Journal*, pp. 221–2.)

42   SW. of Ajuda Palace. Not then open to the public, so Beckford was privileged.

43   Caldas da Rainha, where the Royal Family took the waters.

44   An image of Our Lady of the Cape, on Espichel Promontory.

45   One of *The Episodes of Vathek* which Byron longed to see, and which were intended to be an appendage to Beckford's novel *Vathek*, but were not published until 1912.

46   *i.e.* for Marialva at Court, then held at Caldas.

47   At W. end of the old city, near Alcantara stream. Given to Order of S. Philip Neri (Oratorians), 1747; now H.Q. of army division. Royal Palace (now Foreign Office) adjoins it; with its obelisk-fountain was erected by João V, 1747–50.

48   José Maria de Melo (1756–1818). Succeeded S. Caetano in the position of Queen's Confessor, one of the most influential in Portugal.

49   Nuno José de Mendonça e Moura (1788–99), 6th Count of Val de Reis. Governor of Algarve from 1786, General, Councillor of State.

50   1722–1804. One of the leading Portuguese writers; philosopher, theologian, fashionable preacher and confessor, Oratorian. One of first to introduce study of experimental physics into Portugal. Exiled under Pombal, 1768–77.

51   Chapman, op. cit., p. 214 n., explains this reference. In May–June 1787 a House of Commons Committee, reversing previous decisions, ruled that the franchise of Borough of Saltash was not vested in Corporation of Saltash, but in the burgage-holders, who thus had a say as to who should represent this "rotten" borough in Parliament. Under the Committee's ruling, the burgage-holders' nominee, Major Lemon, remained M.P.

52   Thomas Wildman of Lincoln's Inn, Beckford's solicitor.

53   Jeronimo Francisco de Lima (1741–1822), noted for his operas and religious compositions.

54   Monastery of S. Antonio dos Capuchos, i.e. of Franciscans of Province of S. Anthony; NW. of Campo de Santana, in N. of city. Since 1836 a Beggars' Home (Asilo de Mendicidade).

55   Marvila is half a mile beyond Lafões' palace of Grilo; its site is now occupied by a big factory, but there is a Pateo Marialva, inhabited by workers, on the site of the stables.

56   The Cape Jasmine, *Gardenia jasminoides*, first cultivated *c.* 1750, and thought to be native to Cape of Good Hope, though actually from China and Japan.

57   Built 1729–49 to supply Lisbon with water, crossing Alcantara valley at Campolide by a viaduct half a mile long.

58   A heavy deletion of 4 lines follows, ending "corrodes and preys upon my mind." The words "every care" were added to the text by Beckford when he made this erasure.

59 At S. Apolonia, on the then E. outskirts of Lisbon. One of the most fashionable
    literary salons in Lisbon was held there.

60 Antonio Leal Moreira (1758–1819). Chapel-Master of Royal and Patriarchal Chapels.
    His religious anthem *Pax Jerusalemi* was performed and known in England. His
    operas were very popular then in Portugal.

61 A Portuguese Judge chosen and paid by the English Factory (i.e. the association
    of British merchants in Lisbon) to guard their interests. The Judge, João Xavier
    Teles de Sousa (*b.* 1732), had in 1787 been appointed one of the Councillors
    (Desembargadors) of the Supreme Court of Justice (Mesa do Desembargo do
    Paço) after having held, during twenty years, several of the highest legal posts. He
    was a member of the Tribunal decreed in 1780 to review sentences passed on the
    Tavora plotters, which led to their rehabilitation. By taking Beckford's side against
    Walpole and his own employers, the Factory, he probably hoped to get Marialva's
    influence with the Queen for further advancement; or perhaps he only wanted a
    bribe.

62 Manoel Teles da Silva (1727–89), heir of 4th Marquis of Alegrete and, through his
    second wife, 2nd Marquis of Penalva; Captain of the Royal Guard, and patron of
    writers and poets.

63 Fernando Teles da Silva (1754–1818), 3rd or "young" Marquis. Became a General,
    Colonial Governor; author of dissertations on constitutional law.

64 Lord Chancellor, and Beckford's former guardian.

65 William Hudson, of the Lisbon firm of Hudson, Harrison & Gonne.

66 *Praça do Comerçio*, also called *Terreiro do Paço*. India House and the Exchange
    overlooked it. In the centre is an equestrian statue of José I.

67 The Patriarchal Seminary was a College of Music where Franchi and all the leading
    Portuguese musicians and singers were taught. In 1787 it was housed in monastic
    buildings of S. Vicente da Fora. It should not be confused with the other Patriarchal
    Seminary for training priests, which moved to Santarem in 1780.

68 Amorous songs inclining to the sentimentally lascivious, introduced into Portugal in
    mid 18th cent. from Brazil.

69 Joana Jozepha de Menezes (*b.* 1723), daughter of 4th Marquis of Alegrete; married
    heir of 4th Marquis of Minas.

70 Eugenia Mariana de Menezes e Silva (*b.* 1731), 2nd Marchioness in her own right.

71 S. Anthony of Padua (*b.* Lisbon 1195; *d.* Padua 1281), principal patron saint of
    Lisbon. Beckford's prestige in Portugal was partly due to his devotion (real or
    assumed) to S. Anthony, and it was this that probably first recommended him to the
    attention of the Marialvas.

72 John Burton (1730–85), one of best harpsichordists and organists of his day.
    Patronised by Beckford.

73 Antonia Margarida Esmeraldo Vilela e Sá; wife of José de Brito (see note 85).

74 Antonia Basilia Heredia de Betencourt (1777-1887), later 1st Countess of Porto Santo by marriage, her husband becoming Foreign Minister.

75 Called Savoyard nuns because they were brought from the Convent of the Visitation of St. Mary at Annecy in Haute-Savoie. Invited to Lisbon by Theodore de Almeida, 1782. First installed near Cordoaria Nacional (Rope Factory) on the Junqueira, in the street called after them, R. das Freiras de N. Sa. da Visitacao.

76 Maria Justina de Mendonça Escarlate (Beckford gives the Italian form of her name, Scarlatti); daughter of Sargento-mor (Major) Caetano Escarlate. 1790, married Joaquim Guilherme da Costa Posser, one of the Principal Clerks in the Ministry of Interior. She lived in the Junqueira, with her maternal grandfather, Cristovam Pato de Mendonça Furtado.

77 Houyhnhnms—horses with human characteristics (*Gulliver's Travels*).

78 David Perez (*b*. Naples 1711; *d*. Lisbon 1779), violinist and composer. His best sacred music was that which so moved Beckford on November 26—his Mattutino de' Morti, printed in London,1774.

79 J. de Sousa Carvalho (*d*. 1798); a leading Portuguese composer of operas. 1779, succeeded Perez as Music Master to Royal Family.

80 Ansano Perracuti, an Italian castrate contralto of Royal Chapel, who also sang in operas.

81 The Judge Conservator of the English Factory.

82 José Street Arriaga Brum da Silveira (1747–1802), born in the Azores; nephew of Mme Arriaga, the Queen's favourite; had a legal career overseas. His wife, Ana Joaquina da Cunha (*d*. 1808), perhaps a Brazilian mulatto, was nicknamed *The Mountain of Gold*, and was the widow of the great capitalist Joaquin da Cruz Sobral (*d*. 1781). Beckford visited them at Carnide, N. of Lisbon, at what is now the *Quinta dos Condes de Carnide* (Street's nephew being created Count).

83 "Meagre" a Lenten diet containing no meat.

84 *S. Antonio da Sé*, adjoining the present Cathedral (Sé), and destroyed in the 1755 earthquake. The existing church, which Beckford describes, was not finished till 1812. The building was paid for by Lisbon children, who collected money by raising altars with the Saint's image on doorsteps of their houses. This was the origin of the custom noted in the previous entry.

85 José de Brito Leal Heredia (*c*. 1745–1805), Chevalier of the Order of Christ. In 1780 in Madeira he was denounced to the Inquisition as a Freemason, for mixing and dining with English Protestants, and for irreverence at Mass. In 1792 he fled to New York for political reasons.

86 On S. side of R. do Sacramento; now used for military and Government purposes; founded for Dominicans.

87 The 3rd Marquis of Tancos by marriage; his eldest son was Duarte Manoel de Noronha (1775–1838), 4th and last Marquis.

88   A *moeda de ouro* equalled £1 7s. 0d.

89   George Whitefield, one of the founders of Methodism.

90   Henrique de Aguilar e Menezes, prelate at the Patriarchate.

91   Luis Teles da Silva (1775–1828), 5th Marquis of Alegrete; son of 3rd Marquis of
     Penalva and his first wife. Became a General and Governor.

92   José Palomino y Quintana (1755–1810), Spanish violinist and composer in Maria I's
     service.

93   Joaquim de Oliveira (*b.* 1749), tenor; the greatest singer of his day in Lisbon.

94   Nickname for 2nd Viscount Courtenay, father of William Courtenay.

95   Nickname for Alexander Wedderburn (1733–1805), 1st Baron Loughborough and 1st
     Earl of Rosslyn, Chief Justice of Common Pleas and Lord Chancellor 1782, married
     as his second wife Charlotte Courtenay (*b.* 1750), aunt of William Courtenay and
     once close friend of Beckford. For Powderham scandal, to which this refers, see
     Introduction.

96   Luis Pinto de Sousa Coutinho (1735–1804), 1st Viscount of Balsemão. Ambassador
     in London (1774–88), when Marialva tried to enlist his help over Beckford's
     presentation to Maria I; later Secretary of State.

97   i.e. a veil that blindfolds. Scarf is also an ecclesiastical term for a band round the
     neck, worn by 18th-century Anglican clergy; the idea would still be the same—the
     renunciation of Protestantism. The reading scarf is uncertain.

98   Beckford's first travel-book, which his family forced him to suppress: see
     Introduction.

99   Miguel Caetano Alvares Pereira de Melo (1765–1808), 5th Duke. Later he was
     Steward of Royal Household and Councillor of State.

100 Almost certainly Mrs. *Hake* (Beckford usually spells names as pronounced), mistress
     of Mr. Burn the codfish merchant. The firm was Christopher Hake & Co., long
     established in Lisbon. Perhaps her husband was Richard Hake, admitted to Factory,
     December 1787.

101 More properly called Gian Francesco di Majo (1740–71), opera composer.

102 His house, built by Viscount de Barbacena in 18th cent., is on R. da Junqueira, at E.
     corner of Calcada da Boa Hora.

103 Colonels of Foot.

104 Monastery of *Vallis Misericordiae*, at Laveiras, near Caxias; now a reformatory.

105 Witham Friary, a former Carthusian monastery between Bruton and Frome.

106 John Forbes-Skelater (1783–1808), later Adjutant-General of Portuguese army.

107 1st Marquis of Marialva (as he later became) raised the Spanish siege of Elvas in
     1659.

108 Martinho de Melo e Castro (1716–95), one of the few able Portuguese 18th-century
     administrators. In 1787 he was Prime Minister, as well as Secretary of State for
     Foreign Affairs, War, and the Colonies and Navy.

109 José Francisco Xavier (1761–88), eldest son of Maria I. In 1777 he married his maternal aunt, Maria Francisca Benedicta (1746–1829). See Introduction and Note on the Manuscript.

110 José Thomaz de Menezes (*b.* 1745), son of 4th Marquis of Marialva. An intrepid daredevil, he was drowned in the Tagus some time before 1796.

111 4th Count of Tarouca.

112 Mme du Noyer: *Lettres historiques et galantes, avec ses Memoires.*

113 Francisco Duarte, chronicler of Jesuits in Portugal. At this time was tutor to "the little Penalva" (later 5th Marquis of Alegrete).

114 In *H.P.*; dated Caldas, 23 June 1787. Horne reports Marialva as saying of Beckford:

> On my return to Lisbon I will spend all the time that I can spare
> with him. I will attend him in his carriage and he shall accompany
> me in mine, we will drive through all the public streets and by the
> Palace frequently. I will give a grand dinner and will invite such
> of the first Nobility as are worthy to be introduced, and when I
> have done this I will once more attack Her Majesty to permit me
> the honour of introducing him. If after this I am refused and Melo
> is deemed the proper person, I will fetch him from his house and
> accompany him to Court, and in the antechamber deliver him up
> to Melo.

115 Built in 1756–61 to house the Royal Family after the earthquake; constructed of wood to withstand further tremors. Burnt down 1794; present 19th-century Palace on its site. It had an opera house and a Botanic Garden.

116 Town Hall of Lisbon, at NW. corner of Praça do Comerçio; burnt down 1863.

117 *Motassem-Billah*, son of Haroun-al-Raschid, reputedly had 130,000 piebald horses in his stables.

118 Dried codfish was the staple food of the Lisbon poor. The tax had been upon its sale within Portugal; remission of this tax helped the trade of fishermen, who therefore decorated their boats. Coaches were waiting to take the Royal Family to their Palace in Praço do Comerçio, but her unexpected welcome decided her to walk, which was probably unprecedented.

119 Head of the Convent of the Most Sacred Heart of Jesus (whose Church is now popularly called the Estrela); she was one of the most influential persons in Portugal.

120 Pedro de Lencastre (1763–1828), 7th Count of Vila Nova de Portimão and 3rd Marquis of Abrantes; President of the Council of Regency, 1807. Member of the Commission sent to Bayonne to meet Napoleon, 1808. Part of the site of his Palace and garden, better known as the Royal Palace of Santos, is now occupied by French Embassy in R. Santos-o-Velho.

121   In Portuguese, *cruzados*. An old crown equalled 2s. 3d. and a new crown 2s. 8½d.

122   Henrique José de Carvalho e Melo (1749–1812), 2nd Marquis of Pombal; see Introduction.

123   A slip for Arrabida Mountains.

124   Frei Inacio de S. Caetano (1719–88), titular Archbishop of Thessalonica and Confessor to Maria I. Son of a small farmer or peasant, he enlisted in the ranks, but ran away to study, and became a Carmelite friar. In 1787 he was also Inquisitor-General, and entered the Cabinet on August 22 as *Ministre assistente ao despacho*.

125   *José I*, father of Maria I.

126   Beckford means 1755 and refers to the opening performances then at the new opera house, the *Teatro do Paço da Ribeira* (also called Teatro do Tejo), where the Naval Arsenal now is on shore of Tagus. The opera was Perez' *Alexander in India*: 400 cavalrymen came on the stage as a phalanx of Macedonian soldiers.

127   The remains of this Palace, which fronted Largo de Loreto on its W. side, were demolished in 1860 to make way for the new Praça de Camoes.

128   Secretary of State's office was Quinta do Meio (also called Palacio do Patio das Vacas) on Ajuda Hill; today it houses the Museum of Colonial Agriculture in the Square (largo) of that name; its gardens are now the Jardin Colonial.

129   José Joaquim Lobo da Silveira, son of 1st Marquis of Alvito; lived at Bom Succeso.

130   The Irish revolutionary who died of wounds in 1798.

131   Barefoot Capuchins of the Order of St. Paul, First Hermit; their church, founded in 1736 and demolished after the Dissolution, was S. Jesus da Boa Morte e Caridade, and stood on W. side of the present Largo da Boa Morte.

132   *Almanacs* call him *Diogo Scares de Noronha*. He was probably the son of Rodrigo Antonio de Noronha e Menezes (son of 3rd Marquis of Marialva).

133   The *Quinta do Marquez de Belas*, NW. of Lisbon.

134   Mariana Joaquina Apolonia de Vilhena Pereira Coutinho, widow of Pombal's colleague Miguel de Arriaga; Lady of the Bedchamber to the Queen, and one of her principal advisers. A great beauty, who had a literary salon, and to whom some of Portugal's leading poets dedicated poems.

135   Now the Tribunals Militares, at Campo de S. Clara, in NE. Lisbon.

136   Later 3rd Marquis of Lavradio.

137   Edmund Foxhall, of Foxhall & Fryer, Old Cavendish St., London, upholsterers, interior decorators, etc.

138   Philippe Jacques de Loutherbourg, R.A. (1740–1812), was a successful artist who, as Garrick's chief designer of scenery at Drury Lane, effected a revolution in scene-painting and helped Garrick in his reform of theatrical costume.
       John Bacon, A.R.A., Thomas Banks, R.A.

139   The MS. looks like "effervase".

140   Symbolic key of office of a Gentleman of the Bedchamber.

141   Composed by Ferdinando Guiseppe Bertoni (1725–1818) and first produced in 1778.

142   José de Assis Mascarenhas, 4th Count.

143   The mob.

144   In the Salitri bull-ring, next to Salitri Theatre.

145   On Sintra-Estoril road; Street Arriaga sold it to Princess Carlota Joaquina, c. 1794.

146   Not, as has long been thought, Seteais, but *Quinta do Marques de Valada* at S. Pedro; see Appendix I.

147   Jean-Baptiste Pillement (?1728–?1808). Visited Lisbon c. 1748, 1766, and 1780-6. His decorations are rococo, and consist of *chinoiserie* and *singeries*.

148   Probably the Hotel Lawrence, where Byron first conceived *Childe Harold*. The funeral described on August 29 started here.

149   The 18th-century *Quinta Mazziotti*, S.W. of Colares.

150   The largest monastery in Portugal, built by João V for monks of the Order of Arrabida, 1717–35. Occupied by Regular Canons of St. Augustine, 1772–92. Architect was J.F. Ludwig (Ludovici) of Ratisbon.

151   Preliminary jotting runs (for this type of entry, see Introduction, pp. 19–20): "The servants bore flaming torches and the wind drove clouds of sparks on the mules. The two last were milk-white and looked like apparitions."

152   Daniel Gildemeester (1727–93), many years Dutch Consul-General in Lisbon until his death, when he was succeeded by his son Daniel. Pombal gave him the monopoly contract for the export of diamonds, 1760–71, and he became one of the wealthiest men in Portugal. Built *Quinta da Alegria* (now called Palace of Seteais) at Sintra (see Appendix I), the opening of which on July 25 Beckford describes.

153   Pedro de Almeida Portugal (1754–1813), 5th Count of Assumar. Better known as 3rd Marquis of Alorna, and perhaps the ablest Portuguese soldier of his day. Fought under Napoleon.

154   Bernardo José Maria de Lorena e Silveira (1756–1818), 5th Count of Sarzedas. He had just been appointed Governor of São Paulo in Brazil, and was later Viceroy of Portuguese India.

155   Diogo José Antonio de Noronha (1747–1806), 8th Count of Vila Verde. He had just been made Ambassador to Madrid, and was later Prime Minister and Foreign Secretary.

156   Preliminary jotting adds "and more like a fencing master than a young man of fashion."

157   Preliminary jotting runs "trying to excite me by every means in my power to drive them out of every great society in Lisbon."

158   His elder daughter, *b.* 1785, later Mrs. Orde.

159   Lourenço José das Brotas de Lencastre e Noronha (1735–1801), 5th Marquis of Minas by marriage, General and Councillor for War, with reputation as a soldier. Beckford's preliminary jotting explains his phrase "puppyism" by saying "I have

heard him accused of the loftiest pride, giving himself unsufferable airs, but tonight he was upon his good behaviour."

160   Walpole's despatch of July 21, 1787, runs: "We have had in this river the French *escadre d'Evolutions* under the command of the Marquis de Neuilly, they have been at sea some weeks and were all admitted up this river. The French ambassador has at a considerable expense entertained the officers during their stay here ... These ships are returned to Brest, from which they are to be despatched to the different destinations of the West Indies, to relieve some of the ships there, and to Toulon."

161   Preliminary jotting runs "Franchi came sneaking in at tea time and I felt confused and guilty (?)."

162   Preliminary jotting runs "I have no trees to plant, ... no strange original (?) animals like Pigott to amuse me with new schemes and systems." Robert Pigott (1736–94) was a Shropshire squire who sold up his estates and settled on the Continent. He ardently supported the French Revolution, and had eccentric ideas on food and dress.

163   The complete preliminary jotting runs: "The Marquis at night, laying close siege, and exerting his utmost abilities to get me to stay."

164   Preliminary jotting adds, "The Marquis looked as yellow as a quince, and I suggest has been mortifying himself at his beloved convent of Boa Morte. He was up at the fire last night which burnt half the Opera House at the Ajuda."

165   Preliminary jotting runs: "At tea time Franchi came in and we played like kittens."

166   Philip Astley, equestrian and circus-founder.

167   Domenico Cimarosa (1749–1801), opera writer.

168   Joana Rita and Maria Micaela de Lacerda Castelo Branco, *açafatas* to the Queen.

169   Diogo Inacio de Pina Manique (1733–1805), the greatest 18th-century Portuguese administrator next to Pombal. In 1787 he was Intendant-General of Police and of the Realm, and Superintendant of Customs.

170   Now *Quinta do Relogio*, and largely rebuilt. The cork tree, also mentioned by Southey, is still there.

171   Now incorporated in Pena Palace.

172   An order of monks whose life was modelled on that of St. Jerome.

173   Seteais.

174   Manoel Carios da Cunha e Tavora (1730–1795), 6th Count of S. Vicente; married daughter of 3rd Duke of Cadaval, and so was "young" Marialva's brother-in-law. Councillor of War, President of Court of Admiralty, and Inspector-General of Marine. 1774, accused of assassination of Col. J.L. Teixeira Homem, his rival in the affections of a *comédienne*, Francisquinha the hat-Maker's Daughter.

175   The wine *Vinho do Cabo*.

176   His firm was James Burn & Sons; a William Burn was admitted to the Factory in 1772.

177   Octaviano Acciaoli (*b.* 1731), of the Madeira branch of Italian family of Acciajuoli.

178   Also called *Convento dos Capuchos*, after the Franciscans who founded it in the
       mountains above Sintra, 1560.

179   For the probable date of this entry, see *Note on the Manuscript*.

180   *Teatro da Rua dos Condes*, demolished 1882, on what is now corner formed by R.
       dos Condes with Av. da Liberdade (S. end of E. side of *Passeio Publico*). Lisbon's
       principal theatre, where Italian opera was played.

181   Parish Church of *S. Pedro-em-Alcantara*, i.e. in suburb of Alcantara, in street now
       called Calcada da Tapada da Ajuda, near its junction with R. da Alcantara. Begun
       after earthquake; its main structure finished in 1788.

182   José Domingos Antonio Totti Mencarelli (died *c.* 1832). Italian contralto.

183   João José Alberto de Noronha (1725–1804), 6th Count by marriage, brother of 3rd
       Marquis of Angeja. From 1750, a Gentleman of the Bedchamber to Prince Pedro,
       later Pedro III (Maria I's consort). A witty opponent of Pombal, who therefore
       imprisoned him in Junqueira, 1760; was only released on the new Queen's accession,
       1777, but refused to come out until his innocence was confirmed, and thought his
       old friend (now King) should come in person to release him; so when Pedro sent
       him his key of office as a Gentleman of the Bedchamber, he threw it into the privy
       at Necessidades Monastery, where he was by then staying. This ended his official
       career.

184   Neither the reading nor the meaning are certain. Mr. John Carter suggests that L-S.
       Mercier, author of *Tableau de Paris*, edited, or saw through the press, this 1787 Paris
       edition of *Vathek* (*The Library*, 4th Series, Vol. 17).

185   Tomas Antonio de Noronha Ribeiro Soares (1744–1809), Brigadier, and Governor of
       Setubal.

186   1697–1736. Son of Pedro II.

187   The *Mesa Censoria* (Censorship Office).

188   On the old Sintra-Colares road. João de Castro, Viceroy of India, retired here,
       1542. He built the various chapels; the heart buried in front of chapel of Our Lady
       of the Mount is that of Castro's kinsman Saldanha. Here the orange tree was first
       introduced into Europe.

189   14th Viscount, commonly called *Visconde Ponte de Lima*; 1st Marquis of Ponte de
       Lima.

190   The phrase striking . . . Paris was inserted above by Beckford.

191   Linho, SW. of Ramalhão.

192   Philip Thicknesse, author of *A Year's Journey through France and part of Spain*, 1777,
       etc.

193   Penha Longa, founded 1355.

194   Swiss artist.

195   After caresses, a whole line is too heavily deleted to decipher.

196   A grandee of a Mahometan Court, especially the Great Mogul's.

197   At Christie's, 19 April 1787.

198   Alexander Cozens, the artist, who died about a month before Beckford's wife (Lady Margaret) in 1786.

199   The Marquis, Grand Master of the Horse, and Rich Gentleman.

200   A fussock is a fat, unwieldy woman.

201   *Crown Vetch* or *Scorpion Senna*.

202   Beckford also spells her *Steets*. *Almanacs'* list of foreign merchants gives Francis Steets.

203   Nicholas Conolly is shown in census of British residents in Lisbon in 1755 as the owner of a business. He was the Lisbon agent of the East India Company.

204   See Introduction.

205   That this is Monsenhor Gomes Freire de Andrade (1761–1831) is proved by the 1786 *Almanac*, which records him in the list of prelates (*Monsenhors*) of the Patriarchate, styling him *Mons. Freire, na Quinta das Picoas*—his father's celebrated Lisbon Palace. He became Head of the State in 1820.

206   This may have been his first cousin. General Gomes Freire de Andrade (1757–1818), an able soldier who served under Napoleon and was shot for alleged treason. He was the kind of man whom Beckford would have liked, for he was good-looking, had been educated abroad, could paint, and spoke several languages.

207   Books here mentioned are: C. Cullen's 2-vol. translation of Abbé D.F.S. Clavigero's *History of Mexico*, 1787; Corneille de Pauw's *Recherches philosophiques sur les Americains*, Berlin, 1768–9, 2 vols.; William Robertson's *History of America*, 1777, 2 vols.; A. de Solis, *Historia de la Conquista de Mexico*, Madrid, 1684.

208   Literally, *Commander-in-Chief*, but here, apparently, the civil or military Governor of the District of Mafra.

209   Beckford's preliminary jotting, pencilled in the green pocketbook on the spot next day (August 28), names them: Mr. Burn the codfish merchant, and Sir John Swinnerton Dyer, 6th Bart. The jotting adds: "I took care to behave in a dignified devout manner."

210   This sentence was jotted in the pocket-book. João V bought the site in January 1713 (after which it was cleared for the new building), so that the Abbé's memory went back at least 74 years. The new foundation-stone was laid in 1717.

211   The patent for the Barony about to be granted to Beckford in 1784 was withdrawn because of the Powderham scandal; see Introduction.

212   Luiz Manoel de Menezes Mascarenhas, prelate of Patriarchate.

213   5th Viscount.

214   See note on his wife, Maria I.

215   See Introduction.

216   Catherine, first wife (*d.* 1782) of Sir William Hamilton, envoy at Naples.

217 Hitherto called *D. José de Mateus,* or *D. José,* by Beckford (see note 18).

218 The arms of the Tavoras in Sala dos Brasões were erased by Pombal, because the Marquis of Tavora was one of the ring-leaders in the Tavora-Aveiro conspiracy of 1758 to shoot José I.

219 Alfonso VI (reigned 1656–67), brother of Catherine of Bragança, was imprisoned after his abdication, but not until 1674 in Sintra Palace, where he remained until his death in 1683.

220 Antonio Maria G. Sacchini (1734–86), born near Naples, was one of the favourite composers of the day. His other aria which Beckford sang, described later, *Poveri affetti miei celatevi nel cor,* comes from Scene V, Act I of his opera *Creso.*

221 José de Sousa Botelho: see note 18.

222 From *Aeneas in Thrace* (1781). According to post-Homeric tradition, Polydorus was son of Priam and Hecuba. When Troy was about to fall, Priam entrusted him, and some treasure, to Polymnestor, King of Thracian Chersonese. For the sake of the money, Polymnestor killed Polydorus and cast his body into the sea, but it was washed up on the Thracian shore. The cry *Avenge my wrongs* was also Beckford's own throughout his life.

223 Portuguese laurel.

224 The context makes it fairly clear that Beckford, under great mental stress, wrote the opposite of what he meant, and that D. Pedro paid him *little attention.* For a similar significant slip of the pen, see p. 204.

225 This ends pencil jotting made on the spot in the green pocket-book. The written-up entry follows, but it was not finished at the time; the last paragraph, asterisked, was added much later to complete it: see p. 21.

226 Luis Joseph Xavier de Miranda Henriques (1726–93), 3rd Count of Sandomil, friend of Prince of Brazil, and later a Major-General.

227 Robert Winson's death produced a typically Beckfordian comment in an unpublished letter in *H.P.* in Italian to Franchi, dated 7 December 1826:

> The other day Wilson, the acolyte of the accursed Sill, died as he
> was coming out of his own cellar with two bottles of port in his
> belly and two in his hand (no exaggeration!). He has left £45,000
> to a cousin, not fresh *(fresca)* but freshly *(frescamente)* arrived
> from Cork. Hardly was the infamous miser dead than fires of
> jubilation—were lit throughout the house—where previously all had
> frozen. They opened up the vinous sanctuary which hitherto none
> had entered save his High Priest of Bacchus and drank to the full to
> his passing—including Coombes the apothecary, and English the
> under-taker and grave-digger. The villain was 71.

He became partner in the firm (Horne, Sill, Lynes & Wilson), and may have been the Robert Wilson admitted to the Factory in 1795, who in 1811 was a hardware and jewellery merchant in England.

228   João Antonio Pinto da Silva, Chevalier of the Order of Christ, and Director of the Royal Theatres. He may be the *J. Antonio* (mentioned in next entry) connected with Patriarchate, for *Almanacs* show him as Secretary to its *Fazenda* (which has fairly wide meaning, not necessarily confined to finance).

229   Manoel Joaquim Bandeira, who was *Corregedor do Crime da Corte e Casa real*—one of the Great Officers of State. A *Corregedor do Crime* is a Judge in criminal causes.

230   José da Rocha; Beckford gives his various posts.

231   The Royal Palace at Sintra, where the Court was in residence.

232   Beckford wrote "at" instead of "had."

233   Beckford wrote "and" for "at."

234   Constance Manoel (1719–94), 1st and last Duchess of Tancos, and 2nd Marchioness in her own right and Principal Lady of Bedchamber to Maria I.

235   Joaquim da Nobrega Cão de Aboim (with variants), a Monsenhor of Patriarchate; published a Life of S. Julian, Lisbon, 1790. *S. Julião* was one of Lisbon parishes and its Prior was Royal Chaplain.

236   Letter 29 of Portugal states that it was *Mortier's* Dutch Bible, by which may be meant the folio edition printed by Pieter Mortier at Antwerp in 1700 of David Martin's *Histoire du Nouveau Testament,* which has engraving of Massacre of Innocents (Vol. 2, p. 18), with legend *Herod fait massacrer les petits enfants à Bethéem.* The Dutch version (1700) of this book was sold in Hamilton Palace Sale, 1st Beckford Portion, Item 896.

237   The Grua were Italian musicians well known in 18th-century Germany. A Peter Grua is mentioned as a violinist at Mannheim in 1763.

238   José do Rosario Garcia, Head of Portuguese Dominicans, with rank of prelate; Deputy of Lisbon Inquisition.

239   Presumably the unpublished *Episodes of Vathek.*

240   His coming-of-age celebrations, Michaelmas 1781.

241   Maria do Carmo de Lima Botado, *açafata* to Princess of Brazil; Maria de Penha de França et Laçerda, another *açafata.*

242   The later version is printed here, but for all practical purposes it is the same as the original entry, parts of which are in note form.

243   *Sala dos Cignos* (swans) in Sintra Palace.

244   Joseph Sill.

245   Francisco Xavier de Assis Pacheco e Sampaio, an eminent Crown lawyer. His journey to Pekin (where he stayed 5 weeks, May–June 1753) is described in 1785 pamphlet by E. Brazão; *Noticias das couzas succeeded na embaixada que levou a Corte de Pekim, Francisco de Assiz Pacheco de Sampayo, mandado pelo Senhor Rey D. José I no 1752.*

246 The later version, but similar to original skeleton entry, which is in note form.

247 Original entry adds "at ½ past four." Brizida Mascarenhas de Melo, *açafata* to Princess of Brazil. Emily O'Dempsy, *açafata* to Carlota Joaquina.

248 Carlota Joaquina (April 1775–1830), daughter of Charles IV of Spain; 1785, married João (see note 270), younger son of Maria I. She was always of diminutive stature.

249 Swearing and supperless the Hero sate,

Blasphem'd his Gods, the Dice, and damned his Fate;

Then gnaw'd his pen, then dash'd it on the ground,

Sinking from thought to thought, a vast profound!

Plung'd for his sense, but found no bottom there;

Yet wrote and floundered on in mere despair.

(Pope's *Dunciad*, I, 115–120.)

250 On September 13, the Prussian army crossed the Dutch frontier in support of the Stadtholder's Orange party (favoured by England), and against the Republican party of the Estates of Holland (backed by France).

251 The Portuguese form of embrace on meeting between friends and relations. It indicates that Beckford was on friendly and familiar terms with the real ruler of Portugal. The interview took place in Sintra Palace.

252 In Letter 27 of *Portugal* (under the fabricated date of September 12), Beckford pretended to have dined with the Archbishop.

253 For his Parliamentary duties.

254 Erected 1782, demolished 1879 for construction of Av. da Liberdade; was at E. end of R. do Salitiri, on N. side. National comedy was acted here.

255 By Voltaire; translated into Portuguese, 1785.

256 Maria Rita de Castelo Branco (1769–1832), 6th Countess in her own right, and Lady-in-waiting to the Queen. Married, 1783, José Luis de Vasconcelos e Sousa, diplomat, 1st Marquis of Belas.

257 Entry unfinished.

258 This monstrance or pyx, called *custodia dos Jeronimos*, was chiselled by Gil Vicente from the first gold brought from the Indies by Vasco da Gama after his second voyage to India; the gold was tribute money from Quiloa (Kilwa), an island 150 miles S. by E. from Dar-es-Salaam. Perhaps the finest piece of metal work in Portugal, it is now in the Museum of Ancient Art at Janelas Verdes (Lisbon).

259 Almost certainly *Voyage Pittoresque ou description des royaumes de Naples et de Sicile* by J.C. Richard, Abbé de St-Non, 5 folio vols., Paris, 1781–6 (which Beckford mentions later, and which was in Hamilton Palace Sale of his books). The author, a renegade clergyman who visited Italy with Fragonard, presented Beckford with 32 etchings of the Views.

260 *History of Lady Julia Mandeville* (anon., 1763), by Mrs. Frances Brooke.

261 *Voyage de Bourgogne* (Paris, 1777), a somewhat erotic book in prose and verse by E.D. de Forges, Chevalier (later Vicomte) de Parny.

262 Peasant women in Lisbon district.

263 *N.S. de Covadonza*, the Spanish treasure ship whose capture in 1743 created a sensation: see Anson's *Voyage Round the World*.

264 This paragraph is Beckford's preliminary jotting. The written-up entry follows.

265 Spanish for *roadside inn*.

266 A kind of chintz bed-cover made in India.

267 Beckford wrote "of."

268 The second wife of 1st Count of Lumiares.

269 1st Count.

270 João, b. 1767, younger son Maria I; married Carlota Joaquina. Succeeded elder brother as Prince of Brazil (heir), 1788. Governed from 1792, when his mother became insane, but did not receive the title of Prince Regent till 1799. Reigned as João VI, 1816–26.

271 Emily O'Dempsy (see note 247).

272 Maria do Resgate Portugal (1771–1823), 3rd Countess in her own right. She gave birth to 4th Count, January 1788.

273 Marialva's second daughter.

274 Beckford's housekeeper.

275 Martinho Antonio Castro's system of street-lighting was inaugurated December 1780 in Lisbon and was superior in some respects to those in London and Paris.

276 Preliminary jotting adds: "Both D. Pedro and the Grand Prior stayed late. The Grand Prior cried out *Vous aimez donc beaucoup le petit Don Pierre* etc."

277 Lay brother.

278 This ends the preliminary jotting. The uncompleted final entry follows.

279 Text breaks off unfinished in mid-sentence.

280 The preliminary jotting, which has about 4 illegible words, runs: "It blew cold and Verdeil had no mind to ride. However we got out and found the day < >. I called at the Marquis'; both of us loathe to part. D. Pedro clings round me. The Grand Prior came (?) < > Bezerra, the Abbade."

281 J.A. Colmenar, *Délices de l'Espagne et de Portugal*, 6 vols., Leyden, 1715; and Udal ap Rhys, *An account of the most remarkable places and curiosities in Spain and Portugal*, London, 1749.

282 Cormorant.

283 All the above was jotted on the spot in the green pocket-book. The final entry follows.

284 D. Pedro.

285 A 16th-century house near Colares, on the Sintra side between the old and new Sintra-Colares roads.

286 Father Antonio Pereira de Sousa Caldas (1762–1814), a Brazilian who was in his day an influential and esteemed lyric poet and preacher. In *Portugal* Beckford substituted the name of Bocage: see Note on the Manuscript, p. 24.

287 The Court had now left Sintra for Lisbon; the Queen had evidently stopped *en route* at Queluz.

288 The preliminary jotting ends here; the contemporary entry follows as the next paragraph; the third paragraph, asterisked, is a later addition.

289 The chapel was the Ermida da Piedade, and the villa Quinta da Piedade.

290 *Quinta das Laranjeiras* (Orange trees); later called Burnay Palace; its grounds are now the Zoological Gardens.

291 Joaquim Pedro Quintela (1748–1817), 1st Barão de Quintela; one of the wealthiest Portuguese merchants. See also note on *Casa dos Milhões*, 297.

292 The fountain in front of Necessidades Palace.

293 Santos Velhos Parish Church, near Tagus and adjoining Vila Nova's Palace.

294 The Chiado (Rua Garrett).

295 *Bairro Alto* is the name of a quarter in the city, but Beckford here seems to mean *Largo (*Square*) do Loreto*, in which Marialva's ruined Loreto Palace stood (see note 127).

296 Loreto Church is on N. side of what is now called *Largo das duas Igrejas* (in map, Largo do Loreto). The Church was badly damaged in the earthquake, and its reconstruction was finished in 1785. It was Parish Church of Italian community in Lisbon.

297 *Casa dos Milhões* (The Millionaire's House), in Largo do Barão de Quintela; also called *Palacio Quintela*.

298 The earliest entry (printed here), which Beckford erased, ended here. Up to this point, the slightly later second entry followed this draft very closely; the remainder of second entry now follows as paragraph 2, continuing the narrative. At a later date he finished the entry off with the third and last paragraph, asterisked here.

299 João Ferreira (*d.* 1788), one of the wealthiest Portuguese merchants, whose State Contracts included hide and leather, and leatherwork for Army. His house is on N. side of Chiado, but was practically burnt down in 1889.

300 Marialva's Palace, the Quinta da Praia.

301 Later 4th Marquis of Tancos.

302 The original entry runs: "Morning: the Marquis; conversation about Melo. Grand Prior and him at dinner. We drove to see Quintela's house, the cathedral, Crows and St. Anthony. Returned to tea: Polycarpo and Lima. Polycarpo went with me to the theatre <in the> Rua dos Condes to hear my favourite *modinha* in the intermezzo, but it was not so well sung as before. Polycarpo entertained me at supper with many curious anecdotes of the Portuguese nobility."

303 *The Sé* (Lisbon's original and present Cathedral), which Beckford has not hitherto mentioned—in his day it was of little account, having been eclipsed and usurped by the Patriarchate.

304 He was martyred at Valencia in Spain in A.D. 304; his remains were transferred to Cape St. Vincent only when the local Christians fled from Moorish persecution.

305 In the manuscript it looks like "canal."

306 Robert Arnauld d'Andilly (1589–1674); wrote several lives of Saints.

307 Preliminary jotting has "the turkey poult stretching out his neck." The turkey poult was Sill.

308 Gabriel, younger son of Charles III, had married Mariana Vitoria, daughter of Maria I. The illuminations were for their daughter (born November 4), who only lived 3 days, and who was therefore dead before news of her birth reached Lisbon.

309 Pedro III.

310 The Rossio (Rocio).

311 Verdeil.

312 Perhaps Bras Biaggio de Lima: see notes 326.

313 Pinto's reply (in *H.P.*) dates Marialva's letter November 9.

314 Near the Tagus opposite the former Monastery of St. John of God.

315 Also known as the *Palace of Counts of Lavradio*, it stands at the corner of R. da Junqueira and R. das Casas do Trabalho; its courtyard is now the Largo do Marques de Angeja.

316 Pedro José de Noronha (1771–1804), 5th Marquis of Angeja.

317 The earlier part of the entry is missing.

318 Convento dos Clerigos Regulares de S. Caetano (or, dos Caetanos Theatinos) de Na. S. da Divina Providencia. Not named on map, but shown there as a small black square SW. of Collegio dos Ingelezes. The Conservatory of Music now occupies its site.

319 Presumably *Collectiones Peregrinationum in Indiam occidentalem et … orientalem*, Frankfurt, 1590–1634 folio, commonly known as *Grands et petits Voyages*, published by the de Bry family.

320 Tomaz Caetano do Bem (1718–97), author of a History of his Order in Portugal and India.

321 *Illustraçao hist. à genealogia dos Reis de Portugal*, published in Lisbon, 1789.

322 *Almanacs* mention this collection as one of the *curious and interesting* things to be seen in Lisbon.

323 Federico Guilherme de Sousa (to which *Calhariz* or *Holstein* may be added), 1737–90. Viceroy of Portuguese India (i.e. Goa), 1779–86.

324 In the present Largo do Intendente (called after him)—not marked in map, but just E. of Desterro Convent (N. part of city).

325 In the Largo de S. Domingos, at NE. corner of Rossio.

326 Bras Biaggio (often called *Bras Francisco*) de Lima (*d.* 1813), younger brother of Jeronimo de Lima. Sent to Italy for further study of music, 1790. On his return, he gave up music, went into business, and became the head of a firm. It is not clear whether this was his first meeting with Beckford; if not, it is probably he whom Beckford describes as *a gawky, pedantic owl* on November 10, p. 176.

327 F. de Sousa, the Viceroy (see note 323).

328 Perhaps Manoel Antonio Ribeiro de Motta, President of the Inquisition at Coimbra, and later Extraordinary Deputy of General Council of the Inquisition.

329 Off the Chiado on its S. side; dedicated to the English and Frankish Crusaders killed capturing Lisbon from the Moors, 1147. Rebuilt after the earthquake, 1769–84.

330 The guild of Lisbon musicians was called *Irmandade de S. Cecilia,* patron-saint of musicians, whose Feast is on November 22.

331 Redlynch in Somerset, seat of 1st Earl of Ilchester.

332 Lord Ilchester's picture (still in his possession) is an 18th-century copy by R. Barret of the original at Sherborne Castle by Marcus Gheeraerts Junior. Beckford follows Vertue in wrongly describing it as the Queen's visit to Lord Hunsdon: it is her visit to Blackfriars in 1600 for a wedding. The original was in the R.A. 1953 Exhibition *Kings & Queens* (No. 100).

333 Rev. the Hon. Charles Redlynch Fox-Strangways, son of 1st Earl of Ilchester.

334 Beckford took this dream down in pencil. When copying it out much later, there was one phrase he was unable to read (part of which I cannot read either); so I have printed his copy. But I have added as the next paragraph, in brackets, the comment (minus the last two or three illegible words) which he wrote in pencil after the dream but did not repeat in his copy.

335 Preliminary jotting runs: "Bright sunshine. Too late for Mass. Verdeil gone to see the Bull published at S. Roque. Dined with the Marquis at the Palace *en famille*: the Marquis, D. Anita (?), D. Henriqueta, the two infants, D. Pedro. Passed the evening at the balcony with D. Pedro and Duarte and his mother: crowds of beggars. Then went to the Theatre Salitri: Queen there etc." All that follows the asterisk was written years later.

336 This Papal Bull, published annually, granted indulgences to the faithful, nominally in return for their help in wars against Infidels; in practice it was a general financial levy.

337 The much corrected manuscript of this late draft looks like a literary composition. It is included here because it is full of authentic details; for literary reasons Beckford erased some of them as he wrote, but I have restored two of them in square brackets.

338 From Milton's *Il Penseroso*.

339 Part of the manuscript is missing: see p. 21; these two lines have been supplied from Letter 5 of *Spain*. Beckford is on his way to Madrid from Lisbon, having been

travelling since November 28. He had just left Talavera de la Reina, about 80 miles
SW. of Lisbon. N.S. del Prayo is a monastery.

340   Sam Derrick's *Letters written from Leverpoole, Chester, Corke*, etc., 2 vols., 1767. Tom
Amory's anon.: *Life of John Buncle, Esq.*, 2 vols., 1756 and 1766. Tom Hull's *Select
Letters between the late Duchess of Somerset . . . Mr. Whistler . . . W. Shenstone and
others*, 2 vols., 1777. Will Bray's *Sketch of a Tour into Derbyshire and Yorkshire*, 2nd
edn., 1783. J. Heely's *Letters on the beauties of Hagley, Envil, and the Leasowes*, 2 vols.,
1777. E. Clarke's *Letters concerning the Spanish Nation*, 1763. Maj. W. Dalyrymple's
Travels through Spain and Portugal in 1774, 1777.

341   The river on which Madrid stands. Beckford kept all these books, which were sold a
century later by his descendants in the Hamilton Palace Sale.

342   Brother of Charles III; Cardinal-Primate until he left the Church to make a
mésalliance; *d.* 1785.

343   See p. 19. Beckford arrived in Madrid on December 12.

344   Beckford was staying at the Cruz de Malta, an inn near the E. end of the Calle de
Alcala; his windows were opposite the Carmelite Church, now S. José's.

345   Caroline Augusta de Stolberg (1755–1828), daughter of Prince of Stolberg-Gedern;
married Carlos Fernando Stuart (*d.* 1787), 4th Duke of Berwick.

346   Liria Palace, in Plazuela del Duque de Liria, NW. Madrid; built 1770.

347   Jacobo Felipe Carlos Fitzjames Stuart (1773–1794), 5th Duke of Berwick. His second
surviving son (7th Duke) united the Houses and titles of Alba and Berwick when in
1802 he succeeded his aunt as 14th Duke of Alba.

348   Detail added from Letter 7 of *Spain*.

349   Maria Fernanda Stuart; 1790, married Duke of Aliaga, later 11th Duke of Hijar.

350   Georgina Seymour, later Countess of Durfort, daughter of Henry Seymour.

351   There were three brothers: Francisco Javier de Rojas, Marquis of Villanueva de
Duero; Fernando; and José, a Knight of Calatrava, who was presumably Beckford's
friend.

352   (Sir) Robert Liston (1742–1836), distinguished diplomat. Minister at Madrid, 1783–
8; Beckford calls him *Chargé* because he was due for recall. The English Legation
was in Beckford's street, Calle de Alcala.

353   Then flanking E. side of Prado walk, and forming E. extremity of Madrid;
abandoned by Charles III, 1764.

354   A carriage hired from a livery-stable. Beckford had left his two carriages behind in
Lisbon, and was trying to sell them to Maria I.

355   Ahmed Vassif Effendi (1740–1808) was one of the most distinguished Turks of his
day, and eventually became Foreign Minister. His second Spanish Embassy lasted
from July 1787 to March 1788. The Sultan commissioned his edition of works of
earlier Turkish historians, which appeared in Constantinople in 1804 as *Annals of
the Ottoman Empire*.

356 Perhaps the saloon of the *Cason de Felipe IV*, famous for its ceiling frescoes by L. Giordano, and now the main hall of Museo de Reproducciones Artisticas. Letter 8 of *Spain* states that the Turk's apartments had once been Farinelli's.

357 Inserted from Letter 8 of *Spain*.

358 The great printer Ibarra had died in 1785, but his business was continued by his widow.

359 A. Ponz: 3rd edn. of his *Viage de España,* Madrid 1787; his foreign travels are *Viage Fuera de España,* Madrid, 2nd edn., 2 vols., 1785.

360 This entry is unfinished. Subsequent movements that day are noted in the preliminary jotting printed in full as the next paragraph.

361 Prado Museum. Begun in 1785 as a collection of Natural History.

362 Portuguese Ambassador.

363 Almoro Pisani (1753–1808), Venetian Ambassador in Madrid until 1790.

364 A royal hunting box and park NW. of Madrid.

365 Manoel Salvador Carmona, well-known engraver.

366 Carlo Ferrero-Fieschi (*d.* 1837), last Prince of Masserano, Captain of Flemish Troop of Royal Bodyguard, and later Spanish Ambassador in Paris. He was almost a hunchback.

367 Church of Carmelites descalzados, also called S. Hermengildo, and now Parish Church of S. José, off Calle de Alcala.

368 Phillipp Peter Roos (*b.* Frankfurt, 1657; *d.* Rome, 1705), called *Rosa da Tivoli*, where he principally worked. All trace of this picture has been lost: it may have been one of the 500 looted from the monastery by Joseph Bonaparte in 1809, or removed at the time of the suppression of the monasteries in 1835.

369 Probably the most famous bookseller and printer Antonio de Sancha.

370 Beckford left a blank.

371 The Spanish voyage to Society (Friendly) Islands was commanded by Domingo de Boenechea, who arrived off Tahiti in November 1774, and who died there in January 1775. He was buried at the foot of a wooden Spanish mission cross, which Captain James Cook saw during his last voyage in 1777 (he was also there in April–May 1774, *before* the Spaniards: Sanchez slightly misinformed Beckford). The manuscript which Sanchez had was either the *Diario de Navegacion* submitted by Boenechea's second-in-command and successor, Gayangos, or *Descripcion de las islas … reconocidas ultimamente por D. Domingo Boenechea* (1772–4).

372 No such expedition is known, and penetration to 80° N. is almost out of the question. But Beckford probably refers to an expedition to Alaska, which is connected to Kamchatka by the long chain of the Aleutian Islands, and which at that time were still being explored by the Russians. The Alaskan expedition nearest to Beckford's date is that in 1779 by the two Frigates *Princesa* and *Favorita*, commanded by Lieutenants Ignacio de Arteaga and Juan Francisco de la Bodega y de la Quadra, which penetrated to 60 ° N.

373   Count Graneri.

374   The wrong date, *19 December* (instead of 20), is understandable, since this first
      paragraph was jotted on the spot in pencil in the green pocket-book. When
      Beckford started to write it up (paragraph 2), he copied down the same wrong date.

375   This inexplicable word is clear in the manuscript.

376   Raphael's *Holy Family*, now in the Prado. Philip IV paid £2,000 for it from Charles
      I's collection and called it *the pearl* of the Raphaels.

377   Federigo Barocci (or Baroccio) of Urbina (1528–1612).

378   Francisco Javier de Rojas, Marquis of Villanueva de Duero.

379   Eugenio Izquierdo de Ribera y Lezaun. The "new Museum" is now the Prado
      Museum.

380   Marie Antoinette Rosalie de Pons de Roquefort (*d.* 1824), Duchess of La Vauguyon.

381   Marie Antoinette Rosalie Pauline de Quélen de la Vagabond (*b.* 1769). Married in
      May 1787, aged 18, the 14-year old Prince of Listenais, later Duke of Bauffremont (see
      note 396). According to Marquis of Bombelles, Ambassador in Lisbon in Beckford's
      time, she was pretty, "pleasant, and gesticulating less than her mother, whose charming
      features and fine figure she has inherited" (Marquis' diary for 3 August 1788 at
      Versailles). Her love affair with Beckford obliged her father to pack her off out of his
      reach, but they corresponded clandestinely through her brother Carency.

382   At W. end of city, overlooking R. Manzanares; built 1738–64.

383   Maria Anna Walstein Wurtemburg Liechtenstein (*b.* 1756), daughter of the Prince of
      Lichtenstein; 1781, married as second wife the aged 9th Marquis of Santa Cruz. Her
      love-letters to Beckford are in *H.P.*

384   Pedro Pablo Abarca de Bolea (1719–99), 1st Count of Aranda, famous Spanish
      statesman.

385   13th Duchess.

386   Maria del Pilar de Silva Abarca de Bolea; married her uncle, Count of Aranda, 1784,
      as his second wife, and had no children.

387   William Carmichael (*d.* 1795), went to Madrid in 1779 as Secretary to the American
      Resident, John Day, who ws unsuccessfully trying to obtain a treaty with Spain.
      Carmichael remained on as *Chargé d'Affaires* until recalled in 1794.

388   11th Duchess, and 14th Countess.

389   Perhaps Udima in Peru.

390   Abbé G.T.F. Raynal was one of the *philosophes*, well-known then for his book on
      India.

391   Fernando Selma (1750–1810).

392   *Madonna of the Fish* is by Raphael.

393   Count Leopold von Beust (1740–1827), Inspector-General of Saxon salt mines.

394   Three heavily deleted and indecipherable lines follow, which begin "We were
      followed by a < > of a soldier who kept ogling and."

395 Paul François de Quélen de Stuer de Caussade (1746–1828), Duke of La Vauguyon. Ambassador to Madrid, 1784–90.

396 Alexandre Emmanuel Louis (1773–1833), Prince of Listenais; created Duke of Bauffremont, 1818.

397 Paul Maximilien de Caussade (1768–1824), Prince of Carency, who later became at traitor, spy and smuggler, and died insane.

398 Carency's younger brother was only 10, so the youth mentioned was presumably someone else.

399 Persian and Turkish poets.

400 The new Royal Palace at W. end of city.

401 Preliminary jotting runs: "Walked in the Prado. Rojas at dinner. Palace. Mme de Santa Cruz, Mme de Osuna, and Mme de Aranda. Midnight Mass at the Descalzas Reales: wretched music, vile stink." See p. 23. Mme de Osuma was 9th Duchess of Osuna.

402 From about this point Beckford uses "M." indiscriminately, regardless of sex; where a woman is evidently meant I have expanded to "Mme."

403 Perhaps Beckford means the Count de Kageneck, Austrian Ambassador; Liston's despatches in Public Record Office similarly describe his character.

404 This was not Angelica Kauffman's nephew, as Beckford stated in *Spain*. Her uncle Anton Kauffman, also a painter, had three sons who served in Charles III's Bodyguard, and it was probably one of these. Young Kauffman painted Beckford in Madrid for the Marchioness of Santa Cruz.

405 José Freire da Silva, Secretary of Portuguese Embassy.

406 There were 3 denominations in *doblons* (doubloons)—of 2 escudos, 4 escudos, and the gold doblon of 8 escudos, which was called a *medal* and was then worth £3 12s. od.

407 John Skey Eustace (1760–1805), an American from New York State. He was in Madrid in connection with his plans to emancipate Venezuela from Spanish rule; later became a general in the French revolutionary armies.

408 Juan Pereyra Pacheco was a Minister in the Exchequer, the King's Majordomo, and a Knight of Santiago.

409 Cardinal Francisco Antonio de Lorenzana, Primate of Spain.

410 Agustin Rubin de Cevallos, Bishop of Jaen.

411 Italian for *refreshment*.

412 This song suddenly swept France when it was used to lampoon Mme du Barry, Louis XV's mistress. Usually called *La Belle Bourbonnaise*; Beckford probably names it from a line in the last verse.

413 Pedro Alcantara de Toledo Salm-Salm (1773–1841), 12th Duke of Infantado; late President of Council of Regency, and Prime Minister.

414 Madrid Court Almanac (*Kalendario Manual*) for 1788 calls him Sidi Amora Coggia; born 1765; eldest son of the First Minister of the Barbary State of Tripoli, which

had thrown off Turkish rule. Beckford spells the brother's name variously but I have standardised it to Mohammed.

415   The writing of *conserved* for *conversed* shows under what emotion Beckford was labouring. For a similar slip of the pen in similar circumstances, see first paragraph of Sunday September 9, p. 137.

416   Letter 16 of *Spain* calls them the two little Sabatinis, half Spanish, half Italian, so they were perhaps grandchildren of Charles III's favourite architect, an Italian who migrated to Spain in 1760, General Francisco Sabatini (1722–95).

417   Entry unfinished.

418   French Ambassador's secretary.

419   The Imperiali were a noble Genoese family with branches in Naples.

420   Presumably pet name for some young person.

421   One of the greatest of the *castrati* singers, a male soprano.

422   Carl August, Baron de Ehrenswärd (1749–1805), envoy at Madrid, 1783–99.

423   Luis Fernandez de Cordoba, Marquis of Cogolludo, became 13th Duke of Medinaceli; Master of the Horse to Charles IV.

424   The British garrison surrendered to Spaniards, 1782, and Britain subsequently lost Minorca.

425   Manuel Antonio Fernandez de Cordoba, 5th Duke of Arion by marriage; his father became Duke of Medinaceli.

426   Heavy deletion makes only approximate reconstruction possible here.

427   Claude Henri, Count of St.-Simon (1760–1825), celebrated political thinker and economist. He was in Spain with a scheme to revive the old project of connecting Madrid to the Atlantic by canal. He was captured by the English on de Grasse's flat-ship, 1782, and imprisoned in Jamaica.

428   In Church of N. Sa. De Carmen.

429   *i.e.* the Portuguese Ambassador.

430   Pablo Sangro y de Merode (1740–1815), Prince of Castel-franco.

431   Stefan Zinovieff.

432   In those days called *Quintra da Alegria*; *Seteais* (variously spelt) was the area and in particular the flat common field in front of the Palace. To avoid confusing the reader, I shall here use the present name *Seteais* for the Quinta da Alegria.

433   *Na caza feita pelo Pileman em S. Pedro.*

434   Antonio A.R. da Cunha, *Cintra Pinturesca ou memoria descriptiva*, 1905, p. 75.

435   Escriptura de Aforamento, printed in *Jornal de Sintra,* 6 June 1934.

436   Dr. de Matos Sequeira has seen a statement that Gildemeester sent instructions from England to sell Seteais.

437   Printed in *Syntra—Archivo Historico*, 1908, No. 4, p. 32.

438   Article *Quelques artistes français en Portugal,* in *Gazette des Beaux Arts*, New York, February 1952.

INDEX

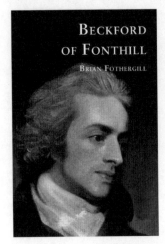

William Beckford could have been remembered for the fact that he was the son of a Lord Mayor of London, the godson of William Pitt, was extremely rich or at one point was Britain's most eligible bachelor. Instead, his spectacular hedonism and disregard for convention led to his epic fall from grace in a homosexual scandal. *Beckford of Fonthill* is Brian Fothergill's account of a sensational life, a history of the celebrated and vilified 'Fool of Fonthill'.

1 84588 085 4
£18.00
384 pages with 16 illustrations

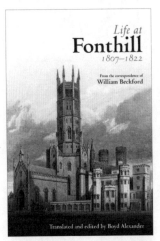

William Beckford was one of the most controversial figures of his time. He was the author of the Gothic novel *Vathek* and the builder of Fonthill Abbey, his monstrosity of a house, which had a tower 300 feet high, was set in 6,000 acres and protected by an eight-mile-long, twelve-feet high 'Barrier' topped by iron spikes. *Life at Fonthill* contains extracts from Beckford's journal for the years 1807–1822 and offers an insight into the life of this eccentric and unforgettable character.

1 84588 069 2
£18.00
352 pages with 16 illustrations

Sir William Hamilton is perhaps best-remembered for the lives adjacent to his own. British Ambassador to the Court of Naples during the rise of Napoleon, his claim to a place in history comes from his involvement in the notorious love triangle between him, his wife Emma and Horatio Nelson. Brian Fothergill's biography reveals a man whose talent for diplomacy was matched only by his dedication to antiquity, who was fêted across Europe as both art-collector and dilettante.

1 84588 042 0
£18.00
352 pages with 16 illustrations

For sales information please see www.nonsuch-publishing.com